The

Chinese &

Asian

Cookbook

The
Chinese &
Asian
Cookbook

Sallie Morris &
Deh-Ta Hsiung

LORENZ BOOKS

First published by Lorenz Books in 2001

© Anness Publishing Limited 2001

Lorenz Books is an imprint of Anness Publishing Limited
Hermes House, 88–89 Blackfriars Road, London SE1 8HA

Published in the USA by Lorenz Books, Anness Publishing Inc.
27 West 20th Street, New York, NY 10011

www.lorenzbooks.com

A CIP catalogue record for this book is available from the British Library.

Publisher: Joanna Lorenz
Managing Editor: Linda Fraser
Editor: Susannah Blake
Jacket and Text Design: Chloë Steers
Typesetting: Jonathan Harley
Illustrations: Angela Wood
Recipes: Yasuko Fukuoka, Deh-Ta Hsiung, Sallie Morris, Steven Wheeler

1 3 5 7 9 10 8 6 4 2

NOTES

Bracketed terms are intended for American readers.

For all recipes, quantities are given in both metric and imperial measures and,
where appropriate, measures are also given in standard cups and spoons. Follow
one set, but not a mixture, because they are not interchangeable.

Standard spoon and cup measures are level.
1 tsp = 5ml, 1 tbsp = 15ml, 1 cup = 250ml/8fl oz

Australian standard tablespoons are 20ml. Australian readers should use 3 tsp in
place of 1 tbsp for measuring small quantities of gelatine, flour, salt, etc.

Medium (US large) eggs are used unless otherwise stated.

CONTENTS

INTRODUCTION

Some of the world's most exciting cuisines come from the Far East and South-east Asia. From the vastness of China to the island states of Indonesia and the Philippines, food is prepared with pleasure and keen attention to detail. Each country has its own unique style of cooking, coloured by climate, local crops, cultural mores and the impact of historical events, but there are common threads too. Throughout this region, the emphasis is always on serving the freshest food, and presentation is paramount, particularly in Japan and Thailand.

Rice is the staple food of the region. It has been cultivated in southern Asia for over five thousand years, is eaten at every meal, and is the basis of both sweet and savoury snack foods, as well as a being a source for wine and vinegar.

Fish forms an important part of the diet. Every country, with the exception of Laos, has miles of coastline, as well as inland waters. The lower reaches of the Yangtze River are traditionally known as the land of fish and rice, a term that is used to indicate the well-being of the local inhabitants.

The Japanese cooks' skill in preparing and serving fish is legendary. This is partly due to the fact that the country has abundant fish stocks and only limited land for grazing, but is also because for many years, meat was off the menu, due to a government decree that prohibited its consumption by any but the sick on the grounds that it increased aggression. Very fresh fish is sliced thinly and served raw or marinated, for example *sashimi* and *escabèche*, but fish is also poached, grilled (broiled), cooked on skewers and battered and fried.

In Thailand fish is always served as fresh as possible. In restaurants it is usual for diners to choose their own fish from tanks, and nobody objects to waiting while the grouper or snapper is prepared for the table. Fish bought at market is often live and is carried home in a bucket of water.

The Asian preoccupation with the freshest possible food can be a little disconcerting for the Western visitor. Before enjoying the Hong Kong dish drunken prawns, for instance, the diner must first watch as the live prawns are marinated in Shao Xing rice wine, then cooked in fragrant stock.

At the other end of the spectrum, salted and cured fish is a valuable source of food throughout the area, but particularly in South-east Asia. All sorts of fish and seafood are prepared in this way, either in brine or by being dried in the sun. Fish sauce and shrimp paste are essential ingredients that go under various names, and contribute a subtle but unique signature to many dishes. Even more important is soy sauce, which was invented by the Chinese. Tofu was originally peculiar to the region, but is now widely used in the Western world, as are noodles.

The countries of China and South-east Asia share a similar approach to food. All prepare, cook and serve their daily meals according to the long-established principle the Chinese call *fan-cai*. *Fan* is the main part of the meal, usually rice or another grain, while the *cai* includes the supplementary dishes such as fish, meat, poultry and vegetables. These elements and ingredients must be perfectly balanced, so that aromas, colours, textures and tastes are in absolute harmony.

Harmony dictates that all the dishes be served together. Guests begin by taking a portion of rice, and then one of the supplementary dishes on offer, relishing it on its own before taking another portion of rice and a second choice. Soup is enjoyed throughout the meal. Harmony extends to presentation as well, especially in Japan. In Thailand, too, food is beautifully served. Thai girls learn the art of fruit and vegetable carving and can create birds, flowers and butterflies from these ingredients.

Tourism is one of the major reasons why Asian food has become so popular in Europe, America, Australia and elsewhere. Travellers discovered that Chinese food was not a single cuisine, but many, ranging from Peking cooking in the north, to the hot and spicy Sichuan-style in the west and Cantonese in the south. Visitors to Vietnam and Thailand wanted to be able to continue eating the meals that had been so much a part of their holiday. In major cities the world over, it is now possible to enjoy authentic Thai, Vietnamese, Indonesian, Malaysian and even Filipino food, and lesser-known cuisines are following quickly.

Asian ingredients, once only available in Asian stores, are now found in many supermarkets. There's never been a better time to discover the joys of Asian cuisine, and this book is the very best place to start.

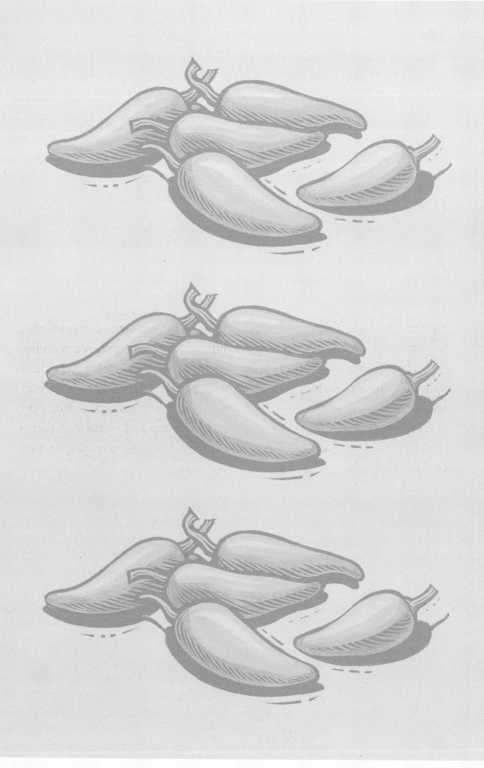

THE CHINESE & ASIAN KITCHEN

The cuisines of China and South-east Asia use hundreds of ingredients, some of which may be more familiar than others to Western cooks. This chapter guides you through every type of Asian food, from the daily staples such as rice and noodles, to unusual vegetables and fruit such as mooli, chayote and durian, and the aromatic herbs and spices that play such an integral part in Asian cooking. These many and varied ingredients are all explained in full and the information includes hints on preparation and cooking, along with instructions for storage.

Equipment & Utensils

Although the equipment in the average Western kitchen will be adequate for most of the recipes in this book, there are some items such as a cleaver, wok and bamboo steamer that will make cooking Asian food easier and more pleasurable. Start to build up your store of specialist items slowly, with a few basics, then gradually add extra pieces as you need them.

CLEAVERS

The heaviest cleaver, known in China as number one, can cut through bone, yet is also delicate enough to create paper-thin slices of raw fish. The flat, broad blade is ideal for crushing garlic or bruising ginger, and can be used to convey crushed items to the pan. It is 23cm/9in long, 10cm/4in wide, and weighs 1kg/2¼lb. Number two is a medium-weight cleaver, which is ideal for chopping, slicing, shredding, filleting and scoring. The back of the blade is used for pounding and the flat for crushing and transporting. The handle can be used as a pestle. Number three has a much shorter, narrower blade and is lighter. It is mainly used for slicing.

Cleavers can be made of stainless steel or carbonized steel. A stainless steel cleaver will need frequent sharpening. To prevent a carbonized steel blade from rusting, wipe it dry after use then coat with vegetable oil.

CHOPPING BLOCK

The traditional block is a cross-section of a tree trunk. The ideal size for domestic use is 30cm/12in in diameter and 5cm/2in thick. Season a new block to prevent splitting. Let it absorb as much vegetable oil as it will take, then clean with salt and water and dry. After use, scrape with the back of a cleaver and wipe down. Never immerse in water.

A 5cm/2in thick, hardwood cutting board or an acrylic board can be used instead.

WOK

This versatile pan conducts and retains heat evenly and, because of its shape, the food always returns to the centre where the heat is most intense. This makes it good for stir-frying, braising, steaming and boiling. The wok is ideal for deep-frying as it requires far less oil than a flat-based deep-fryer and has more depth and a greater frying surface. It is also safer to use than a pan as a wok has a larger capacity at the top and is less likely to overflow and catch fire.

There are two basic types of wok: the double-handled wok is suitable for all types of cooking; the single-handled wok is best for stir-frying. Both types are available with flattened bases for use on electric or gas hobs (stovetops).

The best woks are made from lightweight carbonized steel. Cast-iron woks are too heavy, and woks made from other metals, such as stainless steel or aluminium, are not as good for Asian cooking.

A carbonized steel wok must be seasoned before use. Place the wok over a high heat until the surface blackens, then wash it in warm, soapy water. Clean with a stiff brush, rinse in clean water and place it over a medium heat to dry, then wipe the surface with vegetable oil. After each use, wash under hot running water without detergent. Scrub with a stiff brush or non-metal scourer, rinse then dry over a low heat. Wipe with a little oil before storing.

Clay Pot

Also known as the sand-pot or Chinese casserole, this earthenware cooking pot comes in several shapes and sizes, most glazed on the inside only. With care, the pots can be used on top of the stove, but they are prone to cracking.

Rice Cooker

Electric rice cookers are a good investment but a deep, heavy pan with a tight-fitting lid is just as good for cooking rice.

Mongolian Firepot

Also known as a Chinese hotpot or steam-boat, this utensil allows food to be cooked at the table. It consists of a central funnel, which is filled with burning charcoal, surrounded by a moat of hot stock. Diners cook small pieces of meat and vegetables in the stock. Once these are eaten, the stock is served as a soup. There are several models available, from expensive brass to cheaper aluminium or stainless steel.

Japanese Omelette Pan

A rectangular omelette pan or *makiyaki-nabe* is useful for making Japanese rolled omelettes but a large non-stick, heavy frying pan or a flat, heavy griddle will work well.

Steamers

A traditional Chinese bamboo steamer has a tight-fitting lid. Several sizes are available, and you can stack them in tiers over a wok of boiling water. The modern steamer is free-standing and made of stainless steel, but the food cooked in a metal steamer lacks the subtle fragrance that a bamboo one imparts. If you do not have a steamer, place a trivet in a wok, fill it one-third full of water and bring to the boil. Place the food in a heatproof bowl on the trivet, cover the wok with a lid and steam.

Wok Tools

Some wok sets come with a spatula and ladle. These are very useful. The ladle can be used for stirring and measuring liquids. A dome-shaped lid and a metal draining rack that fits over the wok to keep food warm are also useful. Short chopsticks are ideal for beating eggs and long ones for deep-frying, as stirrers or tongs. A wok stand will protect the table when serving.

Strainers

The most useful strainers are the slotted spoon or perforated metal scoop and the coarse-mesh wire skimmer, which is used for removing food from hot oil.

Mortar and Pestle

Asian cooks prefer granite or stone mortars and pestles. Rough, flat-bowled mortars are good for making spice and herb pastes.

Spice Mill

If you are going to grind a lot of spices, a spice mill is useful. An electric coffee grinder works well for this purpose.

Grater

Traditional graters are made from wood or bamboo, but a stainless steel cheese grater can also be used.

Sushi Equipment

To make sushi properly, you will need a bamboo mat (makisu or sushimaki sudare). This mat is used for rolling sheets of nori seaweed around vinegared rice and other fillings when making norimaki, a type of sushi.

Sushi chefs spread the rice on the nori with their fingers, but a rice paddle (shamoji) makes it easier. For pressed sushi, wood or plastic moulds are useful.

Rice

This grain has been cultivated in southern Asia for over five thousand years and is the region's staple food. There are more than four thousand different strains grown in China alone. Since rice requires a wet and warm climate for its cultivation, 90 per cent of the world production of rice is grown in the monsoon regions of Asia. A small amount is cultivated on dry land in northern China.

Broadly speaking, rice can be classified as being either *Oryza sativa indica* or *Oryza sativa japonica*. Varieties of both types are cultivated in Asia. Long-grained indica rices are the most common. Long grain white rice has had its husk, bran and germ removed, taking most of the nutrients with them and leaving a bland rice that is light and fluffy when cooked. Long grain brown rice has had only its outer husk removed, leaving the bran and germ intact, which gives it a chewy, nutty flavour.

Culinary Uses

It is impossible to think of Asian food without rice. Rice is served in one form or another at every meal, including breakfast. Although wheat – in the form of dumplings or noodles – is eaten more often than rice in some parts of Asia, such as northern China, Asians everywhere regard rice as their staple food. Some languages use the same phrase for eating rice as for eating food.

The most common way of serving rice throughout Asia is boiled or steamed; fried rice does not normally form part of an everyday meal, but is either served as a snack on its own, or reserved for a special occasion. Unlike India pilau, Italian risotto or Spanish paella, Asian fried rice dishes are never based on raw rice, but always use cooked rice (either boiled or steamed). For the best results, the rice should be cold and firm, not soft.

Throughout Asia, breakfast is a creamy, moist rice dish, which is known as *congee* or rice pudding. It is considered highly nutritious and is often given to babies and people with digestive problems as well as the elderly. Coconut milk is used instead of water in many South-east Asian countries. Because it takes over an hour to make a creamy *congee*, many Japanese cooks (and some Chinese) cheat by simply adding hot water to cold cooked rice.

Preparation and Cooking Techniques

There is no definitive way of cooking plain rice. Some types benefit from being rinsed in cold water first, while others should be soaked before use. Some need to be cooked for longer than others, and the amount of liquid required varies too. The general rule is to use double the volume of water to dry rice. However, if the rice has been washed or soaked first, less water will be needed otherwise the rice will become soft and sticky rather than firm and fluffy.

Asian cooks often add a teaspoon of vegetable oil to the water to prevent the rice from sticking to the base of the pan. Adding salt is a matter of choice. It is usually added when cooking regular long grain rice, but not for Thai fragrant rice. The width, depth and material of the pan used will also affect the final result. One of the best ways of cooking perfect boiled rice is in an electric rice cooker, and a microwave is good too.

MAKING PLAIN BOILED RICE

Use long grain rice, basmati rice or Thai fragrant rice. Allow 50g/2oz/generous ¼ cup raw rice per person.

1 Put the dry rice in a colander and rinse under cold running water. Tip into a large pan, then add cold water to cover the rice by 2cm/¾in. Add a pinch of salt, and, if you like, about 5ml/1 tsp vegetable oil. Stir once and bring to the boil.

2 Stir once more, reduce the heat to low and cover with a tight-fitting lid. Cook for about 12 minutes, then turn off the heat and leave the rice to stand, tightly covered, for about 10 minutes.

Storing Rice

Store raw rice in an airtight container in a dry, cool place away from strong light, and use it within 3–4 months of purchasing.

TYPES OF RICE

A number of different varieties of rice are used in China and Sout-east Asia. Each is valued for it's own distinctive qualities.

PATNA RICE

At one time, most of the long grain rice sold in Europe came from Patna, and the term was used loosely to mean any long grain rice. Today, it is generally used to describe variety of long grain rice from the Bih region of India.

BASMATI RICE

This slender long grain rice is grown northern India, the Punjab areas of Pakist and the foothills of the Himalayas. Af harvesting it is aged for a year, which giv it a characteristic flavour and a light, flu texture. Basmati rice has a cooling effect hot and spicy curries.

THAI FRAGRANT RICE

This wonderfully delicate rice has quite a distinctive scent of jasmine, and is highly prized by South-east Asian cooks. Once cooked, the grains become slightly sticky.

SHORT-GRAINED JAPONICA RICES

These rices are less fragrant than indicas but tend to taste slightly sweeter. Japonica rices are cultivated in northern China, Japan, Korea and surrounding areas. They are higher in amylopectin than long grains, and are therefore more starchy. The grains cling together when cooked, which makes them ideal for *sushi* and similar dishes.

GLUTINOUS RICE

Also known as sweet or waxy rice, this rice is even more sticky than Japonica rice. This makes it very popular with South-east Asian cooks because the cooked rice can be shaped or rolled, and is easy to pick up with chopsticks. White glutinous rice has fat, opaque grains and is the most common type, but there is also a black glutinous rice, which retains the husk and has a nutty flavour. Less common are a pinkish-red glutinous rice and a purplish-black variety. Glutinous rice has a high sugar content, and is used in Japan for making rice crackers (*senbei*), rice cakes (*mochi*) and rice wine. It is also used to make lotus leaf parcels and rice pudding.

Flours

Numerous flours made from locally grown cereal grains, starchy vegetables and pulses are used in Chinese and Asian cooking. Different flours have different cooking properties. For example, cornflour (cornstarch) and tapioca flour are used as thickening agents, while other flours such as rice flour are used to make batters, rice papers, noodles, dumplings, cakes and breads.

CORNFLOUR/CORNSTARCH
This very fine white powder is made from ground corn (maize) and is used to thicken sauces, soups and casseroles.

WHEAT FLOUR
Ground from the whole grain, this may be wholemeal (whole-wheat) or white. Hard or strong wheat flour is high in gluten. It is often added to rice flour to make bread.

RICE FLOUR
This is more finely milled than ground rice, this is also known as rice powder. The texture is similar to that of cornflour. Rice flour is used for thickening sauces, and to make rice papers and dumpling dough. It is often used to make sticky Asian cakes and sweets, but because rice flour does not contain gluten, the cakes made with it are rather flat. Rice flour can be combined with wheat flour to make a crumbly bread.

SOYA FLOUR
This is a finely ground, high-protein flour made from the soya bean. It is used as a thickener in a wide range of sauces and soups, and is often mixed with other flours such as wheat flour to make bread and pastries. It has a pleasant nutty flavour.

POTATO FLOUR
This is made from cooked, dried, ground potatoes and is used as a thickening agent.

TAPIOCA FLOUR
This granular flour is extracted from the cassava root. It is used as a thickening agent for sauces, soups and casseroles.

ARROWROOT
This delicate starch is usually made from the roots of *Maranta arundinacea*. It has little taste, will set to an almost clear gel and is less starchy than cornflour. It is used to thicken clear sauces and soups.

WATER CHESTNUT FLOUR
This powdered starch is made from dried water chestnuts. It is used to thicken clear sauces and soups and in cakes.

MUNG BEAN FLOUR
This fine flour is made from ground mung beans. It is used to thicken clear sauces and to make cellophane noodles.

CHICKPEA FLOUR
This very fine flour is also called gram flour or besan. It is mainly used in India but was taken to Malaysia by Indian immigrants.

NOODLES

Whether Marco Polo actually introduced noodles from China to Italy is a debatable point, but we do know that some kind of noodle made from wheat flour appeared in China as early as the first century BC, around the time of the Roman Empire. Noodles rapidly became a popular food, not only in China but throughout the whole of Asia.

Up to the end of the nineteenth century, when modern machinery was first imported from Europe, noodles were always made by hand, and even today certain types of noodle are still hand-made, such as the "hand-pulled" or "drawn" noodles made by chefs in northern China. It takes more than ten years to master the technique.

Noodles form an important part of the daily diet in Asia. Unlike rice and steamed buns, which are served plain as part of a meal, noodles are usually cooked with other ingredients and eaten on their own as light meals or snacks. In Vietnam, rice noodle soup is the standard breakfast. In Japan there are restaurants specializing in noodle dishes such as plain noodles served with dipping sauces; bowls of steaming noodle soup; and noodles cooked with sliced vegetables and seaweed. Thailand has its noodle stalls, noodle boats and even noodle meals available from bicycle vendors.

Preparation and Cooking Techniques
Noodles are very easy to prepare. Some types benefit from being soaked before being cooked, so see individual recipes for advice, read the instructions on the packet or seek advice from someone in the store where you bought them. Both dried and fresh noodles have to be cooked in boiling water before use. How long for depends on the type of noodle, the thickness of the strips and whether (as is usual) the noodles will be cooked again in a soup or sauce. Most types of dried noodle require about 3 minutes' cooking, while fresh ones will often be ready in less than a minute. After the initial cooking, noodles are then usually served in soup, braised or fried.

Noodles in soup This dish usually consists of noodles served in bowls of clear broth with pieces of cooked meat, poultry, fish, shellfish and/or vegetables, sometimes with a sharp sauce on the side.

Braised noodles The difference between this dish and noodles in soup is that braised noodles are first cooked in a broth, then served with a thickened sauce.

Fried noodles This has to be one of the most popular Chinese dishes in the West (and in South-east Asia, but not so much in north China or Japan). The two basic types of fried noodles are dry-fried (crisp) or soft-fried. Generally speaking, only the fine vermicelli-type of noodles are used for dry-frying; the thicker round or flat noodles are more suitable for soft-frying.

Storing Noodles
Packets of fresh noodles carry a use-by date, and must be stored in the refrigerator. Dried noodles will keep for many months if kept sealed in the original packet, or in airtight containers in a cool, dry place.

Types of Noodles

Asian noodles are made from a wide variety of different flour pastes, including wheat, rice, mung bean, buckwheat, seaweed, corn and even devil's tongue, which is a plant related to the aurum lily.

Wheat Noodles

There are several different types of wheat noodles. They can be plain, enriched with egg or flavoured. Dried wheat noodles are often referred to as longevity noodles, being associated with long life.

Plain Noodles

These are made from strong (bread) wheat flour and water. They can be flat or round and are available in various thicknesses. In Japan, they are known as *udon* and are available fresh, pre-cooked or dried. Somen are thin, white Japanese plain noodles, made by pulling the dough (rather than rolling and cutting into thin strips). They are sold in bundles, held together with a narrow paper band.

Egg Noodles

These are far more common than plain wheat noodles. In China they come in various thicknesses and are sold fresh or dried. *Ramen* are the Japanese equivalent and are usually sold in coils or blocks. Very fine egg noodles are called *Yi* noodles in China, after the family that originally made them. They resemble vermicelli and are popular in hakka-style cooking.

Unusual Noodles

As well as the common types of noodles, there are a number of other noodles that are less easy to find in the West. Japanese **Shirataki** *are made from a starch derived from the tubers of the devil's tongue plant, which is related to the arum lily.* **Bijon**, *made from corn, are produced throughout South-east Asia.* **Canton** *are Chinese wheat noodles that may be plain or enriched with eggs.*

Shrimp Noodles

These seasoned egg noodles are lightly flavoured with fresh shrimp and/or shrimp roe. They are usually sold dried, in coils of various widths.

Instant Noodles

Packets of pre-cooked egg noodles are a familiar sight in the West. They come in various flavourings, such as mushroom, chicken, prawn and beef.

Rice Noodles

Wheat noodles must have preceded rice noodles by several centuries, since there were no written records of the existence of rice noodles until well into the Han Dynasty in the third century AD. Not surprisingly, rice noodles are very popular in southern China and South-east Asia where not much wheat is grown.

Unlike most other noodles, which are made from flour of one type or another, rice noodles are made from whole grains of rice, which are soaked and then ground with water into a paste. This is drained through a sieve to form a dough, which is divided into two. One half is cooked in boiling water for 15 minutes before it is kneaded with the raw half to make a firm dough. The dough is then put through a press, which cuts it into various shapes and sizes. The finished strands are blanched in water, drained and rinsed before being sold fresh, or dried in the sun before packaging.

Types of Rice Noodles
Although they are known by different names, the rice noodles sold in southern China, Thailand and Vietnam are all quite similar. Like wheat noodles, they come in various widths, from the very thin strands known as rice vermicelli, or *sen mee* in Thailand, to rice sticks, which start at around 2mm/$\frac{1}{16}$in and can be as wide as 1cm/$\frac{1}{2}$in, as in the case of *ho fun*, a special variety from south China reputedly made with river water rather than tap water. In Thailand it is possible to buy a rice noodle enriched with egg. It is called *ba mee* and is sold in nests. A wide range of dried rice noodles is available in Asian supermarkets, and fresh ones can occasionally be found in the chiller cabinets.

MUNG BEAN/CELLOPHANE NOODLES
Also known as transparent noodles, bean thread vermicelli or glass noodles, these noodles are very fine, rather brittle strands made from green mung beans. Although very thin, the strands are firm and resilient, never becoming soggy when cooked, which doubtless contributes to their popularity.

Cellophane noodles are almost tasteless unless cooked with other strongly flavoured foods and seasonings, but they do have a fantastic texture. They are never served on their own, and are always used as an ingredient in a dish, most notably in vegetarian cooking and in hotpots, as well as in Vietnamese spring rolls. They are only available dried. In Japan, cellophane noodles are called *harusame*, which means spring rain; in China they are *fensi*; and in Vietnam they are *bun*.

BUCKWHEAT NOODLES
The best-known buckwheat noodles are the Japanese *soba*, which are usually sold dried in bundles of fine strands. *Soba* are much darker in colour than wheat noodles. There is also a dark green variety called *cha-soba* (tea *soba*), which is made of buckwheat and green tea. Korean cooks use buckwheat noodles, too, preferring a very thin variety.

PREPARING RICE AND MUNG BEAN NOODLES
Unlike wheat noodles, which need to be cooked in boiling water, rice noodles and mung bean noodles need only be soaked in hot water.

Rice noodles These should be soaked in hot water for a few minutes to soften them. If they are soaked for too long, they will become soggy and lose their texture.

Add the noodles to a large bowl of water that has been recently boiled and leave to stand for 5–10 minutes until softened, stirring occasionally to separate the strands as they soften.

Mung bean noodles These can be soaked in warm or hot water and will not become soggy if left to soak for too long.

Place the noodles in large bowl of hot or warm water and leave to stand for about 10 minutes, or until soft. Use a pair of kitchen scissors or a sharp knife to chop the noodles into shorter strands for easier handling.

These often delicate dough rounds or squares feature prominently in Chinese and Asian cooking. Pancakes can be thick or thin, while wrappers are always paper thin and need to be handled with care. Both are usually made from a simple dough and are used to enclose either sweet or savoury fillings. The best known of these "packages" are spring rolls and wontons.

PANCAKES

Asian pancakes are quite different from their counterparts in the West. For a start, they are almost always made from plain dough, rather than a batter, and they are more often than not served with savoury fillings rather than sweet.

There are two types of pancakes found in China, either thin or thick. Thin pancakes, called *bobing*, are also known as mandarin or duck pancakes because they are used as wrappers for serving the well-known dish Peking duck. They are also served with other savoury dishes, most notably the very popular *mu-shu* or *moo-soo* pork, which consists of scrambled egg with pork and wood ears (dried black fungus).

REHEATING CHINESE PANCAKES

Ready-made thin pancakes for serving as wrappers with dishes such as Peking duck are quick and simple to prepare.

1 Stack the pancakes, interleaving them with squares of baking parchment.

2 Carefully wrap the stacked pancakes in foil, folding over the sides of the foil so that the pancakes are completely sealed.

3 Put the foil parcel in a steamer and cover. Place the steamer on a trivet in a wok of simmering water. Then steam for 3–5 minutes until the pancakes are hot.

The dough for thin pancakes is made of wheat flour and very hot water, which is then kneaded and rolled out very thin. Two oiled layers of dough are rolled out together, then cooked on a dry griddle before being peeled apart. Making pancakes demands considerable skill and dexterity, so cooks often prefer to buy frozen pancakes from Chinese and Asian supermarkets.

Thick Chinese pancakes are made with lard and are usually flavoured with savoury ingredients such as spring onions (scallions) and rock salt. In northern China, thick pancakes are eaten either as a snack or as part of a main meal, rather like the Indian paratha. Both thin and thick pancakes are sometimes served as a dessert, with a filling of sweetened bean paste.

Indonesian sweet pancakes, called *dadar gutung*, are made from batter, similar to that used for making pancakes in the West, rather than dough, and filled with coconut flesh cooked with a little water, brown sugar, cinnamon and lemon juice.

NONYA SPRING ROLL PANCAKE WRAPPERS

These thin pancake wrappers are typical of the Singaporean style of cooking known as Nonya. They are made from an egg, flour and cornflour (cornstarch) batter, rather than the dough used for Chinese pancakes. Nonya spring roll pancakes are filled with a selection of savoury ingredients.

SPRING ROLL WRAPPERS

These paper thin sheets are essential for creating the crispy shell of spring rolls (also known as egg rolls in the US and pancake rolls in many other parts of the world). The spring roll wrappers are usually made from a simple flour and water dough, except in Vietnam where wrappers are made from rice flour, water and salt. They are wrapped around a tasty savoury filling, traditionally lightly cooked spring vegetables, then deep-fried for a few minutes to produce a very crisp, golden case.

Spring rolls must be one of the best-known and most popular Chinese snacks all over the world, including in China itself. While the fillings may vary slightly from region to region, or even between different restaurants and fast food stalls, the wrappers are always more or less the same.

There are three different sizes of ready-made spring roll wrappers available from the freezers of larger supermarkets and Chinese and Asian stores: small, medium and large. They are all wafer-thin. The smallest of these wrappers, which are about 12cm/4½in square, are used for making dainty, cocktail-style rolls. The standard-size wrappers measure about 21–23cm/8½–9in square, and usually come in packets of 20 sheets. The largest wrappers, which are 30cm/12in square, are far too big for general use, so they are usually cut in half or into strips for making samosas and similar deep-fried snacks.

As soon as spring roll wrappers have thawed, they should be covered with a dampened dishtowel until ready to use. If they are allowed to dry out, the wrappers will become extremely brittle and almost impossible to fold without cracking. Any unused spring roll wrappers can be returned to the freezer, then thawed again and used at another time.

MAKING SPRING ROLLS

Use medium-size spring roll wrappers (or, for cocktail snacks, use the smallest size). To make the filling, stir-fry ingredients such as beansprouts, bamboo shoots, water chestnuts or canned and dried mushrooms, with chopped prawns or finely minced pork.

1 Allow the spring roll wrappers to thaw at room temperature, then peel off the top wrapper. Cover the remaining wrappers with a clean, damp dishtowel to prevent them drying out.

2 Spoon the spring roll filling diagonally across the wrapper, leaving enough room to fold up the ends.

3 Fold one corner of the wrapper across the length of the filling.

4 Using a pastry brush, moisten the edges of the wrapper with a little cornflour (cornstarch) and water paste.

5 Fold the two ends over the filling, then roll up in to a neat parcel.

6 Heat oil for deep-frying in a wok to 190°C/375°F. Deep-fry the spring rolls, a few at a time, for 2–3 minutes until crisp and golden. Lift out of the hot oil with a slotted spoon or wire skimmer and drain on kitchen paper. Keep them warm while you cook the remaining spring rolls.

WONTON SKINS

These wrappers are made from a flour and egg dough, which is rolled out to a smooth, flat thin sheet. The sheet is then usually cut into small squares, although round wonton wrappers are also available. Ready-made wonton skins are stacked in piles of 25 or 50, wrapped and sold fresh or frozen in Asian or Chinese stores.

Unlike spring roll wrappers, which have to be carefully peeled off sheet by sheet before use, fresh wonton skins are dusted with flour before being packed. This keeps each one separate from the others making them very easy to use. Frozen wrappers must, however, be thawed thoroughly before use, or they will tend to stick together. Any unused skins can be re-frozen, but should be carefully wrapped in foil so that they do not dry out in the freezer.

There are several ways of using wonton skins. They can be deep-fried and served with a dip, filled and boiled, steamed or deep-fried, or simply poached in a clear broth. On most Chinese restaurant menus in the West, this last option is listed under soups, which is misleading, as in Asia wonton soup is always served solo as a snack, never as a separate soup course.

PREPARING WONTONS

Place a spoonful of the filling in the centre of the wonton skin and dampen the edges with water. Press the edges of the wonton skin together over the filling to create a little purse shape, sealing the filling completely.

RICE PAPERS

These wrappers, which are used in Vietnam and Thailand, are quite different from the rice paper that is used for writing and painting in China and Japan, nor do they bear any resemblance to the sheets of rice paper Western cooks use as lining when baking macaroons.

These round, tissue-thin crêpes are made from a mixture of rice flour, water and salt, and then dried on bamboo mats in the sun. Drying in this way results in the distinctive cross-hatch pattern that is found embedded on each sheet of rice paper.

Rice paper sheets are used for wrapping Vietnamese spring rolls and small pieces of meat and fish to be eaten in the hand. The sheets are rather dry and brittle, so must be softened by soaking in warm water for a few seconds before use. Alternatively, they can be placed on clean damp dishtowels and brushed with water until they are sufficiently pliable to be wrapped around food or enclose a filling.

Spring rolls are usually deep-fried, but this is not always the case. Vietnamese cooks also make a fresh version. Cooked pork, prawns, beansprouts and vermicelli are wrapped in rice paper, which has been dipped in cold water until it is pliable and almost transparent. The filling can clearly be seen through the wrappers, and the rolls look very pretty.

Rice papers are usually packaged and sold in 15cm/6in, 25cm/10in and 30cm/12in rounds. They will keep for months in a cool, dry place, provided the packages are tightly sealed. When buying, look for sheets that are of an even thickness, with a clear, whitish colour. Broken pieces are a sign of bad handling, and make the rice papers quite useless for wrapping, so avoid any packages that look as if they have been damaged in transit.

DUMPLINGS

Commonly referred to in the West as *dim sum*, dumplings are eaten throughout Asia. There is a wide variety of shapes and sizes, with fillings ranging from pork and vegetables to mushrooms and bamboo shoots. Some enclose the filling in a very thin dough skin while others use a dough made from a glutinous rice flour. There are also steamed buns filled with meat or a sweet bean paste.

Dumplings are particularly popular in China, and there is a wide variety of different shapes and sizes, with fillings ranging from pork and vegetables to mushrooms and bamboo shoots. Some, known as *jiao zi*, enclose the filling in a very thin dough skin while others use a dough made from a glutinous rice flour. There are also steamed buns, which are known as *bao zi*, filled with meat or sweet bean paste.

The best way to experience the diversity and delicious flavours of dumplings is to indulge in *dim sum*, a wonderful procession of tasty morsels that the Cantonese have elevated almost to an art form. Although dumplings originated in northern China, it was in Canton that the practice developed of enjoying these snacks with tea at breakfast or lunch time.

Dim sum literally means dot on the heart and indicates a snack or refreshment, not a full-blown meal. Although the range of dishes available on a *dim sum* menu now embraces other specialities (spring rolls, wontons and spare ribs, for instance), dumplings remain the essential items.

What is more, unlike the majority of *dim sum*, which are so complicated to make, dumplings are comparatively simple to make at home. Both *jiao zi* and *bao zi* are available ready-made from Asian or Chinese stores – the former are sold uncooked and frozen, and the latter are ready-cooked and sold chilled.

Preparing and Cooking Dumplings

Frozen *jiao zi* should be cooked straight from the freezer. There are three different ways of cooking and serving them.

Poaching In China, the most common way of cooking dumplings is to poach them in boiling water for about 5 minutes. Add the dumplings to a pan of boiling water. Return to the boil, add a cupful of cold water and bring to the boil again. Repeat twice more, by which time the dumplings will be ready. Serve hot with a vinegar and soy sauce dip, chilli sauce or chilli oil.

Steaming The best way to do this is by using a bamboo steaming basket. Place the dumplings on a bed of lettuce or spinach leaves on the base of the steamer. Cover with a tight-fitting lid and cook for about 8 minutes. Serve hot with a dip.

Grilling/Broiling Dumplings cooked in this way are often called pot stickers. "Grilling" is a slightly misleading description because the dumplings are not actually grilled at all. They are fried, then steamed, in a flat frying pan. The result is dumplings that are crispy on the base, soft on top and juicy inside. Shallow-fry the dumplings in a frying pan, then add a small amount of boiling water and cover with a bamboo steamer lid. Cook until all the liquid has evaporated. Serve hot with a dip.

PEKING DUMPLINGS

These crescent-shaped dumplings are filled with minced pork, greens and spring onions (scallions) and seasoned with salt, sugar, soy sauce, rice wine and sesame oil. In northern China they are eaten for breakfast on New Year's Day, but are available all year round and are often served as snacks.

RICE DUMPLINGS

These are found in many parts of Asia. In China, *t'ang t'uan*, meaning boiled ball, are made of a kneaded glutinous rice dough. They usually have a savoury filling, such as pork, and are poached.

Yüan hsiao, which is traditionally eaten on the 15th day of the Chinese new year, are made from glutinous rice flour. They have a sweet, solid filling, made of crushed nuts, sugar and fat. The filling is rolled into a ball, dampened, then rolled in glutinous rice flour until well coated and then poached.

Mochi are sweet dumplings eaten at Japanese new year. They are made of glutinous rice dough, wrapped around red bean paste. They are always steamed.

PRAWN CRACKERS

Also called shrimp chips, these are made from fresh prawns (shrimp), starch, salt and sugar. They are popular as cocktail snacks, and some restaurants serve them while you wait for your order. The raw crackers are grey in colour. The small Chinese ones are not much bigger than a thumbnail, while those used in Indonesia are much larger. Once deep-fried, both types of cracker puff up to four or five times their original size, and become very pale. Ready-cooked crackers are also available. They are sold in sealed packets, but do not keep once opened, so should be eaten as soon as possible.

STEAMED BUNS

These are to Asia what baked bread is to the West, and *bao* (filled buns) are considered the Chinese fast food equivalent of Western hotdogs, burgers and sandwiches. There are two main types of steamed buns, either plain or filled.

The plain, unfilled buns are made from leavened dough and are treated in much the same way as plain boiled rice. They are intended to be eaten with cooked food.

The filled buns known as *bao zi*, meaning wraps, can be savoury or sweet. The sweet filled buns may contain either a lotus seed paste or a sweet bean paste filling and are usually eaten cold. Savoury *bao zi* come with a wide range of different fillings, the most common being pork, and a very popular type is filled with honey-roasted pork. Savoury buns are available ready-made, and are at their best eaten while they are still piping hot.

Also widely available ready-made, but uncooked, are what are known as Shanghai dumplings. These are small and round, much smaller than the steamed buns filled with honey-roasted pork. They consist of minced (ground) pork wrapped in a thin skin of unleavened dough.

hinese and Asian cooking makes great use of the wonderful array of fresh, exotic vegetables that are grown in the region. Some such as spring onions (scallions) and pak choi (bok choy) will be familiar, while others such as chayote and bitter melon may be unfamiliar. Many of these unusual vegetables can now be found in Chinese and Asian supermarkets.

CHINESE LEAVES

In the West, this member of the brassica family is generally called Chinese leaves, but it is also known as Chinese cabbage, Napa cabbage (in the US) or celery cabbage. It has long, pale green, crinkly leaves with a chunky white core. Chinese leaves are available in abundance from November through to April, but can be found all year round. There are three common varieties, which all look similar.

Chinese leaves have a crunchy texture and a delicate, slightly sweet aroma with a mild cabbage flavour that disappears when cooked. This versatile vegetable can be used in stir-fries, stews, soups or salads. It will absorb the flavours of any other ingredients with which it is cooked. Braised Chinese leaves are often served as a base for roasted meats or duck.

To prepare Chinese leaves, discard the outer layer of leaves and trim off the root, then cut the head crossways into shreds. You may prefer to wash the leaves before using in a salad, for instance. When stir-fried, Chinese leaves develop dark scorch marks. Restaurant chefs usually blanch the vegetable in boiling stock, which enhances the flavour, before frying.

Store Chinese leaves in the salad drawer of the refrigerator and they will stay fresh for up to 12 days. Tiny black specks on the leaves are quite normal.

PAK CHOI/BOK CHOY

This is another member of the brassica family. In the West it is sometimes known as horse's ear (from the shape of the leaves) or Chinese white cabbage. The glossy, dark green leaves are a distinctive feature of this vegetable. The stalks, however, are pale, and range from light green to ivory white. Pak choi is a perennial, and several varieties are available throughout the year.

Although pak choi is less delicate than Chinese leaves and does not taste as sweet, it has a distinctive flavour that is a sort of cross between a mild cabbage and spinach. Pak choi can be used in soups and stir-fries, and is delicious when quickly braised, but should not be subjected to prolonged stewing. It is interchangeable with Chinese leaves in most dishes, even though their colour and flavour are quite different.

Pak choi is prepared in much the same way as Chinese leaves, except the stems are as important as the leaves. It is a good idea to separate them for cooking, as the stems take slightly longer to cook. Baby pak choi can be cooked whole or in halves or quarters. Only when very young and tender can pak choi be eaten raw.

Try to use pak choi as soon as you buy it because the leaves will start to wilt, and the outer leaves will turn yellow after 2–3 days, much sooner than lettuce and spinach.

CHOI SUM

This is a Cantonese word, meaning cabbage heart. Choi sum is a member of the brassica family and is related to oilseed rape. It has bright green leaves and thin, pale green stalks that are slightly grooved. The bright yellow flowers at the centre are responsible for its common name of flowering cabbage.

Choi sum has a pleasant aroma with a mild taste, and remains crisp and tender when correctly cooked. It is very popular is Asian cooking and can be used for soups or stir-fries, either on its own or cooked with other ingredients.

To prepare choi sum, wash under cold running water, then shake off the excess water and separate the stalks before use. Cut the leaves into large pieces or leave whole. Most restaurant chefs leave the stalks whole, blanch them in boiling stock for just a few minutes, then serve hot with oyster sauce.

Choi sum can be kept in the salad drawer of a refrigerator for about 3 days if bought fresh, but ideally should be used as soon after purchase as possible.

MUSTARD GREENS

Although this vegetable is related to choi sum it looks and tastes completely different. In shape, it resembles a cos or romaine lettuce. Unlike many Asian vegetables, which were relatively unknown outside their country of origin until recently, mustard greens have long been cultivated in Europe. However, the dark green, slightly puckered leaves were always thrown away; only the seeds were prized. It took the Chinese to introduce us to the delicious flavour of the leaves. Mustard greens are most abundant during the winter and spring, especially from Asian groceries, but also from specialist producers.

Although the leaves resemble lettuce, the similarity ends there. The leaves have a robust, often quite fiery flavour and can taste rather bitter. Very young leaves can be eaten raw in salads; mature leaves are best stir-fried or simmered in soups. Fresh mustard greens should be blanched in salted water before stir-frying, to preserve the green colour and remove some of their slightly bitter taste. In China, most of the crop is salted and preserved.

Provided they are fresh when you buy them, mustard greens can be stored in the salad compartment of a refrigerator and will keep for several days.

CHINESE BROCCOLI

This vegetable has more in common with purple sprouting broccoli than the plump, tight heads of dark green calabrese broccoli familiar to most Western shoppers. It has long, slender stems, loose leaves and tiny white or yellow flowers in the centre.

Chinese broccoli belongs to the same family as mustard greens, but has a more robust flavour and texture. It has a definite cabbage flavour. Every part of the plant is edible. It is often served as a side dish, but can be combined with other ingredients.

To prepare Chinese broccoli, discard the tough outer leaves, then peel off any tough skin from the stalks. Leave each stalk whole if it is to be served on its own, or cut into two or three short sections if it is to be cooked with other ingredients. Before stir-frying, blanch the vegetable briefly in salted boiling water to enhance the flavour.

Chinese broccoli will keep for only a few days, even if it is very fresh when bought. After that the leaves will wilt and yellow, and the stalks are liable to become tough.

AUBERGINE/EGGPLANT

There are many varieties of this vegetable. Although it belongs to the same family as tomatoes and (bell) peppers that originated in America, the aubergine is actually native to tropical Asia, where it has been cultivated for more than 2,000 years.

The most common variety in Asia – the Asian or Japanese aubergine – is tubular rather than ovoid in shape and is usually straight or slightly curved. As a rule, Asian aubergines tend to be much smaller and more slender than Western varieties – some are only the size of large peas. Aubergines come in a wide variety of colours from black, purple, orange or green to the white egg-shaped vegetables that inspired their American name of eggplant.

Aubergine has a unique, mild flavour that is almost smoky and subtly bitter. Its spongy texture absorbs other flavours well. It can be stir-fried, deep-fried, braised, stuffed and baked or steamed. In Thailand, strips of very young raw aubergine are served like crudités, with spicy dips.

To prepare, wash the aubergine and cut off the chunky stalk, then cut the flesh into slices, strips or chunks. It is very seldom necessary to peel an aubergine.

When buying, select small- to medium-size firm aubergines that have a smooth, blemish-free skin. Large specimens with a wrinkled skin are overmature and are likely to be bitter and tough. Aubergines bought in prime condition will keep for 3–4 days in the salad drawer of a refrigerator.

SALTING AUBERGINES/EGGPLANT
Some recipes advise layering aubergine slices with salt before cooking. This is not essential if the vegetables are young and tender, but in older specimens it will help to reduce bitterness and prevent the slices absorbing excessive amounts of oil during cooking. If you salt an auberine, be sure to rinse and dry it thoroughly afterwards.

Another method that helps to stop the aubergine from drawing up too much oil, but which retains its succulent texture, is to dry fry the slices over a medium heat for 5 minutes before cooking them in oil.

CHAYOTE

This pear-shaped marrow is also known as vegetable pear and custard marrow. In the Caribbean, chayote is called *christophine*. The Chinese call it Buddha's fist because it resembles hands clasped in prayer, with the fingers folded inside. It has a smooth, pale green skin with a subtle aroma. The taste is delicate and the texture is fairly firm not unlike that of courgette (zucchini).

Because of the religious connotations of its shape, chayote is often used as an offering at Buddhist festivals. It can be eaten raw or cooked, and is usually stir-fried or simmered in soups. It does not need peeling but should be washed, cut open to remove the stone, then cut into thin slices or strips. Since chayote has a mild flavour, Asian cooks favour cooking it with strong seasonings such as garlic, fresh ginger, onion and/or chillies.

Chayote keeps quite well and can be stored for up to a week in the salad drawer of the refrigerator.

MOOLI/DAIKON

This large, thin, cylindrical vegetable looks rather like a carrot, but with a thin, smooth, white skin. It is a member of the radish family and is also known as the oriental radish. Believed to be native to China, the mooli is widely cultivated in many parts of the world.

It has an unmistakeable, pungent smell of radish. The texture is crisp and the flavour is quite mild, with a juicy, sweet taste similar to turnip. Mooli can be eaten raw or cooked. Both the Chinese and Japanese also pickle it. Cantonese cooks use mooli to make a stiff pudding with rice flour, which is often served as part of the *dim sum* selection in a restaurant. At home, mooli is usually braised with meat such as pork or beef, but it is also delicious in a stir-fry.

To prepare mooli, scrape or peel, then cut into slices or chunks. The beauty of this vegetable is that it withstands long cooking without disintegrating and absorbs the flavours of other ingredients, and also tastes good raw. When stir-frying, add slices for the last few minutes of cooking so that it stays very crisp and juicy.

Buy mooli with firm, unblemished skin. Store in a cool, dark place or in the salad drawer of the refrigerator for 3–4 days.

BITTER MELON

Also called bitter gourd, this warty-skinned vegetable originated in South-east Asia, and is very popular in Indonesia, the Philippines and Thailand, where it is used as the basis for delicious curries. The plant resembles a wild grape vine, and is grown in the West mainly as an ornament for its attractive foliage and strange-looking fruit.

As its name suggests, the flesh of this vegetable tastes quite bitter, especially when green and immature, but it has a sweet and fragrant smell. The flavour mellows as the vegetable ripens and turns first pale green, then yellow-orange (when it is past its best).

The bitter flavour of winter melon may be an acquired taste, but it has a cooling effect in a hot climate and it is highly regarded throughout Asia. The flesh readily absorbs other flavours and its bitter tang can provide a wonderful accent to a dish.

Since the odd-looking skin is a feature of the winter melon, it is never peeled. To prepare, wash, slice in half lengthways, remove and discard the seeds, then cut into slices or chunks. Blanch in salted water for 2 minutes to remove excess bitterness, then drain before stir-frying or adding to soups.

Firm, green bitter melon will keep for about 3 days (and should be allowed to ripen a little before use), but a soft yellowish one should be used within 2 days.

WINTER MELON

This is one of the largest vegetables grown in Asia, or anywhere else. Winter melons can grow to 25cm/10in in diameter, and weigh more than 25kg/55lb but small ones are available too. The larger specimens are usually sliced and sold in sections.

Winter melon has a subtle, delicate taste rather like courgette (zucchini). Despite its name, it is actually a warm season vegetable and since it is 90 per cent water, it is popular in hot weather as it is juicy yet not too filling. It is always cooked before being eaten.

Winter melon is prepared in much the same way as pumpkin. The rind must be cut off and the seeds and coarse fibres at the centre scooped out before the flesh is cut into thin strips or wedges. It tastes good in stir-fries or soups. It readily absorbs other flavours and is often cooked with strong-tasting ingredients such as dried shrimps, ham and dried mushrooms.

A whole winter melon will keep for days if not weeks but, once cut open, it should be eaten as soon as possible as the exposed surface will deteriorate rapidly.

ONIONS

These are so commonly used in the West that in Asia, the common onion is known as foreign onion, where shallots and spring onions (scallions) are generally preferred. They come in a wide variety of sizes and colours from huge golden-skinned globes to smaller, milder red and white onions.

There is no mistaking the strong aroma and flavour of the onion. It is used as a flavouring ingredient throughout Asia, but seldom served on its own as a side vegetable. It can be fried, boiled, steamed or eaten raw and is an essential component in a great number of sauces, curries and stews. Fried onions are a very popular garnish, especially in South-east Asia.

To prepare, peel the onions and remove the papery skin, then slice and chop as required. To avoid watering eyes, leave the root intact until the last minute and, when the root is exposed, press it down on the chopping board rather than exposing it.

Buy firm onions with smooth, unmarked skins. Store them in a cool, dry place where they will keep for several weeks. If any show signs of sprouting, use them at once.

SHALLOTS

These belong to the onion family and look very like baby onions. They have bulbs that multiply to produce clusters joined at the root end. Shallots tend to be sweeter and milder than large onions and some Thai varieties are actually sweet enough to be used in desserts.

In South-east Asia, shallots are far more popular than onions and spring onions (scallions) for everyday use. Minced with garlic, ginger and aromatics, shallots form the standard marinade and are also essential in curry pastes and satay sauce. Dried shallots are popular in Vietnam.

To prepare, top and tail the shallots, peel off the skin, then prize the bulbs apart. Leave the bulbs whole for braising, or chop thinly. Shallot rings are sometimes deep-fried and used as a garnish.

Shallots can be stored in a cool, dry place for several months.

Spring Onions/Scallions

These are also known as green onions. The leaves are tubular in shape, and are always sold with the bulb attached. Japanese spring onions are larger than the European ones and have blue-green stems.

Spring onions are more subtle in aroma and flavour than onions and the taste can vary from very mild to really pungent. Smaller bulbs tend to have a milder flavour than larger ones. In Asia, spring onions are served as a vegetable as well as being used as a flavouring agent. The vegetable forms a yin-yang pair when used in combination with ginger. Sping onions are ying and ginger is yang.

To prepare, trim off the roots and discard any wilted outer leaves, then separate the green and white outer parts and cut these into short lengths or shreds. If the green part is used, it is usually added at the last moment (the white part takes longer to cook) or simply used raw as a garnish.

Making Spring Onion Curls

These make an attractive garnish. Trim the green to 7.5cm/3in. Finely shred the spring onions to within about 1cm/½in of the root end, then place in iced water. Chill for 15–20 minutes, or until the shredded ends have curled.

It is best not to keep spring onions in a plastic bag, but instead store them loose in the salad compartment of the refrigerator to allow them to breathe. That way, if bought in prime condition, spring onions should remain fresh for 4–5 days.

Chinese Chives

Although related to Western chives, Chinese chives are quite different. Two species are available: one has long, flat green leaves like a small, thin leek, the other has long, tubular stalks with a single bud at the tip. Both have a stronger aroma than chives grown in the West. Their flavour is a cross between garlic and leek.

Chinese chives are served as a vegetable in their own right or used as an ingredient in cooked dishes. A very popular Chinese vegetarian dish features chopped chives cooked with scrambled eggs and tofu.

Chinese chives are always sold without the bulb. The leaves should be uniformly dark green and any turning yellow should be discarded. To prepare, wash well, drain, then chop or slice into short sections. Cantonese cooks often blanch chives for 1–2 minutes before stir-frying.

Fresh chives, stored in an airtight box in the refrigerator, should keep for 4–5 days.

Potatoes and Sweet Potatoes

These are actually unrelated but, when they first reached Asia, they were given the same name. In northern China white potatoes are a staple food; in the south they are less significant. Sweet potatoes are popular in the Philippines.

Several varieties of regular potatoes and sweet potatoes are grown in the East. Sweet potatoes have a red skin and flesh that varies from pale white to yellow-orange.

Potatoes and sweet potatoes generally form part of a braised dish, or are served as a side dish or snack. Thai cooks make a dessert with deep-fried sweet potatoes.

Both types of potato are prepared in the same way. They are first peeled, then sliced or diced and stir-fried or braised.

Potatoes should be stored in a cool, dark, dry place. Sweet potatoes do not keep well.

TAROES

These tubers are widely used in South-east Asia. There are two basic varieties: the more common big, barrel-shaped one with hairy, brown skin, and a smaller variety, known in the West as eddo or dasheen. The flesh is white with purple flecks.

Cooked taro has a subtle flavour that has been likened to floury water chestnuts. They can be used in place of potatoes in most dishes and are good in stews. They are often added to fatty meat dishes.

Taroes contain toxins just below the skin, which are eliminated when the vegetable is cooked. To prepare, peel thickly, wearing gloves, then boil.

Store taroes in a cool, dark, dry place. They have a thick skin so keep well.

YAMS

Thought to have originated in China, yams are now grown in all tropical regions. The Chinese yam has fine whiskers and the flesh is creamy white. They have a mildly sweet flavour and are quite juicy.

Like taroes, yams can be used instead of potatoes. Asian cooks often use them as a substitute for bamboo shoots. To prepare, peel thickly, removing both the outer skin and the layer underneath. They contain a toxin that is eliminated when boiled. Slice or dice the flesh and boil in salted water.

Store yams in a cool, dark, dry place.

LOTUS ROOT

Also known as *renkon*, lotus root is used throughout Asia. Raw lotus root looks like a string of fat sausages covered in black mud. When sliced, a pattern emerges in each cross-section, a result of the narrow channels that run through the root. Fresh lotus roots can be purchased from Asian stores. Canned lotus root is also available, and dried slices are used in soups.

Lotus root has little aroma, the taste is mild and subtly sweet. It has a wonderfully crunchy texture. The root is used as a vegetable and the seeds are eaten as a fruit when fresh, or used as a dessert when dried. They can also be puréed and blended with sugar to make a filling for cakes and buns. Dried lotus leaves are used for wrapping food in a number of Asian dishes.

To prepare fresh lotus root, scrub, chop into sections, discarding the necks, then peel off the outer skin. The flesh is sliced or cut into chunks, but whole roots can be stuffed. Japanese cooks often soak the slices in acidulated water for about 5 minutes before boiling. They cook quickly and make a pretty garnish. Canned lotus root is ready for use. Dried lotus roots are sold sliced, and should be soaked in water for about 2 hours before using in soups or stews.

Fresh lotus root should keep for 4 days. Select firm and unblemished roots. Dried roots will keep almost indefinitely if stored in a dry, cool place.

DRIED LILY BUDS

Known in China as yellow flower or golden needles, these dried buds of the tiger lily are very popular. The unique fragrance of the tiger lily intensifies when the buds are dried. They have a mild sweet flavour and a pleasant crunchy texture.

In Chinese cooking, dried lily buds are often combined with wood ears (dried black fungus.) The buds are also used in Buddhist vegetarian cooking. Before adding to dishes, the dried buds must be soaked in warm water for 30 minutes, then drained and rinsed in cold water. Once the hard ends have been snipped off, the buds can be used whole or cut in half.

Dried lily buds will keep almost indefinitely in an airtight jar away from light, heat or moisture.

BAMBOO SHOOTS

The shoots of the bamboo that are used as a vegetable are dug just before they come above ground. Fresh bamboo shoots are hard to find in the West but canned shoots are available. Pickled bamboo shoots are popular with Vietnamese cooks.

Bamboo shoots have a delicate aroma and a mild sweet flavour, which some claim changes subtly with the seasons. As a result, winter bamboo shoots are highly prized.

In China, they are regarded as the queen of all vegetables. The shoots taste delicious on their own but also complement other ingredients with which they are cooked.

If you manage to find fresh shoots, it is vital to par-boil them before cooking, as they contain an acid that is highly toxic. To prepare, remove the base and the hard outer leaves, then cut into chunks. Boil in salted water for 20–30 minutes, then drain, rinse in clean water and drain again. Slice, shred or cube for further cooking. Canned bamboo shoots should be rinsed and drained before use. Dried bamboo shoots are tastier than canned and must be soaked in water for 2–3 hours before use.

Fresh shoots will keep for up to a week in winter but only 2–3 days in summer. Once opened, canned bamboo shoots can be stored in the refrigerator for several days in a jar of fresh water that is changed daily. Dried bamboo shoots can be stored almost indefinitely in a cool, dry place.

BEANSPROUTS

Several types of beans can be sprouted but the ones most used in Asian cooking are the small green sprouts from mung beans and the larger yellow soya bean sprouts. Fresh sprouts can be found in supermarkets and health food stores, or you can sprout the beans at home. Avoid canned beansprouts, which are limp and tasteless.

Soya bean sprouts have a stronger flavour than mung bean sprouts, but both are fairly delicate, with a crunchy texture. Stir-frying, is the most popular cooking method. Mung bean sprouts can be eaten in salads, while soya bean sprouts are often used in soups.

To prepare, wash the beansprouts in cold water to remove the husks and roots. Some restaurants actually top and tail each sprout, which turns this humble vegetable into a luxurey dish. Since the sprouts are largely composed of water, overcooking will render them limp and fibrous.

Store beansprouts in water in a covered box in the refrigerator. They will stay fresh for 2–3 days.

WATER CHESTNUTS

These are popular throughout Asia. They are not actually nuts but corms, which are about the size of walnuts. There are several varieties, but the Chinese type, which are dark brown and look similar to small dafodil bulbs, are the most widely available outside Asia. They have a soft skin, which, because they grow in water, tends to be covered in dried dirt. Fresh ones are far superior to canned. The snow-white flesh is crunchy and juicy and stays that way no matter how long they are cooked. They have a sweet taste.

Water chestnuts can be eaten raw in both savoury and sweet salads. They are also eaten as a snack. Cooked water chestnuts are good in stir-fries or braised dishes. Fresh water chestnuts should be washed and peeled before use. Canned or fresh, they can be left whole, sliced or diced, and are sometimes minced with fish or meat.

Fresh, unpeeled water chestnuts will keep well in a paper bag in the salad drawer in the refrigerator. Once peeled, water chestnuts can be kept in water in a covered container in the refrigerator for up to a week.

HORNED WATER CHESTNUTS

Often confused with the water chestnut, these have a hard, shiny black shell with two sharp horns. The nuts measure about 5cm/2in and the hard shells enclose pale, sweet-tasting flesh. The nuts are never eaten raw, but can be steamed or boiled, added to soups or braised in stews.

Horned water chestnuts can be bought in Asian and Chinese stores and will keep for several weeks in the refrigerator. Once shelled, use within 2 days.

LUFFA

Also known as angled luffa, silk gourd, silk squash or Chinese okra, this vegetable looks like a large okra pod. The common variety is ridged and dark green. The rarer smooth luffa is larger, more cylindrical, with a thicker base, heavier and paler. Both have a mild, delicate taste, similar to cucumber.

Luffa is used mostly in stir-fries and soups and goes well with chicken, fish, shellfish and other vegetables. To prepare, peel the ridges of older luffas. If the skin is very tough, peel completely. It is always cooked.

Keep luffa in the salad compartment of the refrigerator for 2–3 days.

BABY CORN COBS

These are available both fresh and canned, fresh being superior. Baby corn has a sweet aroma and flavour, and a crunchy texture.

Baby cobs can be used in salads, stir-fries and soups. They are good combined with other vegetables such as (bell) peppers, broccoli and mangetouts (snow peas).

To prepare fresh cobs, wash, then halve or slice large ones. Asian cooks blanch them in salted water for 1 minute before stir-frying. Drain and rinse canned cobs.

Fresh baby corn cobs will keep for a week in the salad drawer of the refrigerator.

SNAKE BEANS

Also called yard-long beans, asparagus beans or Thai beans, snake beans resemble green beans but are much longer. There are two types – pale and dark green, the darker and thinner being the best. When young they are sweeter and more tender than green beans, but mature beans can be tough and need longer cooking.

Snake beans are usually stir-fried, either on their own or with other ingredients, or served cold as a salad after blanching. Wash and cut into 5cm/2in lengths. They go well with pork, chicken or prawns. In Sichuan, they are used in a dish called *kan shao*, with garlic, ginger or chillies.

Use snake beans within 3 days of purchase before they turn yellow and become stringy.

MANGETOUTS/SNOW PEAS

These must be one of the best-known and best loved of all Asian vegetables. The French name *mangetout* means eat all and is an apt description since the vegetable is eaten in its entirety – pod and all. Sugar snap peas are quite similar but have slightly plumper pods. Freshly picked mangetouts have a fresh aroma, but this vanishes quite quickly. The flavour is slightly sweet.

To prepare, simply wash, then top and tail the pods. Leave whole or snap in half. Mangetouts can be stir-fried on their own, or with other vegetables such as carrots and baby corn cobs. Cook briefly and be careful not to overseason. Mangetouts are perfect partners for shellfish.

Mangetouts will keep fresh for 4–5 days in the salad drawer of the refrigerator.

MUSHROOMS

The Chinese and Asian cuisines make good use of the wonderful and unusual selection of mushrooms and fungi that can be found in the region. Many varieties are available, both fresh and dried, and they impart a delicious flavour and aroma to numerous dishes. Some varieties such as oyster mushrooms have an almost meaty texture, while others such as enoki mushrooms are very delicate.

SHIITAKE

These fungi grow on hardwood logs in their native Japan. They resemble brown open-cap mushrooms. Shiitake are available fresh, dried or canned. They have a meaty, slippery texture and taste slightly acidic.

Although small mushrooms can be eaten raw, cooking brings out their flavour. They are used in soups, stir-fries and braised dishes, and go well with noodles and rice.

The stems of fresh shiitake mushrooms are usually removed before cooking. They need a slightly longer cooking time than button (white) mushrooms, but do not overcook or they will toughen. For salad, boil briefly, then toss in French dressing.

Store fresh shiitake mushrooms in a paper bag in the refrigerator for up to 3 days.

OYSTER MUSHROOMS

In the wild, these mushrooms grow in clumps on rotting wood, but they are now grown commercially. The caps, gills and stems are all the same colour, which can be pearl grey, pink or yellow. They have a fairly mild flavour, with a suggestion of seafood.

Oyster mushrooms are used in soups, stir-fries, and noodle and rice dishes. Large mushrooms should be torn, rather than cut. If overcooked, they can become rubbery.

Store oyster mushrooms in a paper bag in the vegetable drawer of the refrigerator, and use as soon as possible after purchase.

ENOKI MUSHROOMS

These delicate mushrooms have long, thin stems and tiny white caps and are popular in China and Japan. Avoid canned ones. Fresh mushrooms have a delicate, sweet, almost fruity flavour, and a crisp texture.

Enoki mushrooms can be added raw to salads or cooked lightly and used to garnish soups or hot dishes. To prepare, cut the mushrooms from the spongy root base. Add to soups or braised dishes just before serving. They are also good in stir-fried dishes but only cook for a minute.

Enoki mushrooms will keep for 4–5 days in the salad compartment of a refrigerator.

STRAW MUSHROOMS

These small, grey-brown mushrooms are grown on beds of rice straw. Fresh straw mushrooms are not readily available in the West, but dried and canned ones can be found in Asian or Chinese stores. Dried ones have a stronger aroma than dried black mushrooms. Canned ones have a delicate, silky surface with a subtle, sweet taste and an unusual slippery texture.

Straw mushrooms can be combined with all sorts of ingredients in soups, stir-fries and braised dishes. They are used for making mushroom soy sauce. Canned straw mushrooms must be drained and rinsed before use. They are usually cut in half lengthways. Straw mushrooms must not be overcooked, especially canned ones.

Fresh straw mushrooms should be used immediately. Dried ones can be stored almost indefinitely.

DRIED BLACK MUSHROOMS/FRAGRANT MUSHROOMS

Sometimes referred to as Chinese mushrooms, these are widely used in Asia and are exported around the world. There are generally three different grades of dried black mushrooms, with caps that range in colour from dark grey, to brown-black or tan. The cheapest are fragrant mushrooms; next come winter mushrooms; the most expensive are flower mushrooms. All three have a dusky aroma and fragrant flavour, much intensified by drying.

Dried black mushrooms can be stir-fried, braised, steamed and used in soups. They are an ideal partner for bamboo shoots, and go well with seafood, poultry and meat. They must be soaked in cold water for several hours or overnight, depending on the thickness of the caps. If short of time, soak in warm water for about 30 minutes. The strained soaking water will enrich the flavour of the dish.

After soaking squeeze dry and discard the stalks. Small mushrooms can be left whole, but larger ones should be halved, quartered or coarsely chopped. The thinner dried mushrooms are usually thinly sliced or shredded, but thicker ones, particularly flower mushrooms are generally left whole.

Dried black mushrooms will keep for over a year in a dry, dark and cool place.

PREPARING DRIED MUSHROOMS

Dried mushrooms have a rich, intense flavour. Once they have been soaked they can be stir-fried, braised, steamed and used in soups. Soaked, dried mushrooms often require slightly longer cooking than fresh ones.

Soak the mushrooms in boiling water for 20–30 minutes, until tender. Drain and rinse well to remove any grit.

WOOD EARS

Also known as cloud ears, tree mushrooms or dried black fungus, these are widely used in China, Thailand and Vietnam. The dried fungi are brittle and look like charred paper. They are almost flavourless, but have a slippery yet crisp texture.

Wood ears are used in stir-frying, braising and soups. They are often paired with dried tiger lily in Chinese dishes. They need to be soaked before cooking and expand to six or eight times their volume after soaking, so use plenty of water in a large bowl. Soak for 30 minutes, then drain, rinse and drain again. Discard any hard roots and sandy bits. Do not cut the fungus but separate into individual ears.

Dried fungus will keep almost indefinitely in a dry, cool place. Keep fungus soaked in water in the refrigerator for up to 3 days.

SILVER EARS

These are also known as dried white fungus. They gained their Chinese name of silver ears because of their rarity, high price and medicinal value. Silver ears are fairly similar in texture to wood ears but have a sweeter flavour.

Silver ears are kept for special occasions, served on their own or cooked with other vegetables. Dried silver ears are prepared, cooked and stored as for dried wood ears.

PRESERVED & PICKLED VEGETABLES

These play an important part in the Asian diet. In the days before refrigeration and rapid transportation, fresh food had to be preserved for the lean months of the year and also so that it could be conveyed to regions that were often a long way from the source of supply. Most vegetables are preserved in salt and are often flavoured with herbs, spices and aromatics.

Some of the best know preserved and pickled vegetables include *kimchee*, the tart, garlicky cabbage pickle that is served at almost every Korean meal and the Chinese sweet mixed pickles that are now an American favourite. In Japan, pickled vegetables are hugely popular, while in Indonesia, cooks relish *atjar kuning*, a mildly hot, yellow mixed pickle.

There are several different ways to presere and pickle food. The most common way is to use salt as a preservative, then dry the food in the sun or by another source of heat. Another age-old method is to partially dry the food, then pickle it in brine or a soy-based solution.

JAPANESE PICKLES

There are many varieties of Japanese pickles, which are known as *tsukemono*. They play an important part in the Japanese cuisine and barrel upon barrel of freshly made *tsukemono* are displayed in the food hall of any department store in Japan. You can sample them before buying.

The most popular types of vegetable used in Japanese pickles are mooli (daikon), pak choi (bok choy), cucumber, aubergine (eggplant), horseradish and the bulbs of spring onions (scallions). Thinly sliced, pale pink pickled ginger (*gari*) is traditionally served with *sushi* and *sashimi*.

Rather than being pickled in brine or vinegar, Japanese pickled vegetables are preserved with salt in wooden barrels. The vegetables are layered with salt then, when the barrel is full, a lid is put on top, and this is weighted down with a large stone or similar weight. The combined effect of the salt and the compression forces the liquid out of the vegetables and they are pickled in their own juices. Salting takes away the coarseness of hard vegetables and makes them soft and digestible as well as preserving them. It also helps to add more depth of flavour.

Other pickling agents include rice bran, miso, sake or mirin pulps, mustard, rice malt (*koji*) or shoyu, together with salt.

Japanese pickles form an essential part of a meal. They may be served as a relish to accompany the cooked food, as a dessert at the end of a meal or, alternativly, as a means of cleansing the palate. They are either served singly or in groups of two or three, always beautifully arranged in small individual dishes.

CHINESE PICKLES

There is a wide range of Chinese pickles available in the West. Some appear in packets, some in jars and some in cans. A pickle may consist of a single ingredient such as ginger, garlic, spring onion (scallion) bulbs, chillies, cabbage, cucumber, gourd, runner beans, bamboo shoots, carrots or mooli (daikon) or a mixture. Individual items are generally pickled in a dark soy sauce solution, while mixed vegetables tend to be pickled in clear brine to which Sichuan peppercorns, distilled spirit, sugar and fresh root ginger have been added, with chillies and vinegar as optional ingredients. The cleaned vegetables are pickled in the brine solution in a sealed earthenware urn. This is left in a cool, dark place for at least a week in summer, or up to a month in winter. The longer the pickling process, the better the taste.

SICHUAN PRESERVED VEGETABLE

This pickle, made from the stems of mustard cabbage, originated in Sichuan province, but is now made in other parts of China. The stems are dried in the sun, then pickled in brine. After being trimmed and cleaned, they are pressed to extract excess liquid (its Mandarin name *zhacai* means pressed vegetable), before being blended with chillies and spices and stored in sealed urns to mature.

Sichuan preserved vegetable has a unique pungent aroma that may not appeal to the uninitiated. It has a smooth and crunchy texture and a salty, peppery flavour.

Unlike most other types of preserved and pickled vegetables, Sichuan preserved vegetable is a very versatile ingredient. It is not merely served raw as a relish to be eaten with cooked dishes, but is also cooked along with other foods in stir-fries, soups and steamed dishes.

Because of its strong hot and salty flavour, Sichuan preserved vegetable is often rinsed in water cold running water to remove some of the excess salt and chillies before use. Place the preserved vegetable in a strainer, rinse under cold water, drain well, then slice or finely shred.

Sichuan preserved vegetable is normally sold in cans, although you may be able to buy the pickle loose in some Chinese and Asian stores. Any unused pickle should be transferred to an airtight container and stored in the refrigerator, where it will keep almost indefinitely.

PICKLED BAMBOO SHOOTS

These are a great delicacy in Vietnam. Sliced shoots are preserved in spiced vinegar, giving quite a sour result. Before use, the shoots should be soaked in water to remove some of the bitterness. They are mainly used in soups and stocks, and are often served with duck.

PICKLED GARLIC

This sweet-and-sour pickle is very popular in Thailand. Small, whole garlic bulbs are preserved in a sweet-and-sour brine.

PICKLED FRUITS

Although used to a lesser extent than preserved and pickled vegetables, pickled fruit such as pickled plums are also important in Asian cooking.

Umeboshi These small pickled plums are a particular Japanese delicacy. This is one of the most important preserved foods in Japan and housewives often still make their own umeboshi *every year. Plums are picked before they are fully ripe and are then pickled in salt, with red shiso leaves to give them their distinctive purplish-red colour. They have a sharp and salty taste and are often chopped and used as a filling for rice balls.*

Pickled limes These are a great speciality in Thailand. Whole limes are preserved in brine or a mixture of soy sauce, sugar, salt and vinegar.

Seaweed

These sea plants are widely used in Chinese and Asian cooking and are particularly popular in Japan. There are many different varieties of edible seaweed, which can be served poached or boiled as a vegetable, added to salads and soups or used to flavour stocks such as *dashi*. Many varieties are sold dried and simply need to be soaked in water before use.

Kombu

This giant seaweed is one of the most common seaweeds used in Asian cooking, especially in Japan and Korea. Known as *kombu* in Japanese, *haidai* in Chinese and kelp in English, this is a large group of brown seaweeds. Kombu is only available in dried form in the West, usually labelled as kombu or konbu.

Kombu is full of vitamins and minerals, and is particularly rich in iodine. It has a strong "sea" flavour and a crunchy texture. It is mainly used in soups in China, but is served poached or stewed as a vegetable in Japan, as well as being used to flavour the fish stock known as *dashi*.

To prepare kombu, just wipe the seaweed with a damp cloth. Do not wash off its pale powdery covering because it contributes to its flavour. Cut the wiped sheet into pieces of the required size, then soak in cold water for about 45 minutes. Both the seaweed and soaking water are used.

Kombu will keep for a long time if stored in a dry, cool place away from strong light.

Nori

This is the wafer-thin, dried seaweed that is mainly used as a wrapping for *sushi*, *nori* being its Japanese name. It is also known as laver. It is a relatively small, reddish brown seaweed with a distinctive shape. It is dried before use and sold in sheets that are dark green to black, and almost transparent in places. The sheet should be grilled (broiled) lightly on one side for making *sushi*, or on both sides until crisp if it is to be crumbled and used as a topping. Nori is sometimes eaten on its own with soy sauce or eaten with rice. It is also used to wrap *omusubi* (rice balls containing a pickled plum).

Ready-toasted sheets known as *yaki-nori* are available from Asian stores. These are seasoned with ingredients such as soy sauce, salt and sesame oil. *Ao-nori* is dried nori seaweed that is crumbled so finely that it looks like powder.

Wakame

This young, dark-coloured seaweed is the most widely eaten seaweed in Japan and, in recent years, has accounted for over half of all seaweed consumed there. Wakame grows in wide fronds, with a thick central rib and lobes on the sides. It has a delicate flavour and soft but crisp texture.

Wakame is available shredded, fresh (vacuum-packed) or dried, and is used in soups and salads. Dried wakame should be soaked in tepid water for 10–15 minutes until it softens and the fronds turn green. At this stage it should be drained, blanched in boiling water for about 1 minute, then refreshed under cold water and drained again. Use as directed in recipes or cool and chop to use in a salad. Only cook wakame very briefly as cooking destroys its large supplies of valuable nutrients.

Hijik

Also called hijiki, this twiggy black marine algae is very popular in Japan. It can grow up to 1m/3ft long and can be found all around the Japanese coast. It has a nutty flavour and a crisp, almost tough texture.

Hijik is cooked and dried and sold in packets in Asian stores. It is usually shallow-fried, then simmered in a soy-based sauce with other vegetables. It is often used with slices of fried tofu. It is also used to garnish rice dishes such as *sushi* and rice balls as its black, twig-like shape provides an attractive contrast to the rice.

Before use it should be soaked in tepid water for 10–15 minutes until soft, then blanched for 1 minute in boiling water and refreshed under cold water.

Agar-agar

This gelatinous substance is also known as *kanten*, grass jelly, seaweed jelly and Japanese or vegetable gelatine. It is obtained from the seaweed known as rock-flower vegetable. Agar-agar is available from Thai, Asian and health food stores as long dried strips or as a fine white powder sold in tubes. It is a very popular setting agent, especially for vegetarians.

Agar-agar has no aroma and is entirely flavourless, but will absorb the seasonings with which it is prepared for serving. Asian cooks sometimes use soaked strips of agar-agar in salads, just as they would any other form of seaweed, but it is more often used as a setting agent, usually to make sweet jellies. Japanese cooks use agar-agar to make a very stiff, coloured jelly, from which pretty shapes such as leaves and fruit are cut. Agar-agar is also used as a thickener for sauces and soups such as bird's nest soup.

To use agar-agar in a salad, soften the strips in lukewarm water for 25 minutes, then drain and dry them on some kitchen paper. Separate the strips and cut them into short lengths. Combine the agar-agar with the other salad ingredients, add a dressing and toss to mix.

To use agar-agar to set a jelly, dissolve it slowly in a pan of water over a very low heat, which may take up to 10 minutes. Heat some milk and sugar, with a flavouring such as almond essence (extract), in a separate pan, then mix with the agar-agar solution. Leave the mixture to cool, then chill in the refrigerator for about 4 hours, or until set. Agar-agar varies in strength, so check the packaging to see how much you should use. As a general guide, 5ml/1 tsp powder will set about 300ml/½ pint/1¼ cups of liquid.

Agar-agar, both in dried strips and in the powdered form, can be stored almost indefinitely in a cool, dry place.

Dashi

This stock, based on kombu and dried bonito flakes, is used as the base of most Japanese soups; it can also be used instead of water in any dish that requires a delicately flavoured stock. This recipe makes 800ml/27fl oz/3½ cups of dashi.

1 Wipe a 10cm/4in square of kombu with a damp cloth; cut it into 3–4 strips and put in a pan. Pour over 900ml/1½ pints/3¾ cups water, making sure that the seaweed is submerged, and soak for about an hour.

2 Place the pan over a medium heat. Just before the water boils, lift out the kombu (shred and use for soup).

3 Stir 40g/1½oz dried bonito flakes into the water, bring to the boil, remove the pan from the heat and leave to stand until the flakes have sunk. Strain through a strainer lined with muslin (cheesecloth).

FRUIT

There are many delicious fruits that are grown in China and Asia. Some such as bananas and mangoes are very common in the West and can be found in any supermarket. Others such as durian and mangosteens are less familiar. However, these more unusual fruits are becoming increasingly available in Asian stores and larger supermarkets and are well worth trying.

BANANAS

These yellow fruits originated in South-east Asia and have grown in the tropics since ancient times. There are hundreds of varieties from very small, squat bananas to the large, curved dessert fruits that are most commonly found in the West.

Under the skin they have pale yellow, smooth, sweet flesh with a mild flavour. They can be eaten raw but are also delicious cooked. Cooking enhances the flavour and gives a very sweet, soft result. In the classic Indonesian dish *pisang goreng*, very small bananas are dipped in batter and deep-fried.

Perfectly ripe bananas have a uniformly yellow skin. Do not buy ones with damaged skins or those with a brown-speckled skin as this indicates they are over-ripe. Unlike other fruit, bananas will continue to ripen at home. Never store in the refrigerator as the skins will blacken. Baby bananas canned in a heavy syrup can be found in Asian stores, but they are extremely sweet.

DURIAN

This tropical fruit originated in Malaysia or Borneo, and is very popular in South-east Asia. Round or oval, it has a dull green shell-like skin covered with pointed spines that turn yellow as the fruit ripens. A typical durian weighs about 2kg/4½lb, but they can grow even larger, up to 4.5kg/10lb.

Durian has a very unpleasant smell, often likened to the stench of raw sewage. The ripe flesh, however, is as delicious as the odour is awful: sweet and creamy, with a hint of strawberries. The fruit is eaten raw, and the seeds are often roasted and eaten like nuts.

Each fruit consists of three, four or five segments. To prepare, use a sharp knife to slit the hard shell of the durian at the segment joints, then press the segments out. Take care not to let the juice drip on to your clothes, as it will stain. The soft, creamy flesh can be eaten with a spoon, or puréed, either for serving as a dessert or as an accompaniment to a curry. Some Asian cooks soak the durian segments in coconut milk for 10–12 hours before eating them, as they claim this helps to eliminate the fruit's very unpleasant odour.

Storing durians is not recommended, as the smell will soon pervade your home however carefully the fruit is stored. When buying durians, look for perfect specimens that are undamaged and get them home as quickly as possible.

MANGOSTEENS

These small, apple-shaped fruits are native to South-east Asia and are cultivated in Thailand. They have a leathery brown skin that turns purple as they ripen. The tough skin surrounds delicious white flesh, which looks similar to that of a lychee. The flesh is divided into segments, each of which contains a large seed.

The pearly white flesh is fresh and fragrant and has a very distinctive sharp-sweet flavour, which some say tastes a little like grapefruit. Mangosteens are always eaten raw, but the related kokum, which has a pleasant sour flavour, is used as a souring agent in some Indian dishes.

To prepare mangosteens, cut the fruit in half and remove the segments, taking care not to include any of the dark pink pith. Be careful of the dark leathery skin when it is cut as it can stain clothing. Serve the segments on their own or in a fruit salad.

Mangosteens keep very well. If they are not over-ripe when bought, they should remain in good condition for 8–10 days.

LYCHEES

These fruits are indigenous to subtropical areas of southern China and Thailand. Lychees grow in clusters on small trees. The ripe fruit is about the size of a small plum, with a scaly red skin. Once this is removed, the pearly white, slightly transluscent fruit, which surrounds a large inedible seed, is revealed. The flesh has a wonderful, clean taste that is quite similar to that of a white grape, but much more scented.

Lychees and their close relatives, longans, "dragon's eyes", are said to boost fertility. In some parts of China it is traditional when a young person reaches puberty to celebrate the event with a meal composed of a young cockerel that has been cooked with dried lychees or longans. On most occasions, however, lychees are eaten fresh, and are good for cleansing the palate after a rich meal. They are also used in fruit salads and for making sorbets (sherbets).

Lychees are very easy to prepare. The brittle skin parts readily, and you can either eat the fruit as is, nibbling the flesh off the seeds, or the fruit can be seeded and sliced before being added to a fruit salad or arranged on plates to serve.

Fresh lychees are seasonal. Store them in the refrigerator, as they taste best chilled. They will remain fresh for up to a week. When fresh lychees are not available, canned fruit can be used instead, but it lacks the subtlety of the fresh fruit. Choose ones canned in natural juice rather than syrup. Once opened, they can be stored, covered, in the refrigerator for 1–2 days.

RAMBUTANS

These small tropical fruits originated in Malaysia, but they are also grown in the Philippines and Thailand. They belong to the same family as lychees, and the flesh is very similar. Rambutans have reddish-brown skins covered with fine green-tipped hairs. Inside, the flesh is similar to the lychee, and hides an oblong seed.

Rambutans are not as strongly scented as lychees. The delicate flesh tastes a little sharper than their cousins. They are usually eaten in the hand, served on the bottom half of the shell, with the top half cut off to expose the flesh. They are used in fruit salads, but are seldom cooked.

To prepare rambutans, cut through the skin, around the equator of the rambutan, then remove half or all the skin. The flesh tends to stick to the seed, so they are more difficult to seed than lychees.

Like lychees, rambutans are best stored in the refrigerator, where they will keep well for at least a week.

DRAGON FRUIT

Also known as *pitihayas*, these brightly coloured fruits are grown extensively in Vietnam. They come in pink and yellow varieties. The pink ones are about 10cm/4in long, and are covered with pointed, green-tipped scales that are rather like the leaves of a globe artichoke. The yellow ones are smaller and look more like prickly pears.

The transluscent pearly-white flesh of both varieties is dotted with a mass of tiny black edible seeds. It is sweet and refreshing, with a slightly acidic melon-like flavour and has the texture of a kiwi fruit. It is best eaten chilled, sprinkled with a little lemon or lime juice to enhance the flavour.

Yellow dragon fruit is ripe when golden all over. When perfectly ripe, both the pink and yellow varieties should yield when gently squeezed. They are best eaten as soon as they are ripe and can be kept in the refrigerator for up to 3 days.

CARAMBOLAS

Also called star fruits because of their shape, carambolas are native to Indonesia. They are yellow or pale amber and have a waxy skin. They are cylindrical in shape, with concave sides and five ridged edges, giving it the appearance of an elongated Chinese lantern. When the fruit is sliced across, the slices are a perfect star shape.

Carambolas have a mild, almost bland flavour but are refreshing and juicy to eat. Some have more flavour than others but there is no way of telling before you taste them, so they are best used with other fruits or reserved for decorating other dishes. To prepare, simply wash and slice across, then remove the flat central seed with the point of a sharp knife.

When buying carambolas, choose firm, undamaged fruits. They can be kept in the refrigerator for up to a week.

MANGOES

These are probably one of the world's most popular fruits. They originated in India and are now widely cultivated throughout South-east Asia, as well as in other tropical and subtropical countries. There are thousands of different varieties. Most are oval in shape, with green, gold or red skin and succulent orange flesh, which can be quite fibrous, although modern varieties are usually smooth and velvety. Canned and dried mango slices are also available although they do not have the same delicate aroma and flavour of fresh mangoes.

The aroma of a ripe mango is unique. Some people say it reminds them of a pine wood in springtime. The juicy flesh is highly scented and tastes deliciously sweet. Apart from being eaten fresh as a fruit, mangoes are used extensively for making chutneys and pickles. Asian cooks also use them in savoury dishes and, when stir-frying a rich meat such as duck, will often add mango instead of pineapple. Mango ice cream is deliciously sweet and creamy, and Thai cooks make a wonderful mango dessert from glutinous rice and coconut milk.

To prepare a mango for eating, first cut off both sides of the fruit on either side of the stone, then scoop the flesh out of the skin with a spoon. After that, strip the skin off the remaining flesh around the central section and suck the flesh off the stone. This may sound rather messy, but in Asia it is the traditional way of eating a mango. If you prefer, you can always peel the mango first,

cut the fruit off the stone and then slice it neatly. Finally – and this often appeals to children – you can cut two large slices from either side of the stone, cross-hatch the flesh on the skin, then press the skin down so that the pieces of mango pop up to make a mango "hedgehog".

Mangoes are usually picked just before they are ripe, and then are packed in straw if they are to be shipped by air to the West. Fruit that is bought when it is still firm can be ripened at home. One of the easiest ways of doing this is to wrap the mango in newspaper, lay it in a box and cover with more newspaper. Colour is not necessarily an indication of ripeness, but touch is. Ripe fruit will just yield when lightly pressed. Eat mangoes as soon as they are ripe.

PAPAYAS

These fruits, which are also known as paw paws, are native to tropical America. It was not until 1600 that they were introduced into Asia, but they rapidly became very popular so that today they are one of the most common and most important fruits in all tropical and subtropical countries.

Papayas can be small and round, but are more often pear-shaped. When ripe, the skin turns from bright green to yellow, and the flesh, which can be deep salmon pink or glorious orange, becomes soft and juicy. The small grey seeds should not be eaten, although Asian cooks use them as a garnish.

The flavour of a ripe papaya is sweet and delicately perfumed and tastes like a cross between a melon and a peach. Some find the flesh sickly, but this can be counteracted by lemon or lime juice. The flesh of under-ripe papaya is pale green, and is not as sweet.

In South-east Asia, papaya is eaten both as a fruit and a vegetable. When ripe, the flesh is usually eaten as it is, sometimes with a squeeze of citrus, but it is also used in fruit

salads and other desserts. Papayas that are not too ripe can be added to soups, curries or seafood dishes. Unripe green papayas are served raw in vegetable salads, especially in Thailand, and can be made into pickles.

To prepare a papaya, slice lengthways in half and scoop out the seeds. To serve raw as a table fruit, slice in wedges, sprinkle with lemon or lime juice, and either cut the flesh off the skin, slicing it into bite-size chunks, or provide small spoons for scooping. To serve raw in a salad, peel slightly unripe fruit, shred the flesh and combine with carrots and lettuce or cucumber, then toss with a spicy dressing. Thai cooks sometimes add dried shrimps.

Green papayas are not often available in the West but, if located, can be kept in the refrigerator for up to a week. Ripe fruit is yellow all over and has a delicate perfume. Do not buy fruit with damaged or shrivelled skin. If the fruit is not quite ripe, check the skin around the stem end and only buy if it is yellow. If it is green, the fruit will never ripen. Fruit that is almost ripe will soften if kept at room temperature for a few days.

YUZU

This Japanese citrus fruit is about the size of a clementine and has a firm, yellowish skin. It has a sharp penetrating aroma. The rind is valued for its flavour and is often used as a garnish. The juice is used in dressings but the flesh is too tart to eat. If you cannot find yuzus, limes make a good substitute.

These are widely used in Chinese and Asian cooking in both sweet and savoury dishes. Nuts are popularly used in vegetarian dishes, but they are also added to many meat and fish dishes. They are used both ground and whole in casseroles and stir-fries, sprinkled over dishes and salads as a garnish, and made into sauces such as the classic spicy Indonesian satay sauce.

PEANUTS

These are also known as groundnuts or monkey nuts. Peanuts are thought to have originated in South America, and were introduced into Asia in the sixteenth century. Today, peanuts are an important world crop, being rich both in oil (40–50 per cent) and protein (about 30 per cent).

Raw peanuts don't have much smell, but once roasted they have a powerful, unmistakable aroma, a crunchy texture and a distinctive flavour. Peanuts play a very important role in Asian cuisine. The smaller ones are used for making oil, while the larger, less oily nuts are widely eaten as a snack, in salads and in main courses. In Indonesia and Malaysia roasted peanuts, pounded to a paste, are the basis for satay sauce, as well as for a dressing in the classic *gado-gado* salad.

Strictly speaking, the peanut is not a nut, but a legume. Its outer shell is the dried fibrous pod of the plant, and contains the seeds or "nuts", which in turn are coated with a thin layer of reddish skin. This skin should be removed before the nut can be used as a food, and the easiest way to do that is to roast or fry the peanuts, then, when they are cool enough to handle, rub off the brittle skins with your fingers.

Raw peanuts in their shells will keep for many months if stored properly. Shelled peanuts will only keep for 7–10 days, even if stored in an airtight container.

GINKGO NUTS

The ginkgo tree is native to China and has been grown in Japan for many centuries where it is called the maidenhair tree. Ginkgo nuts resemble lotus seeds both in appearance and taste, but have a smoother and firmer texture and are less sweet. When cooked, they have a viscous texture.

Ginkgo nuts are used widely in vegetarian cooking in Asia, particularly in China and Japan. They feature in the classic vegetarian casserole called Buddha's delight and are used in a number of Japanese rice and vegetable dishes. In Japan, they are also deep-fried on pine-needle skewers.

Gingko nuts do not travel well. The flesh inside the shells tends to dry up and rot after a time, so usually only dried and canned ginkgo nuts are available in the West. Dried nuts need soaking in water for several hours. Drain before adding to stir-fries, casseroles and soups. Canned gingko nuts are packed in brine so should be rinsed well before use.

Unused soaked or canned ginkgo nuts can be stored in a bowl of fresh water in the refrigerator for 2–3 days.

ALMONDS

These nuts come from the kernel of a fruit closely related to the apricot. However, the fruit of the ripe almond is leathery, dusky green and quite inedible.

Almonds have a unique aroma quite unlike any other nut. There are bitter and sweet varieties, both with a pleasant, crunchy texture. In Asia, sweet almonds are mostly used as garnishes and in desserts and cakes. Bitter almonds, which are not available in the US, contain prussic acid. They must not be eaten raw, but their essence is distilled and used as a flavouring.

Whole kernels should be soaked to remove the thin red skin. This is seldom necessary in the West, however, as shelled or blanched almonds are readily available – whole, sliced, as thin slivers or ground.

Almonds have a high fat content, so they become rancid if stored for too long. Keep unopened packets in a sealed container in a cool, dry place, and use within 2–3 months. Nuts bought loose or in opened packets should be used as soon as possible.

OTHER NUTS

There are a number of other nuts that are also popular in Asian cooking.

Candle nuts *These nuts are native to Indonesia and are similar to macadamia nuts, which can be used as a substitute. In Asia, the pounded nuts are used as a thickener. They are slightly toxic when raw and should always be cooked.*

Chestnuts *These have a robust flavour and meaty texture, which makes them a very popular addition to a wide variety of vegetarian dishes. They are delicious stir-fried with leafy vegetables such as pak choi (bok choy).*

Cashew nuts *In Asian cooking, both raw and roasted cashews are used.*

SESAME SEEDS

The sesame plant probably originated in Africa but has been cultivated in India and China since ancient times. Today, it is grown all over the world in tropical and subtropical countries. Sesame seeds are very small, flat and pear-shaped. Usually, they are white, but they can also be cream to brown, red or black.

Raw sesame seeds have little aroma and are almost tasteless. When roasted or dry-fried, a nutty aroma becomes pronounced and their flavour is heightened.

Sesame oil is used in Chinese and Asian cooking for flavouring. The seeds are used in many Chinese dishes, such as honeyed apples and bang-bang chicken. They are used widely in Singaporean, Malaysian, Indonesian and Japanese cooking. They are often toasted and sprinkled over salads and other dishes.

Sesame seeds are frequently roasted before being used. Place them in a wok or pan over a medium heat. They burn easily so shake the pan constantly to keep them moving and do not leave unattended at any time. To grind the seeds, use a mortar with a pestle or, as in Korea, use two flat plates pressed together. Japanese cooks use a device rather like a pepper mill, which grinds the roasted sesame seeds as finely or as coarsely as needed.

The high oil content of sesame seeds means that they do not keep well. Store them in a cool, dry place and check the use by date on the package.

These are essential ingredients in South-east Asian cooking. There is an old saying that "he who plants a coconut palm, plants food and drink, vessels and clothing, a habitation for himself and a heritage for his children". Once mature, the palms will go on producing coconuts for 75–100 years, which helps to explain why they are so highly prized.

The coconut was called the nut of India until the Portuguese changed its name to coco, meaning clown or monkey, due to its appearance. Fresh coconuts are available at certain times of the year in Asian stores and supermarkets. The liquid you can hear sloshing around inside the nut when it is shaken is coconut juice, not coconut milk. As any traveller who has tasted it will attest, the juice makes a really refreshing drink, especially when tapped from a fresh green coconut. It can also be made into palm wine, which can be extremely potent.

An average size coconut weighs about 675g/1½lb. If it is fresh, it will be full of liquid, so test by shaking well before buying. To open a coconut, hold it in the palm of your left hand, with the "eyes" just above your thumb. The fault line runs between the eyes. Hold the coconut over a bowl to catch the juice, then carefully strike the line with the unsharpened side of a cleaver, or a hammer. If you have done this correctly, the coconut should break cleanly into two pieces. Taste a little of the white flesh to make sure that the coconut is fresh, as on rare occasions the flesh may have become rancid.

To remove the flesh, slip a round-bladed knife between the outer husk and the flesh and prise out the pieces of fresh coconut. The thin, brown papery skin on these pieces can be removed with a vegetable peeler, if you like, although this is a rather fiddly job.

Coconut is widely used in South-east Asian cooking. The milk is often used as a cooking medium instead of stock, and it is also added at the end of cooking to enrich stews and curries. It can be cooked with rice, to make a savoury accompaniment, or as the basis for rice cakes, and also to make a delicious creamy rice pudding. In Thailand, coconut milk is often used to make aromatic soups.

COCONUT MILK
This is a rich, sweet liquid made from the grated flesh of the coconut. In Asia, it is possible to buy bags of freshly grated coconut specifically for making coconut milk. Warm water is poured over the grated coconut, which is then squeezed repeatedly until the mixture becomes cloudy and takes on a delicious coconut flavour. When the mixture is strained, the liquid obtained is coconut milk.

Ready-made coconut milk can be bought in cartons and cans from supermarkets and Asian stores. Even in countries with a plentiful supply of coconuts, cooks often use these products as they are so convenient and can save enormously on preparation time. The quality is excellent, and it is even possible to buy a low-fat version that is 88 per cent fat free.

COCONUT CREAM

If coconut milk is left to stand for a short time, coconut cream will float to the surface in much the same way as regular cream does on whole milk. Coconut cream has a much thicker consistency and richer flavour than coconut milk.

Ready-to-use coconut cream is widely available in cartons and is a wonderful ingredient where a rich coconut aroma and flavour are required. In many Thai curries the spices are initially fried in bubbling coconut cream instead of oil, which is the ingredient more commonly used for frying.

CREAMED COCONUT

This should not be mistaken for coconut cream as it is a somewhat different product. (It can, however, be reconstituted to make coconut milk or cream.) Creamed coconut is solid and is available in 200g/7oz blocks from supermarkets and Asian stores.

It is a very useful ingredient. Small pieces of creamed coconut can be cut off and added to dishes to supply a little richness just before serving.

When only a small quantity of coconut milk is called for, it is not worth opening a can or carton. Instead, dissolve about 50g/2oz creamed coconut in about 100ml/3½fl oz/scant ½ cup hot water. Coconut cream can be made in the same way: dissolve about 75g/3oz creamed coconut in 100ml/3½fl oz/scant ½ cup hot water.

MAKING COCONUT MILK

Coconut milk can be made at home, from desiccated (dry unsweetened shredded) coconut. Although the procedure takes a little time, it has plenty of advantages. Desiccated coconut is readily available, stores well and is an item that many cooks routinely keep in stock. You can make as much or as little as you like – although the method is more practical for large quantities – and coconut milk made this way is less expensive than any of the ready-made alternatives.

1 Tip about 225g/8oz/2⅔ cups desiccated coconut into the bowl of a food processor and pour over 450ml/¾ pint/scant 2 cups boiling water. Process for 20–30 seconds and leave to cool slightly. If making a number of batches, transfer the mixture immediately to a large bowl and repeat with more desiccated coconut and water.

2 Place a sieve lined with muslin (cheesecloth) over a large bowl. Place the bowl in the kitchen sink, then ladle some of the coconut mixture into the muslin.

3 Bring up the ends of the cloth and twist it over the sieve to extract as much of the liquid as possible. Discard the coconut left in the muslin and repeat with the remaining coconut mixture.

4 Before using freshly made coconut milk, leave it to stand for 10 minutes. The coconut cream will float to the top. If needed, skim off the cream using a large spoon, or leave it to enrich the milk.

Any unused coconut milk or cream can be transferred to a plastic tub and stored in the refrigerator for 1–2 days, or poured into a freezer container and frozen for use on another occasion.

There are a large number of soya bean products that are popularly used in Chinese and Asian cooking. They are often used in place of meat as they are a rich, healthy source of protein. The best known is tofu, which is available in many forms including deep-fried, marinated and fermented. Other soya bean products include tempeh and miso, which is often used as a flavouring.

TOFU

Also known as beancurd, this fermented soya bean product is one of China's major contributions to the world as a cheap and healthy source of protein. Highly nutritious and low in fat and sugar, tofu is a much healthier food than either meat or fish and is a fraction of the cost.

The process of making tofu is not unlike that of making cheese but is much less time consuming. The soya beans are first soaked and husked, then pounded with water to make soya milk. The soya milk is then filtered, boiled and finally curdled with gypsum to make solid tofu.

There are two basic types of tofu that are available in the West: soft or silken tofu, and a firm variety. Both are creamy-white in colour and are either packed in water or vacuum packed. The firm type is usually sold in cakes measuring about 7.5cm/3in square and 2.5cm/1in thick. Also available are marinated tofu, deep-fried tofu and pressed tofu.

Good quality tofu should smell fresh with a faint, pleasant beany aroma. On its own, it is quite bland, but the beauty of tofu is that its soft, porous texture will absorb the flavours of other ingredients.

As a vegetable protein, tofu contains the eight essential amino acids plus vitamins A and B and is rich in a number of health-promoting phytochemicals. It is free from cholesterol, so is good for anyone with heart disease or high blood pressure. It is also very easy to digest, so is an ideal food for infants, invalids and the elderly.

Tofu is very versatile and, depending upon the texture, it can be cooked by almost any method, and used with many ingredients, both sweet and savoury.

Soft or silken tofu is delicate so it is mainly steamed or added to soups. It makes a refreshing sweet dessert and is also used to make dairy-free ice cream.

Firm tofu is the most common type available in the West, and is also the most popular for everyday use. Although it has been lightly pressed, it still needs to be handled with care. Having been cut to the required size and shape, the pieces are usually blanched in boiling water or briefly shallow-fried. This hardens them before they are stir-fried or braised. Tofu that has been lightly grilled (broiled) on both sides (*yaki tofu*) is slightly firmer.

Because tofu has such a bland taste, it is important to cook it with strongly flavoured seasonings such as garlic, fresh root ginger, spring onions (scallions), soy sauce and shrimp paste. Although primarily a vegetarian food, tofu also tastes very good with meat. It is often cooked with either pork or beef, but seldom with chicken. It goes well with fish and shellfish, too. One of the most popular tofu dishes is *ma po doufu* from Sichuan, in which cubed tofu is first blanched in boiling water, then braised with minced (ground) beef, garlic, spring onions, leeks, salt, Sichuan pepper, rice wine, chilli bean paste, fermented black beans and sesame oil.

Fresh tofu submerged in water in a sealed plastic container will keep for several days in the refrigerator. Vacuum-packed fresh tofu bought from health food stores and supermarkets will keep for slightly longer, but is unlikely to taste quite as good. Tofu is also available as a powder mix, which has a long shelf life.

Deep-fried Tofu

This is fresh, firm tofu that has been cut into cubes, squares or triangles, then deep-fried until light golden brown. It puffs up during cooking, and underneath the crispy brown skin the tofu is still white and soft. Like fresh tofu, it has little taste of its own but readily absorbs seasonings and the flavours of other ingredients with which it is cooked.

Deep-fried tofu can be used in the same way as fresh firm tofu. As it has been fried in vegetable oil, deep-fried tofu is suitable for vegetarians. Non-vegetarians often stuff the larger squares or triangles with minced pork, chicken, fish and prawns (shrimp), then braise them in a sauce. In Japan, it is a popular addition to a wonderful hotpot called *oden*, which is sold from street stalls during the winter months.

Unlike fresh tofu, which is very delicate, deep-fried tofu can be handled much more roughly without risk of it disintegrating. Larger pieces should be chopped a little to allow the seasonings to penetrate.

Cakes of deep-fried tofu can be found in Asian stores. They are sold in plastic bags either chilled or frozen and have a use-by date stamped on the packaging. They will keep for much longer than uncooked fresh tofu and can be frozen for up to a year.

Pressed Tofu

This is fresh tofu that has been compressed until almost all the liquid has been squeezed out, producing a solid block with a smooth texture. It is usually marinated in soy sauce and seasoned with five-spice powder, which makes it pale brown on the surface but a creamy white inside.

Pressed tofu is usually cut into slices, cubes or fine shreds then stir-fried with meat and vegetables. It offers a contrast in both taste and texture when combined with other ingredients.

Usually sold in vacuum-packed plastic bags in Asian stores, pressed tofu will keep for several weeks in the refrigerator. Check the use-by date on the packaging. Pressed tofu should not be frozen.

Dried Tofu Skins

These are made from soya milk. A large pan of soya milk is gently brought to the boil, the thin layer of skin that forms on the surface is skimmed off and hung up to dry into a flat sheet. Dried tofu sticks are made by rolling the skin up while it is still warm.

Dried tofu skins have neither aroma nor taste until they are cooked with seasonings and other ingredients. The flat skins are used in soups, stir-fries and casseroles, and sometimes to make spring rolls. Dried tofu sticks are used in vegetarian dishes, and are also cooked with meat in braised dishes and casseroles. Before use, dried tofu skins should be soaked for 1–2 hours, and the sticks for several hours or overnight.

Dried tofu sheets and sticks keep well. Store in their packet or in a sealed plastic bag in a cool and dry place.

Fermented Tofu

This is made by fermenting fresh tofu on beds of rice straw, then drying it in the sun before marinating with salt, alcohol and spices. Finally the fermented tofu is left to mature in brine in sealed earthenware urns for six months before being packaged.

Fermented tofu is definitely an acquired taste. It is sometimes referred to as Chinese cheese because it smells very strong and the flavour is rather powerful. There are two types available in the West: white, which can be quite spicy, and red, which is coloured on the surface only. Both types are either served on their own with rice *congee* at breakfast, or used as a seasoning when marinating and cooking other ingredients.

Fermented tofu is available in cans and jars from Asian stores. Once opened, it should be stored in the refrigerator.

TEMPEH

This is an Indonesian speciality. It is made by fermenting cooked soya beans with a cultured starter. Tempeh is similar to tofu but has a nuttier, more savoury flavour and a firmer texture.

It can be used in the same way as firm tofu and also benefits from marinating as it its flavour is so mild. It must be boiled or fried before being eaten.

Tempeh is available chilled or frozen from health food stores and Asian stores. Chilled tempeh can be stored in the refrigerator for up to a week. Frozen tempeh can be kept for 1 month; defrost before use.

MISO

This thick Japanese paste is made from a mixture of cooked soya beans, rice, wheat or barley, salt and water. Miso is left to ferment for up to 3 years. The soya beans retain their original shape. Traditionally, miso was ground at home but now it is available ready ground.

There are three main types: *kome*, or white miso, is the lightest and sweetest; medium-strength *mugi miso*, which has a mellow flavour and is for everyday use; and *hacho miso*, dark chocolate in colour with a thick texture and a strong flavour.

Miso is used to add a savoury flavour to soups, stocks, stir-fries and noodle dishes and is a staple food in Asia.

Miso keeps very well and can be stored for several months but, once opened, it should be kept in the refrigerator.

GLUTEN

Also known as mock meat, gluten is a good source of vegetarian protein. It is usually made from a mixture of wheat flour, salt and water, from which all the starch has been washed out, leaving a gluten with a sponge-like texture. It has little aroma or flavour of its own but can be shaped, coloured and flavoured to resemble meat or fish. Flavoured and cooked gluten is often available in cans from Asian stores. Once opened, it can be stored in the refrigerator for up to a week.

Konnayaku, a Japanese gluten product, is made from the konnayaku *plant, which is a type of yam. It has a dense, gelatinous texture with no aroma or flavour. It may be eaten raw or added to soups and hot-pots. Cakes of* konnayaku *are available in Japanese supermarkets. Once opened, it should be stored in the refrigerator and used within 2 weeks.*

Dried Fish & Shellfish

These are widely used in South-east Asian cooking. They tend to be very strongly flavoured, and many are used as a seasoning or flavouring, or added as an ingredient to composite dishes. Some dried fish are eaten on their own with accompaniments such as rice, while others, such as dried sardines and dried anchovies, are consumed as snacks.

SALTED FISH

Many types of fish, both freshwater and saltwater, are salted and cured for general use in South-east Asia. They range from tiny whitebait to large croakers, usually preserved in salt or brine, although some are dried in the sun.

Salted fish is an acquired taste. It smells so pungent and has such a strong flavour that some people may find it disagreeable. It is, however, very popular is South-east Asia.

Like fermented tofu, salted fish has two basic functions. It is either eaten on its own with rice, or used to season vegetables and meat in steamed dishes, casseroles or soups. It should be soaked in water before use to remove excess salt. Large fish are usually sold without the heads.

Preserved fish in brine are seldom found in the West, but salted and dried fish are available from most Asian stores. They will keep almost indefinitely when stored in a cool, dry place.

DRIED ANCHOVIES

These are a Malaysian speciality. Anchovies are seldom eaten fresh in South-east Asia; they are either used for making fish sauce, or are salted and dried. Fishing for these fish is a huge industry in Malaysia. As soon as the anchovies are hauled in, the fishermen boil their catch in salted water for about 5 minutes. Back on shore, the fish are dried, graded and packed.

Dried anchovies have an overpowering aroma and a very strong flavour. They can be used as a flavouring, as an ingredient in a composite dish, or as a snack food. A very popular Malaysian recipe involves steaming and filleting the fish, then serving them with a sauce made from preserved black beans flavoured with fresh chillies, lime juice and sugar. They are sometimes deep-fried and served either as a snack or as a starter. They also make a tasty accompaniment to curries and chicken *rendang*.

Dried anchovies will keep for a very long time stored in a dry and cool place in an airtight container.

DRIED BONITO

In different parts of the world, the name bonito is given to several different types of fish. For instance, the Atlantic bonito is a relative of mackerel, and is known as Spanish mackerel in Europe, while the Pacific bonito is a small tuna.

The Pacific bonito has a stronger flavour than regular tuna, particularly when dried. In Japan, where the Pacific bonito is very popular and much used, it is cooked and dried in a whole block and then shaved for use. Once it was the Japanese housewife's job, first thing in the morning, to shave the hard block of dried tuna. However, ready-shaved flakes are now widely available in Japanese and Asian stores. The flakes come in various thicknesses.

Fine flakes are one of the main ingredients used in the basic Japanese stock known as *dashi*, and are also used as a topping or garnish for other dishes such as vegetables or fish. It can be mixed with shoyu to make a delicious accompaniment to boiled rice. Powdered bonito is used as a seasoning.

Dried bonito flakes can be stored almost indefinitely in an airtight jar.

Fish Maw

This is the swim bladder or stomach of certain types of large fish and eels, which has been dried in the sun, then deep-fried. It is considered a great delicacy in both China and Thailand.

Fish maw has little aroma, nor does it have a distinctive flavour. It is mainly valued for its texture, which is rather slippery.

Fish maws must be soaked in a large bowl of cold water for 24 hours before use. They will float at first, so will need to be kept submerged with the aid of a plate or dish. As they absorb the water, the maws will swell to four times the original size and slowly sink to the bottom of the bowl. Before use, drain but do not dry the maws, then slice or cube them as required.

Dried Squid

In inland China and other parts of Asia that are far from the coast, where seafood was for a long time unavailable, dried squid and cuttlefish have always been regarded as great delicacies.

Dried squid is pale brown in colour and has a subtle, slightly fishy aroma but a relatively strong flavour. Some people find the texture of dried squid rather tough when compared to fresh but others like the chewiness of the dried version.

Dried squid is used mainly in soups or meat stews. The stronger taste and texture provides an interesting contrast to fresh squid and the two are often stir-fried together in a popular dish that is known as two-coloured squid-flowers.

Before using them for cooking, dried squid must be soaked in warm water for at least 30 minutes, then drained and rinsed in cold running water. If the dried squid is to be stir-fried, score the inside of the flesh with a sharp knife in a criss-cross pattern, then cut it into small pieces. Cooking causes the cuts to open up so that each squid resembles an ear of corn, which is how they came to be called squid flowers.

Dried squid will keep almost indefinitely if they are wrapped tightly and stored in a cool, dry place.

Other Dried Seafood

As well as the more common dried fish and shellfish, there are several unusual dried sea creatures.

Dried jellyfish *Sheets of edible dried jellyfish are available in some Chinese stores. It is a delicacy in China and is valued for its crunchy yet elastic texture.*

To prepare, soak the sheets in a bowl of cold water for several hours, changing the water frequently, and squeezing the jellyfish each time. Drain, squeeze again, then cut into strips.

Strips of dried jellyfish are often added to a stir-fry, but they must be tossed in at the last moment or they will become rubbery in texture.

Dried sea cucumber *This is not actually a vegetable at all, but a marine animal, also known as a sea slug. Before use, dried sea cucumber must be soaked in cold water for at least 24 hours, during which time it will double in bulk and become quite gelatinous. It is mainly used in soups, stews and braised dishes.*

DRIED SHRIMPS

These are very popular throughout Asia, especially in China and Thailand. They are pale pink in colour, having been boiled before being spread out in the sun to dry. There are several different sizes, from tiny shrimps not much bigger than grains of rice (hence their Chinese name sea rice) to large ones 1cm/½in long. The larger ones are sold shelled while the tiny ones are sold whole.

Dried shrimps have a very strong smell that can be detected through the plastic bags in which they are sold. The strong smell dissipates with cooking. Their flavour is sharp and salty. Dried shrimps are used as a seasoning or flavouring, as an ingredient in dishes and as a garnish in salads.

Before use, the shrimps should be soaked for an hour in water or rice wine. The soaking liquid is saved and often added to the dish during cooking.

Dried shrimps keep well when stored in an airtight container in a cool, dry place. Colour is a good indication of freshness as older shrimps tend to fade. Any shrimps that look grey, or start to turn grey while being stored, will be past their prime. Stored dried shrimps may become a bit moist. If this happens, spread them on baking sheets and dry them briefly in a hot oven.

DRIED SCALLOPS

These are another Asian delicacy. They are very expensive because the most sought-after varieties are so scarce. The Chinese variety known as *conpoy*, for example, is only found in the inland sea called Po Hai, and then only during the short summer season. The best scallops are round and golden, with a delicate, sweet flavour. Japan produces fine dried scallops, including the variety *aomori*.

Before being dried, scallops are cooked in their shells in boiling water. The flesh is then removed and cleaned. Dried scallops have quite a distinct aroma with a concentrated flavour. They are seldom used on their own, but are combined with other ingredients in soups and stuffings.

Dried and fresh scallops are sometimes used together in the same dish. Dried ones are the classic garnish for crispy seaweed but, when the dish is served in Chinese restaurants in the West, ground fried fish is often used instead.

To prepare, dried scallops should be soaked in boiling water for at least an hour before use, then drained.

For some unknown reason, dried scallops seem to be available only in large boxes in the West. Should you manage to acquire any, transfer the scallops to clean, dry jars, close the lids tightly and store in a cool, dry place. They will keep indefinitely.

Throughout China and Asia, eggs and meats are preserved and either used as ingredients in other dishes or eaten on their own. Pork is one of the most commonly preserved meats and is used to make wind-dried sausages and belly pork, and crispy pork crackling. Preserved eggs are considered a great delicacy in China. There are two main types: salted duck eggs and thousand-year-old eggs.

CHINESE/WIND-DRIED SAUSAGES

Despite their name, these are actually made throughout South-east Asia, and are widely available in the West. There are two types: pink and white, made from pork and pork fat; and a darker one containing duck liver.

Wind-dried sausages have no aroma, but when cooked become fragrant and sweet. They can be eaten alone, combined with milder meats or cooked with vegetables. They are often cut diagonally into thin slices, steamed on a bed of rice or steamed whole, then skinned and sliced and added to dishes such as fried rice.

Chinese sausages will keep for several months in the refrigerator or can be frozen.

WIND-DRIED BELLY PORK

This Chinese speciality is found principally in the Hunan province and is available in Asian stores. It must always be cooked.

PORK CRACKLING

Also known as *chicaron*, this is made from pork rind that has been deep-fried, forming crisp puffy crackers. It has a meaty aroma and subtle flavour, and a firm yet spongy texture that absorbs other flavours.

It is served with curries or sliced in salads. To use in soups, stews and hotpots, soak in hot water for 35 minutes then drain.

If well wrapped and stored in a cool, dry place, pork crackling will keep for several months. It becomes rancid if kept too long.

SALTED DUCK EGGS

These are made from raw duck eggs, which are coated in a salt and mud paste, rolled in rice husks, then packed into an earthenware urn, which is sealed and stored in a cool, dark place for 30–40 days. They will keep for about a month.

The eggs taste quite salty and can be eaten on their own, or as part of the filling in cakes. To use, remove the outer coating and wash thoroughly, steam or boil, then shell.

THOUSAND-YEAR-OLD EGGS

These are made from raw eggs, which are coated with a mixture of wood ash and slaked lime, then left for up to a hundred days. The whites turn to brown jelly and the yolks become creamy and greenish. They will keep for 4–6 months in the refrigerator.

These eggs have a milder taste than salted duck eggs. They need no cooking and can be served as a first course, or chopped and added to *congee*. They can also be used in an omelette, with pork and hen's eggs. To use, remove the outer coating, wash well, then shell.

Poultry

Chicken, which marries well with a wide variety of flavours, is the most common poultry used in Chinese and Asian cooking, swiftly followed by duck, which is particularly popular in China. The meat is usually chopped or sliced into small, manageable morsels that can easily be picked up in chopsticks and do not require further cutting.

Chicken

This bird is popular in almost every cuisine. It combines well with a variety of different ingredients and this is nowhere more amply illustrated than in Asia, where it is used in soups, salads, stir-fries, curries, roasts and braised dishes. Every part of the chicken is utilized in the Asian cuisine, including the liver, gizzard, heart and even feet, which are used to make a delicious stew.

Chicken can be cooked whole, jointed, or taken off the bone and chopped or cut into thin strips – this is the usual practice if the meat is to be stir-fired. In China, chicken breasts on the bone may be cut into as many as 20 pieces before being stir-fired.

In Japan, chicken is the most important meat on the menu, second only to fish in terms of popularity. Chicken breast is the favourite cut, largely because it cooks so quickly and remains wonderfully tender in dishes such as *yakitori* and *teriyaki*. Skinless, boneless chicken breasts are readily available in Japan, unlike in the rest of Asia, where it is more usual to buy chickens whole; portions are regarded as wasteful, or simply too expensive.

Throughout Asia, frugality is considered a virture, so one chicken might be used to make three different dishes: the breasts may be sliced into strips for a stir-fry; the rest of the meat might be braised in a red-cooked dish or curry; and the carcass used to make a flavoursome stock.

Duck

These birds are a symbol of happiness and fidelity, which doubtless contributes to their popularity in the Chinese cuisine. They are central to celebratory meals such as Chinese New Year. Duck is also popular in Vietnam, Thailand and Indonesia, but is seldom used in Japanese cooking.

The most famous duck dish in the West is probably Peking duck. The prepared and cooked meat is sprinkled with very finely sliced spring onion (scallion) and slivers of cucumber and wrapped in a thin Mandarin pancake with a little plum sauce.

In China, a duck is prepared for roasting by pricking the skin lightly all over with a fork. The bird is then placed on a trivet in the sink and a kettle of freshly boiled water is poured over the top. The bird is drained well, and the cavity wiped with kitchen paper, before the duck is suspended from butcher's hooks and left to dry overnight. Once the bird is dry, the skin is sprinkled with a little salt. The bird is then placed on a trivet in a roasting pan and roasted in a hot oven until the skin is quite crisp and golden brown and the bird is fully cooked.

Game Birds

Small game birds are eaten in China and South-east Asia, but most are caught in the wild. With the exception of quail and pigeon, they are rarely farmed.

MEAT

hroughout Asia, the choice of meat is greatly influenced by religious beliefs and habits. Almost all Chinese, except those who have converted to Islam, love pork. In predominantly Muslim countries such as Malaysia and Indonesia, pork is rarely eaten, while in Hindu communities such as Bali, beef is eschewed in favour of pork or lamb.

PORK

This meat is as popular as chicken in China and in other parts of Asia, which have large Chinese communities. Like chicken, pork goes well with a wide range of ingredients, from vegetables to shellfish, and is equally at home with salted and pickled foods.

Wherever there are Muslim communities, however, pork is off limits and either beef or lamb is served instead. This is the case throughout Malaysia, the only exception being the Nonya style of cooking. This came about because of the intermarriage of Chinese merchants with Malaysian women who then started to cook pork dishes for their husbands. Nonya cooking is very popular in Singapore, the west coast of Malaysia around Malacca, and on the island of Penang in the north.

Pork is rarely used in Indonesian cooking, except where cooked by members of the Chinese communities on the thousands of islands of the Indonesian archipelago. Bali is an exception. The population of this island are mainly Hindu so pork is permissible and widely used. A barbecued suckling pig is often served at the festivals that are such a feature of Balinese life.

For stir-frying, fillet, lean leg or belly are the preferred cuts, along with the meaty parts of chops or spare ribs. The meat is cut into thin shreds so that it responds to really quick cooking over high heat, which is economical in the use of fuel.

For long-cooked casseroles and braised dishes, shoulder, spare ribs or belly pork might be used. In these dishes the meat is often cooked for so long that it forms a luscious jelly-like mixture.

BEEF

It is only relatively recently that beef has been eaten in China and Asia, because cattle were considered beasts of burden and highly valued as such. The buffalo, too, has always been used widely, mainly in the paddy fields to plough the land prior to planting by hand.

Beef is traditionally eaten only in the north of China and in places where there are large Muslim communities. However, because of the proximity of Beijing to the northern provinces and the number of Chinese Muslim restaurants in the capital, beef is becoming increasingly popular there. It is used in a wide variety of different dishes, mainly as a substitute for pork.

LAMB

Like beef, lamb is traditionally only eaten in northern China. It is generally thinly sliced and used for dishes where a quick method of cooking such as stir-frying is required. Because it has a stronger flavour than pork, it works best in dishes that contain aromatic flavouring ingredients such as garlic, root ginger and onions. Lamb is also cooked in Mongolian hotpot.

hina and the countries of South-east Asia have immense coastlines as well as rivers, canals, lakes and flooded paddy fields. Along these waterways, local people catch their daily supply of fish, which can be found in abundance. The fish is steamed, grilled (broiled) with local spices and herbs, served in soups or curries, or added to salads and omelettes.

Fish is exploited and enjoyed all over the Far East. With a coastline of over three thousand miles China has an abundant and varied supply of saltwater fish, some of which are familiar to Westerners, such as bass and sea bass, halibut, mackerel, sea bream, sole, plaice, tuna, cod, salmon, sardines and herring. China also has rivers and lakes, which are a source of freshwater fish, including the ubiquitous carp.

Indonesia, the Philippines and Japan are all island nations, so it is not surprising that fish plays an important role in their cuisines. This is especially so in Japan, where an early moratorium on meat eating was one of the factors that led to the Japanese expertise in preparing this popular food. *Sashimi*, which is very fresh fish that is finely sliced and served raw, is now appreciated worldwide – well beyond the boundaries of its country of origin. Trout, mackerel, tuna, salmon and herring are all popular in Japan. More exotic varieties such as parrot fish or pomfret are also enjoyed.

The most important requirement when buying and preparing, is that fish should be as fresh as possible. When buying fresh fish, the eyes of the fish should be bright and clear, not sunken; the gills should be clean and bright red/coral in colour; the skin should be firm and fresh with a sheen and, when held, the fish should feel almost springy, as if it could swim away at any moment; and the fish should smell fresh.

Cooking Techniques

There are many cooking techniques that are typical of Asian cuisine, all of which give delicious results.

Steaming This is ideal for fresh whole fish that weigh about 675g/1½lb. Rub the skin with salt and scatter with shredded fresh root ginger. Pour over a mixture of rice wine, soy sauce and sugar, then steam over boiling water. Remove the fish when the flesh just flakes. Serve with the juices.

Clear simmering This is usually reserved for larger fish (about 1.5kg/3lb). Use a fish kettle if you have one. Pour in 1.75 litres/ 3 pints/7½ cups water and add salt to taste. Slice a 4cm/1½in piece of root ginger and add to the kettle. Bring the water to the boil. Place a strip of foil under the fish to act as a strap. Lift the fish into the kettle, placing it on the trivet. Return to the boil, lower the heat and simmer for 4 minutes. Reduce the heat further and cook for 6–8 minutes. Lift the fish out and drain. Transfer to a serving dish and pour over 75ml/5 tbsp hot groundnut (peanut) oil.

Frying Fish can be stir-fried, deep fried or pan-fried. It should be cooked quickly.

Braising This is good for whole fish. Fry the fish in garlic and ginger oil, add soy sauce, and flavourings, cover and cook briefly.

Types of Fish

Many different fish can be found in the seas, rivers and lakes of China and Asia. Many are commonly found in the West.

Carp

This freshwater fish is extensively farmed and thrives in ponds, lakes and flooded paddy fields. There are several varieties. Ask the fishmonger to remove the large scales and dorsal fins. The flesh is meaty and moist. Bake carp whole with a stuffing.

Cod

This handsome fish has greenish bronze skin dappled with yellow. Cod can vary in size from 1kg/2¼lb to 30kg/66lb. When properly cooked the flesh is moist and will break into large flakes. It is ideal for grilling (broiling), baking or frying, and is excellent in curries. Add cubes of cod at the very end of cooking so that they keep their shape.

Sea Bass

This family of fish also includes groupers. Sea bass is silver in colour with a dark back and white underbelly. The flesh has a delicate flavour and holds its shape when cooked. The fish can be grilled (broiled), steamed, baked or barbecued whole, or cut into fillets or steaks before being cooked.

Sea Bream

Look for gilt head bream, which have a gold spot on each cheek and a squat, compact body. Sea bream must be scaled before being cooked. The flesh is rather coarse but remains moist if not overcooked. Slash each side two or three times so that the thicker part of the fish will cook more evenly. Sea bream is best baked whole in an oiled or buttered foil parcel with ginger, spring onions (scallions) and seasoning. It is good served with a sweet-and-sour sauce.

Grey Mullet

This fish has dark stripes along the back, lots of thick scales and a heavy head. The flesh is soft and rather coarse but responds well to distinctive flavours. Try it baked, with a stuffing of minced pork and prawns (shrimp) with fresh root ginger and spring onions or soaked Chinese mushrooms, or moisten it with fish sauce and steam it. If you cannot find grey mullet, red snapper or pompano may be used instead.

Salmon

This is often called the king of fish and it is used in many dishes. The skin on a salmon's back is steely blue going down to a silver body. The pink flesh is oily and firm. It is best either clear simmered or poached in a fish kettle, or wrapped in foil and baked. Salmon cutlets can be barbecued and served with Thai salad or used to make the Filipino marinated dish, *escabèche*. In Japan, salmon is rarely used, although it is often served in Japanese restaurants in the West.

Tuna

These enormous fish are the big brothers of the mackerel family. Tuna swim huge distances at speed and this causes the muscles to fill with blood, which produces the deep red colour of the flesh. The skipjack and albacore are much sought after by the Japanese for making *sashimi* and *sushi*. When grilling (broiling) or barbecuing tuna, marinate the fish first and then baste it to keep it moist throughout cooking. It is also good pan-fried.

MACKEREL

These fish are easy to recognize thanks to the wavy dark blue markings that run part of the way down to a silvery green side and pale underbelly. The inside of the mouth is black. Mackerel is an oily fish, with soft, pinkish flesh, and is good grilled (broiled) or poached with miso. Serve mackerel with wedges of lemon or lime. It is also excellent in *laksa* or Thai fish soup.

HALIBUT

This rather chunky flatfish can reach a huge size, sometimes growing up to 2m/6½ft and weighing over 200kg/440lb. It has a brown skin on one side and is pearly white underneath with two eyes on the bridge of the snout. The smaller variety, called chicken halibut, weighs under 1.5kg/3lb and is ideal for poaching or baking.

PLAICE

This distinctive flatfish has dark brown skin with orange spots and a white underside. The flesh is soft and moist. Cook plaice whole, either deep-fried or poached. If filleted, make a stock from the bones with bruised fresh ginger, onion and seasoning. Flounder may be used instead.

SOLE

This is another member of the flatfish family. It has rough brown skin on top and a long lozenge-shaped body. The flesh has superb texture and a delicate flavour. Sole is best grilled (broiled) or fried whole. It may be sold filleted, in which case ask for the bones to make stock for a fish soup.

POMFRET

Malaysian and Thai cooks hold this flatfish in high regard. It is silver grey with a pearly white underside. The best way to preserve its delicate flavour is to steam it with simple flavourings such as ginger, spring onion (scallion), light soy sauce and seasoning. It is also good grilled (broiled) and fried.

SNAPPER

The red snapper, with its distinctive colour, is perhaps the best known of the snapper family. However, there are other colours as well, including silver, grey and silver-spotted grey. The snapper has large eyes and very strong dorsal fins that should be removed before cooking. The flesh is moist and well flavoured. Small to medium snappers are good for steaming or baking whole.

SQUID

Asian cooks are very fond of these sea creatures. In the West, they are usually available ready cleaned, otherwise ask the fishmonger to prepare them for you. To clean squid yourself, pull the tentacles out from the body sac. Squeeze the tentacle in the centre to remove the hard central bone or "beak". Trim the tentacles from the head and set aside. Pull the quill and the innards from the body cavity and discard. Peel off the mottled outer skin, then wash the body inside and out.

To stuff squid, stuff the sac until two-thirds full, then pop the tentacles into the top of the sac. Secure with a cocktail stick (toothpick). To stir-fry, slit the sac from top to bottom and turn it inside out. Flatten it on a board and score the inside surface lightly with a sharp knife, pressing just hard enough to make a criss-cross pattern and cut lengthways into ribbons. These will curl up when cooked.

sian cooks have access to a wonderful assortment of shellfish, not only from the ocean, but also from freshwater lakes, rivers and canals. Shellfish is cooked as fresh as possible and may be steamed, deep-fried and stir-fried, used in soups and made into dishes such as crab cakes. If you have to use frozen shellfish, thaw it slowly and dry before cooking briefly.

ABALONE

This large shellfish is also known as ormer and sea ear. It can grow to about 20cm/8in in length and has a particularly pretty shell, lined with what looks like mother-of-pearl. The flesh of abalone, which has a subtle flavour of iodine, can be tough, and it is usually beaten with a wooden mallet to tenderize it before cooking.

Frozen abalone is available from some Asian stores, and it is also possible to buy canned abalone. This is yellow brown in colour and has a savoury flavour. Canned abalone tends to be rubbery in texture, so it is seldom served in its own, but is usually combined with other ingredients. The can juices can be used in soups and sauces. Dried abalone is an expensive and much sought-after delicacy.

CLAMS

There are many different types of clam. In Japan, the giant clam and the round clam are both used for making *sushi*, and in China clams with black bean sauce are a favourite treat. When buying clams, check that the shells are not broken. Wash them well in cold running water, then leave in salt water before steaming for 7–8 minutes or until the shells open. Clams are delicious served simply, with a dipping sauce based on hoisin sauce, plum sauce or soy sauce with ginger. Clams also make a very good addition to soups.

MUSSELS

This is another shellfish that is widely used in Asian cooking. Farmed mussels are now readily available and have the advantage that they are usually relatively free of barnacles. They are generally sold in quantities of 1kg/2¼lb, sufficient for a main course for two or three people. Look for good-size specimens with glossy shells. Discard any that are not closed, or which fail to shut when tapped. Use the back of a short stout knife to scrape away any barnacles, pull away the hairy "beards", then wash the shellfish thoroughly. The best way to cook mussels is to steam them in a small amount of flavoured liquid in a large lidded pan for 3–4 minutes until the shells open. Use finely chopped ginger, lemon grass, a few torn lime leaves and some fish sauce to add flavouring to the mussels.

CRABS

These are eaten with great relish throughout the East. There are many different species that are exclusive to Asia, found in the sea and in fresh water. Blue swimming crabs are commonly available in Hong Kong and Thailand. This species obligingly moults its shell leaving a soft shell underneath, which allows the crab to be eaten whole. Other species have very hard shells, from which the meat must be removed. The meat is often pan-fried or cooked in a pot of rice.

To cook a crab, place it in a pan of cold water and bring it slowly to the boil. Time cooking from the moment the water boils, and do not cook the crab for more than 12 minutes, whatever its size.

LOBSTERS

In Asia, this luxury shellfish is usually served as a restaurant dish, rather than cooked at home. To cook a live lobster, put it in the freezer for 2 hours to render it unconscious, then place it in a pan of ice-cold water, cover the pan tightly and bring the water to the boil. The shell will turn bright red in colour and the flesh will be tender and succulent when the lobster is cooked. If you buy a ready-cooked lobster the tail should spring back into a curl when pulled out straight. One of the best ways of eating lobster is with a simple dip of soy sauce with grated ginger.

SCALLOPS

Prized for their tender, sweet flesh, scallops are popular throughout Asia. The delicate flesh needs the briefest possible cooking. An excellent way of cooking scallops is to marinate them in a mixture of Chinese rice wine, sugar and soy sauce for 30 minutes, then steam them with the marinade and some slivers of fresh root ginger and spring onion (scallion).

SHRIMPS AND PRAWNS

There are thousands of varieties of these small crustaceans, which can be found in both fresh water and the sea. In Asia, the terms shrimps and prawns tend to be used fairly indiscriminately, while in the US prawns and shrimps are known collectively as shrimp.

Shrimps can be small or large and the same holds good for prawns. Always try to buy fresh raw shellfish whenever possible, choosing specimens that are a translucent grey colour tinged with blue. If using frozen shrimps and prawns, it is preferable to buy them raw rather than cooked. Thaw them slowly and dry them well before using.

Further preparation will depend upon the chosen recipe. The shells may be left on or removed, and larger shrimps or prawns may be shelled but with the tails left intact.

FANTAIL OR PHOENIX PRAWNS

This very pretty way of serving prawns comes from China. The cooked shellfish are served with their bright red tails still intact and are supposed to resemble the legendary phoenix, which is a symbol of dignity and good luck. To served prawns in this way, choose large specimens.

1 Remove the heads from the prawns and peel away most of the body shell. Leave a little of the shell to keep the tail intact.

2 To devein the prawns, make a very small incision along the back of each prawn and remove the black intestinal cord with the point of a sharp knife.

3 Hold the prepared prawns by the tails and dip them lightly in seasoned cornflour (cornstarch), and then in a frothy batter before cooking them in hot oil until the tails, which are free from batter, turn red.

The complex and intriguing flavours of Chinese and Asian cooking rely heavily on spices, aromatics and herbs. Each region uses flavourings in slightly different ways. For example Thai dishes are often heavily spiced with chillies and scented with aromatic coriander (cilantro), while in Japan these flavourings are used to create a much more subtle, but equally enticing result.

CHILLIES

Althought these are grown, and used, all over the world, they are actually native to tropical America. Christopher Columbus introduced them to Europe, having come across them in Mexico while searching for peppercorns. Their fame spread rapidly, and soon they were being cultivated in Africa, India and South-east Asia, where they rapidly became an integral part of their cuisine. There is, however, a wild variety grown in China's Sichuan province, known as towards sky canyon or peacock's eye chilli, which appears to be native to China.

Chillies belong to the same family as sweet (bell) peppers, and there are many varieties. The ones most commonly used in Asia are the *kalyanpur*, *kovilpatt* and *kesanakurru* chillies from India, the Japanese *honka* or *hontaka*, the Korean chilli and the family of Thai chillies, which includes the fiery bird's eye. Like sweet peppers, many chillies start out green and ripen to red, while others change from yellow to red and finally to brown or even black, so what might appear to be a basket of assorted chillies may be the same variety. Chillies range from pea-size to 30cm/12in monsters. Although Asian cooks tend to use them fresh, chillies are also available dried.

Although heat is the quality most often associated with chillies, flavour is important too. They may be described as sweet, smoky and piquant. The degree of heat varies from very mild to quite explosive, but can be moderated somewhat if the seeds and pithy membrane (where most of the heat resides) are removed. The shape and colour give no sure indication of the hotness – for example some large green chillies are very mild, while others are blisteringly hot. Chillies grown in hot climates tend to be hotter than those grown in a cooler climate.

Chillies are the perfect ingredient for hot climates. It may seem surprising but, because they encourage blood to rush to the surface of the skin, they actually promote cooling in the body.

In many Asian countries chillies are eaten out of the hand, as snacks, and cooks often determine the strength of a chilli before buying by nibbling a sample from a market stall. They are used fresh in many sauces and salads, and are essential ingredients in Indonesian sambals (spicy relishes). They are also used in cooked dishes, including stocks, soups, braised dishes and stir-fries, either with or without the seeds. Where just a hint of heat is required, chillies are sometimes added whole to a dish, then removed again just before serving.

Thailand is one of the world's greatest producers of fresh chillies and Thai cooks have developed some of the most exciting and innovative chilli recipes. A popular way of serving whole chillies is to fill them with a pork and prawn stuffing. The chillies are steamed, then fried.

In China, cooks use chillies to stimulate the palate. The regional cuisines of Hunan, Jiangxi, Guizhou and Yunnan all feature chillies, although not as strongly as does the province of Sichuan, which is famous for its spicy food. Even in Sichuan, however, chillies are used with discretion and at least a third of Sichuan dishes do not contain any chilli at all. The Cantonese use chillies in some of their dishes, and chilli sauce and chilli oil are popular condiments.

When buying, look for firm, unblemished fruit. Some types look wrinkled even in their prime, so do not let this put you off fruit that otherwise appears to be in good condition. The best way to store chillies is to wrap them in kitchen paper, place them in a plastic bag and keep them in the salad compartment of the refrigerator. They will keep well for a week or more, but it is a good idea to check them occasionally. If you intend to use them solely for cooking, they can be frozen. There is no need to blanch them if you plan to use them fairly quickly. To dry your own chillies, thread them on a string, then hang them in a warm place for a week or two until they are dry. Crush dried chillies in a mortar with a pestle.

PREPARING CHILLIES

Chillies must be handled with care. They contain capsaicin, which can cause intense irritation to sensitive skin. Wash your hands immediately after handling chillies. Some people wear rubber (latex) gloves when preparing them.

To prepare fresh chillies, *remove the stalks, then slice the fruits lengthways in half. Scrape out the pith and seeds, then slice, shred or chop the flesh. The seeds can be added to the dish for extra heat.*

To make chilli flowers, *hold a fresh chilli by the stem and slit it in half lengthways. Keeping the stem end of the chilli intact, cut it lengthways into fine strips. Put the chillies in a bowl of iced water, and chill for several hours. Drain on kitchen paper and use as a garnish.*

To make chilli paste, *halve and seed fresh chillies, then purée until smooth in a food processor. Add a chopped onion for bulk. Store in the refrigerator for up to 1 week, or freeze for up to 6 months. Sambal oelek, an Indonesian chilli sauce, is made in a similar way using blanched chillies.*

To prepare dried chillies, *remove the stems and seeds and snap each chilli into 2–3 pieces. Put these in a deep bowl, pour over hot water to cover and leave to stand for 30 minutes. Drain, reserving the soaking water if it can usefully be added to the dish, and use the pieces of chilli as they are, or chop them more finely.*

To roast dried chillies, *heat a heavy frying pan without adding oil. Press the chillies on to the surface of the pan, but don't allow them to burn. Remove from the pan and leave to cool, then crush or grind in a mortar with a pestle.*

GARLIC

This pungent bulb is a member of the onion and leek family. It is believed to have originated in Asia, and is mentioned in very early Chinese texts, which date back over three thousand years.

There are several varieties of garlic, from tiny heads to the aptly named elephant garlic. The colour of the skin varies from white through to pink and purple, and the flavour can be anywhere from mild to extremely pungent. The most common variety in South-east Asia has a purple skin, a distinctive aroma and a fairly strong flavour with a hint of sweetness. In South-east Asia, cooks use a miniature variety of garlic. There are only four to six cloves in each bulb, and both the aroma and flavour are much more concentrated. Thai cooks favour small garlic bulbs whose cloves have such thin skins that it is seldom necessary to remove them for cooking. The cloves are simply smashed with the flat side of a cleaver, then added to the pan, where the skins dissolve to become part of the dish.

In Chinese cooking, particulary in Beijing and Sichuan, garlic forms a trinity of flavours with spring onion (scallion) and ginger in thousands of dishes. It is a basic ingredient in much of Asia, including Korea, but it is less popular in Japanese cooking and is mainly used for medicinal purposes. Vietnamese cooks use a great deal of garlic, and in Thailand an aromatic mixture of crushed garlic, coriander (cilantro) root and pepper is the foundation of many dishes. Garlic is an essential ingredient in Thai curry pastes. Raw garlic is often used in dips, marinades and dressings.

Garlic is usually peeled before use. To do this, crush it with the flat blade of a cleaver. The skin will separate from the flesh easily. For whole cloves of garlic, or slices, just cut off the root end of the clove and remove the peel with your fingers. If the garlic is to be used in a spice mix, put the whole clove in a mortar and hit it with a pestle to release the skin. Remove the broken skin, then crush the garlic with the other ingredients. Recipes indicate whether garlic is to be sliced, chopped or crushed.

Asian cooks usually purchase bulbs of garlic or minced garlic in jars. Dried garlic is also available, as granules or flakes. Flakes need to be reconstituted in water before stir-frying, but can be added directly to braised dishes with plenty of liquid.

When buying, look for firm, plump bulbs (also called heads) with clear, papery skins. Avoid any that are sprouting. Garlic bulbs keep well in a cool, dry place.

MAKING GARLIC OIL

Throughout Asia, garlic is used to flavour oil for frying. This is partly due to the wonderful flavour that it imparts, but also because it helps to reduce the oily flavour of fried dishes.

To make garlic oil, heat about 120ml/4fl oz/½ cup oil in a small pan. Add 30ml/2 tbsp crushed garlic. Cook gently for 5 minutes, or until the garlic is pale gold, stirring occasionally. Leave to cool, strain and use as required.

GINGER

This is believed to be indigenous to the tropical jungles of South-east Asia, and was introduced into China by way of India more than two thousand years ago. The portion of the plant popularly called ginger root is actually a rhizome or underground stem. The colour ranges from pale pink (when very young) to a golden beige, with a dry, papery skin. Ginger is highly valued throughout Asia, not only as an aromatic, but also for its medicinal properties. It is believed to aid digestion, check coughs and quell nausea.

Fresh root ginger, also known as green ginger, has a refreshing scent, reminiscent of citrus, and a pleasant, sharp flavour. Young ginger is tender and mild enough to be stir-fried as a vegetable, while older roots become fibrous and tends to be more pungent. Root ginger is available dried, but tastes quite different from fresh. It is used mainly as a pickling spice. Asian cooks would not consider it an acceptable substitute for the fresh root. Ground ginger tastes quite different again and, in Asia, its use is limited to mixing with other ground spices such as when making curry powder.

Root ginger is an indispensable ingredient in Asian cooking. In China, it is usually paired with spring onions (scallions) to create a harmonious yin-yang balance in a wide variety of dishes; the cool spring onion provides the yin and the hot ginger the yang. Together, they go with the flavour of some meats and seafood.

Ginger is sometimes used on its own to counteract the oily flavour of some cooking oils and marinades. In Thailand, sticks of young ginger are often served as dippers with spicy sauce, while Indonesian cooks make a wonderful sambal by grinding chillies, shallots and garlic with ginger, and stirring in sugar, salt and rice vinegar.

Pickled ginger also plays an important role in Asian cooking. It can be served solo as a side dish, or combined with other ingredients such as beef or duck. Chinese pickled ginger is packed in sweetened rice vinegar and is quite hot. Japanese pickled ginger has a more delicate flavour. The pale pink type called *gari* is always served with *sushi* or *sashimi* to refresh the palate between mouthfuls.

Root ginger is usually peeled before use. The flesh is then sliced, grated or chopped. When ginger is used as a flavouring, then discarded after cooking, it must be bruised first with the flat blade of a knife or cleaver.

Fresh root ginger is readily available in supermarkets. Look for firm pieces with smooth skin. It will keep well for up to 2 weeks in a cool, dry place, away from strong light. It can also be frozen, then grated straight from the freezer and will thaw on contact with hot food.

MAKING GARI

This pale pink pickled ginger is a great delicacy in Japan and is served with sushi *and* sashimi. *It is easy to make and will keep for several months.*

1 Thinly peel 200g/7oz fresh root ginger. Lightly rub 5–10ml/1–2 tsp salt on to the the peeled ginger and leave for 24 hours.

2 In a small bowl, mix together 250ml/ 8fl oz/1 cup rice wine vinegar, 120ml/ 4fl oz/1/2 cup water and 45ml/3 tbsp sugar, and stir until the sugar has dissolved. Rinse and drain the salted ginger and add to the vinegar mixture. Cover and leave to marinate for a week.

To serve, use a sharp knife to slice the ginger very thinly along the grain, cutting only as much as you require.

TURMERIC

This comes from the ginger family but does not have the characteristic heat associated with fresh ginger. The plant is a rhizome and is indiginous to hot, humid, hilly areas of South-east Asia. Frequently referred to as Indian saffron, it shares with saffron the capacity to tint foods yellow, but is nowhere near as subtle. The world's largest producer of turmeric is India, but Indonesia and China also grow significant quantities of this spice. The bulk of the turmeric crop is used for domestic consumption or ground and sold as powder.

Fresh turmeric is available from Asian stores. When cut, the bright orangy-yellow flesh is revealed. It has a peppery aroma with a hint of wood. It imparts a warm, slightly musky flavour and a rich colour to any food with which it is cooked. The dried spice has similar properties.

Ground turmeric is an essential ingredient in curry powders. It is also used in some blends of mustard powder. Kedgeree contains turmeric, and it is also used in pilau rice, dhals and vegetable dishes. It has a natural affinity with fish, and is often used in Malaysian recipes.

To use fresh turmeric, slice off the skin, then slice, grate or chop the flesh. Grind with other ingredients to make a curry paste. Wash hands after handling as it can stain the skin. Some people prefer to wear gloves when preparing fresh turmeric.

OTHER USES OF TURMERIC
The bright yellow colour, that can clearly be seen when the rhizome is sliced, is used as a dye of silks and cottons, including the fabric used to make robes for Buddhist monks. When mixed to a paste, turmeric is sometimes smeared on the cheeks to protect the skin from the sun.

Fresh turmeric will keep for 2 weeks, if stored in a cool, dry place away from strong light. It can be stored in the refrigerator, but must be well wrapped as its pervasive smell can be absorbed by other foods. Ground turmeric will lose its potency quickly. Store in an airtight container away from strong light. Whole pieces of dried turmeric are used in some pickles.

GALANGAL

Like fresh root ginger and turmeric, this is a rhizome that grows underneath the ground. The finger-like protruberances of galangal tend to be thinner and paler in colour than ginger, but the two look similar and are used in much the same way. Fresh galangal is widely available in the West. There are two types: greater galangal, also known as *lengkuas*, is a native of Indonesia, while lesser galangal originated in southern China. It is not as widely used as its larger relation but is popular in Thailand, where it is known as *krachai*.

Greater galangal has a pine-like aroma with a correspondingly sharp flavour; lesser galangal is more pungent and tastes similar to a cross between ginger and black pepper.

Laos powder is dried ground galangal. Although it does not taste the same as fresh galangal, it is required for many South-east Asian recipes. As a general guide, about 5ml/1 tsp of Laos powder is equivalent to 1cm/½in fresh galangal, which has been peeled and chopped.

Galangal is an essential flavouring in South-east Asia, particularly for seafood and meat. It is often pounded with shallots, garlic and chillies to make a spice paste for dips or curries. The Thais add sliced galangal to soups, with shreds of lemon grass and lime leaves, while the Vietnamese add it to a peanut and lime sauce used to dress meat and vegetable salads.

Fresh galangal should always be peeled. The flesh is usually thinly sliced or cut into matchsticks for cooking. It is quite hard, so should be sliced before trying to crush it. It needs to be cooked slightly longer than ginger if it is to become tender.

Fresh galangal will keep for up to 2 weeks if stored in a cool, dry place. It can be stored in the refrigerator but must be wrapped in greaseproof (waxed paper) to keep it moist.

LEMON GRASS

At one time, this scented grass was little known outside South-east Asia; today it is widely available in the West. Lemon grass is a perennial tufted plant with a bulbous base. It grows in dense clumps in tropical and subtropical countries and is cultivated commercially on a grand scale. The cut stems are about 20cm/8in long, and look a little like fat spring onions (scallions) or very skinny leeks.

It is only when the lemon grass stems are cut that the distinctive citrus aroma can be fully appreciated. This is matched by the clean, intense lemon flavour, which has a hint of ginger but none of the acidity associated with lemon. Lemon rind is sometimes suggested as a substitute but it lacks the lively intensity of lemon grass, and will give disappointing results.

Ground dried lemon grass, also known as serai powder, can be used instead of fresh, although the flavour is not as good. As a guide, about 5ml/1 tsp powder is equivalent

MAKING A LEMON GRASS BRUSH

The upper part of the lemon grass stem can be made into a brush and used to baste meat, fish or vegetables that are to be grilled (broiled) or barbecued. This imparts a subtle flavour of lemon grass.

Keep the dry part of stalk that is left after the bulbous part has been used for a recipe. Using a cleaver or pestle, flatten the cut end of the stalk to produce a fibrous brush-like tip.

to one fresh stalk. Whole and dried chopped stalks are also available in jars from Asian stores and larger supermarkets, as are jars of lemon grass paste.

Lemon grass is widely used throughout South-east Asia, in soups, sauces, stir-fries, curries, salads, pickles and marinades. Its tangy citrus flavour is a perfect partner for coconut milk, especially in fish, seafood and chicken dishes. Thai cooks often start a stir-fry by adding a few rings of lemon grass and perhaps a little ginger or galangal to the oil. This flavours the oil and will fill the kitchen with a glorious aroma. A very popular Vietnamese dish consists of sea bream coated in a lemon grass paste, which is left to stand until the flavour penetrates the fish, and then fried.

There are two main ways of using lemon grass. The stalk can be bruised with a pestle or the flat side of a cleaver, then cooked slowly in a soup or stew until it releases all its flavour and is removed, or the tender portions of the lemon grass (usually the lower 5cm/2in of the bulbous end of the stem) can be sliced or finely chopped, then stir-fried or used in a salad or braised dish.

Fresh lemon grass stalks should be stored, wrapped in a paper bag, in the salad drawer of the refrigerator. They will keep for about 2 weeks.

KAFFIR LIMES

These fruit are not true limes, but belong to a subspecies of the citrus family. Native to South-east Asia, they have dark green knobbly skins, quite unlike smooth-skinned limes. The fruit itself is inedible. The rind is sometimes used in cooking, but it is the leaves that are most highly prized.

Kaffir limes yield very little juice, and what there is is extremely sour. Malaysian and Thai cooks sometimes use it to heighten the flavour of citrus-based dishes. However, it is more commonly used by Vietnamese women as a hair rinse.

The scented bouquet of kaffir limes is unmistakably citrus, and the full lemony flavour is released when the leaves are torn or shredded. The leaves are synonymous with Thai cooking, and are also used in Indonesia, Malaysia, Burma and Vietnam. They are torn or finely shredded and used in soups (especially hot-and-sour soups) and curries. The finely grated rind is sometimes added to fish or chicken dishes.

Fresh kaffir limes and leaves can be found in Asian stores and large supermarkets. They will keep for several days, or can be frozen for several months. Freeze-dried kaffir lime leaves are also available and make a reasonable substitute for fresh. These are used in much the same way as bay leaves and do not have to be soaked in water first. Stored in a sealed container in a cool, dry place, the dried leaves will keep their flavour for only a few months.

ORANGE OR TANGERINE PEEL

Both oranges and tangerines originated in China, where they were held in high regard for centuries before traders introduced them to the West. The sun-dried peel of both of these citrus fruits is often used as a spice, particularly in the cooking of Sichuan and Hunan. The dried peel is brown and brittle, but retains a citrus fragrance. When used in cooking, it imparts a tangy flavour.

Originally, dried citrus peels were used only medicinally. Today, however, they are a popular seasoning and are often combined with star anise and cinnamon in braised meat and poultry dishes. In braised dishes, pieces of dried peel are used in much the same way as star anise, and are discarded after cooking. When peel is used in a stir-fry, however, it is first soaked in water until soft, and the white pith is scraped off before the peel is shredded or sliced.

Orange and tangerine peel are available in sealed plastic bags in Asian stores. Once opened, the bags should be resealed and stored in a cool, dry, dark place. The peel will keep for many months.

JAPANESE CITRON PEEL

In Japan, very thin slices of citron peel are used to garnish soups. The ground peel is used to flavour miso.

CURRY LEAVES

These are the shiny green leaves of a hardwood tree that is indigenous to India. They are widely used in Indian cooking and were introduced into Malaysia by Tamil immigrants. The spear-shaped leaves grow on a thin stem. They are slightly serrated, with a pale underside, and quite similar to small bay leaves.

Curry leaves have an intriguing warm fragrance, with just a hint of sweet, green pepper or tangerine. The full flavour is released when the leaves are bruised. When added to curries and braised dishes, they impart a distinctive flavour. Dried curry leaves are greatly inferior to fresh and rapidly loose their flavour.

The leaves are used whole or torn in Indian, Malaysian and Indonesian curries. Fried in ghee, with mustard seeds, they make a good addition to dhals. To use, rinse the leaves and then strip them from the stems. Use the leaves whole or chopped.

Fresh curry leaves can be bought from shops selling Indian and Gujerati produce. They will keep for several days in the vegetable compartment of the refrigerator, but should be tightly wrapped to prevent their flavour being transferred to other items. Alternatively, open freeze the leaves, then transfer a plastic box. If you buy dried leaves, choose vacuum-packed ones as they have a better colour and flavour.

MINT

This herb originated in the Mediterranean region, but it spread rapidly throughout the world. There are many types of mint grown in Asia, but the most commonly used is a tropical variety of spearmint, which has grey-green oval leaves.

All mint has a very distinctive fresh, stimulating aroma. Asian mint tends to be more strongly flavoured than European varieties, and is slightly sweet. It has a wonderfully cool aftertaste that goes well with spicy foods.

Mint is an essential herb in Vietnamese cooking and it is they who introduced the herb to Thai cooks. Its fresh flavour is enjoyed in many salads, and in the delicious rice paper rolls called *goi cuon*. Thai cooks often add a large handful of mint leaves to some of their soups and highly spiced dishes just before serving.

As mint has such a dominant flavour, it is seldom used with other herbs. To prepare fresh mint, simply wash the leaves on the stem under cold water, shake then pat dry on kitchen paper.

To store, wrap mint loosely in kitchen paper and keep in the salad compartment of the refrigerator, or stand the stems in a jug (pitcher) of water covered with a plastic bag and keep in the refrigerator.

BASIL

This is one of the oldest herbs known to man. It is an annual and is believed to have originated in India. In Vietnam, Laos and Cambodia it is an important ingredient, but it is in Thailand that basil is most widely used, and it is the varieties of basil favoured by the Thais that you will find most frequently in Asian shops in the West.

Sweet basil (*bai horapa*) comes closest to the Mediterranean varieties. It has shiny green leaves and the stems are sometimes purple. Holy basil (*krapow*) is another sweet basil, but with narrower leaves that tend to be dull rather than shiny. The leaves have serrated red or purple edges. Thais also use a lemon-scented basil (*manglak*), sometimes known as hairy basil, but this does not travel well and is seldom seen outside Thailand. If you cannot obtain Asian basil when cooking Asian dishes, Western varieties can be used instead, but the flavour will not be the same, and you should use a little more than the recipe states. Basil is best used fresh.

Of the Asian basils, sweet basil has a faint aniseed flavour and is added to curries or salads both as an ingredient and also as a garnish. It imparts a fresh spicy flavour. Holy basil is more pungent. It only releases its full flavour when cooked so is frequently used in stir-fries. Hairy basil has a lemon scent and is slightly peppery.

To use basil, strip the leaves from the stem and either tear them into pieces or use the leaves whole. Avoid chopping as this bruises the delicate leaves.

To store, wrap bunches of fresh basil loosely in kitchen paper and keep them in the salad compartment of the refregerator. Alternatively, stand the stems in a jug (pitcher) of cold water covered with a plastic bag and keep in the refrigerator. Change the water every day.

GROWING BASIL

If you have difficulty locating supplies of fresh basil for Thai or Vietnamese recipes, it might be worth growing your own from seed. Many garden centres and hardware stores sell the full range of Asian varieties, and they do well wherever the climate is relatively mild. Start them off in pots on a warm window sill, and move them to a sunny patio after the threat of frost has passed.

SHISO

Also known as *perilla*, this annual herb is grown in China, Korea, Laos and Vietnam and is very well known in Japan. The leaves can be green or a reddish-purple and often appear slightly wrinkled. When crushed, the leaves release a pungent aroma, similar to that of mint. Japanese cooks use shiso in *tempura* and when making *umeboshi* (pickled plums). In the presence of an acid, the red-leafed variety dyes fresh root ginger red. Shiso flowers are used as a garnish.

CORIANDER/CILANTRO

Also known as Chinese parsley, coriander is one of the most popular herbs in the world. Although a native of southern Europe, fresh coriander has become an indispensable ingredient throughout Asia, the Middle East and Latin America.

The fresh leaves have a very distinctive, wonderfully aromatic, scented flavour. When dry-fried, the seeds smell rather like burnt orange, and the ground seeds impart a warm, spicy aroma to food.

Asian cooks use every part of the plant: the stems are used for flavouring; the leaves in stir-fries, soups and noodle dishes, and as a garnish; the seeds for spice pastes and in curries. Ground coriander is widely used, often in combination with ground cumin. In Thailand, the roots are used, too. If you cannot obtain roots, use the bottom portion of the stem instead.

When using fresh coriander, try not to chop it too finely. Never overcook the leaves or they will become limp and unpalatable; either use them raw as a garnish, or add them to a dish at the very last moment. If a recipe calls for ground coriander, dry-fry and grind the seeds yourself for superior aroma and flavour.

Fresh coriander will keep for 3–4 days if stood in a jug (pitcher) of cold water covered with a plastic bag and stored in the refrigerator. Coriander roots can be frozen. Dried coriander seeds keep well, but the ready-ground powder rapidly loses its aroma and flavour.

Star Anise

This is the unusual star-shaped fruit of an evergreen tree native to Vietnam and Southwest China. The tree has yellow flowers that resemble narcissus. These give way to the star-like fruits, which are harvested before they ripen. The tree bears fruit after 6 years initially, but then has a productive life of up to a hundred years. The points of the star contain amber seeds. Both the seeds and the husk are used for the ground spice. In China, one section of the star, which is known as a point, is often chewed after a meal as a digestive.

Star anise smells and tastes like liquorice and the flavour can also be detected in drinks such as pastis and anisette. It is very popular in Chinese cuisine, especially with pork and duck dishes, and it is often used to flavour beef soups in Vietnam. It is also sometimes used in sweet dishes such as fruit salads. Ground star anise is included in five-spice powder.

Star anise can be added to dishes whole, and looks so attractive that it is often left in a dish when serving, even though it no longer fulfills a culinary purpose. When only a small quantity is required, the spice can be broken and just one or two points or segments can be added. It is possible to grind star anise at home, but it should be used sparingly as it is quite powerful.

As a whole spice, star anise has a long shelf life. However, the ground spice does not keep well so buy in small quantities from a store with a high turnover of stock. It should be stored in a cool, dry place, away from direct light, to retain maximum aroma and flavour.

Five-spice Powder

This reddish brown spice mixture is classically composed of equal quantities of Sichuan peppercorns, cassia or cinnamon, cloves, fennel seeds and star anise. Sometimes ginger, galangal, black cardamom and liquorice are included. Ginger gives the spice blend a sweeter flavour, and this version is used in desserts. Five-spice powder is very popular in China, and is particularly good with duck, pork, red cooked meats (cooked in soy sauce) and barbecued meats such as spare ribs. Make your own powder by grinding equal amounts of the five spices with a mortar and pestle, or buy the ready-ground powder. A five-spice paste is now available in small jars from many of the larger supermarkets.

Japanese Seven-spice Powder

This wonderful spice mixture is known as shichimi-togarashi *in Japan, seven-flavour seasoning or seven-taste powder. The Japanese use it as a condiment in the same way that Westerners use salt and pepper. It is popular as a seasoning for soups and noodles and other dishes such as* sukiyaki *and* tempura. *Seven-spice powder is made from ground chilli, hemp seed, poppy seed, rape seed, Sichuan peppercorns, black and white sesame seeds, and dried ground tangerine peel. Ground nori seaweed is added to some mixes.*

CLOVES

These are the dried unopened flower buds of a tree that is a member of the myrtle family. They originated in the Spice Islands in Indonesia but now the biggest producer of cloves is Zanzibar, where the fresh pink buds are picked twice a year. The buds are dried on palm leaf mats or over a gentle heat when they turn reddish brown. They have an intense fragrance and an aromatic flavour that can be fiery.

In Asia, cloves are mainly used in savoury dishes, and their warm aromatic flavour complements rich meats. Thai cooks use them to cut the rich flavour of duck, and with tomatoes, salty vegetables and in ham or pork dishes. Ground cloves are an essential ingredient in many spice mixtures, including five-spice powder.

When buying cloves, look for plump specimens. Whole cloves have a long shelf life if kept in a cool place. Ground cloves lose their flavour quite quickly so should be bought in small quantities and stored in an airtight jar away from strong light.

CINNAMON

This spice is actually the bark of a bushy tree that is a member of the laurel family that flourishes in Asia. After three years, the branches are cut off and a long incision is made in the bark, so that this can be lifted off. This is carried out during the rainy season, when the high humidity speeds the peeling process. The bark is then dried in the sun and hand rolled to produce the familiar quills or sticks. Ground cinnamon is also produced.

Cinnamon has a delightfully exotic, sweet and fragrant bouquet. The warm, aromatic. flavour has universal appeal in sweet and savoury dishes and in cakes and breads. In Asia, the sticks are used in spicy meat dishes, often with star anise, with which

cinnamon has a great affinity. In Indonesia, cinnamon is used in *rendang*, a spicy beef and coconut stew.

To use, add the whole or broken cinnamon stick as directed in the recipe. The sticks are difficult to grind at home, so buy ready-ground cinnamon.

Cinnamon sticks will keep for a year or more in an airtight container. Ground cinnamon loses its flavour quite quickly.

CASSIA

This is sometimes known as Chinese cinnamon. Like cinnamon, it comes from the bark of a tree that is related to laurel. It is harvested in much the same way as cinnamon, but the bark is not as fine so, although it curls, it will not form the fine quills that we associate with cinnamon sticks. Cassia smells like cinnamon, but is rather more pungent.

Chinese cooks make much use of cassia. It is one of the constituents of five-spice powder and is also an important ingredient in the elaborate spiced stock known as *lu*, which is used throughout China for simmering foods. Cracked cassia quills and cassia buds, which look like cloves, are used in the East to give a warm aromatic flavour to pickles, curries and spiced meat dishes.

To use, break the pieces as required with the end of a rolling pin or put them in a mortar and shatter them with a pestle. Buy ready-ground cassia when required.

Cassia should be stored in an airtight jar and will keep for about a year. Ground cassia will lose its aroma quite quickly.

CARDAMOM

This native of South India belongs to the ginger family. It is largely grown for its pods, although Thai cooks sometimes use the leaves for flavouring. The pods are either added whole to spicy dishes, or opened so that the tiny dark seeds can be extracted. The most familiar pods are pale green, and there are also white pods, which are actually just bleached green ones. Black cardamoms, which come from Vietnam and India, are larger and coarser than green ones, and taste quite different.

Cardamoms are sweet, pungent and highly aromatic. They have a pleasantly warm flavour, with hints of lemon and eucalyptus. Indian cooks often use them to flavour curries, pilaus and desserts.

The pods can be used whole or bruised and dry-fried to enhance the flavour. If just the seeds are required, discard the outer husks. For ground cardamom, grind the seeds in a mortar using a pestle.

When buying, choose whole pods and store in an airtight jar in a cool dry place.

CUMIN

This is a member of the parsley family and has been cultivated since the earliest times. Only the seeds, which can be either whole or ground, are used in cooking. It has a sweet spicy aroma and the flavour is pungent and slightly bitter.

Cumin is often partnered with whole or ground coriander seeds. Indian cooks are particularly partial to cumin, and it was they who introduced the spice to Singapore, Malaysia and Indonesia. To bring out their full flavour, the seeds are often dry-fried.

Store cumin in a cool place away from bright light. For best results dry-fry and grind the whole cumin seeds as required. You can buy ready-ground cumin, but it loses its flavour rapidly.

FENNEL SEEDS

This plant is a member of the parsley family and is widely grown in India and Japan. The small ridged seeds are sage green in colour and have a warm aroma and an anise flavour.

Fennel seeds are a constituent in many spice mixtures, especially in those for fish or shellfish. Ground fennel is used in five-spice powder. Before grinding fennel seeds, dry-fry to release their full flavour.

Buy small quantities of the seeds at a time and store in an airtight jar in a cool place, away from strong light.

PEPPER

Referred to as the king of spices, pepper is a perennial climbing vine indigenous to the Malabar coast of India where it is said that the best pepper is still produced. It grows best near the equator and is cultivated intensively in Sarawak and Thailand, as well as in tropical Africa and Brazil.

Pepper berries are harvested when they are still unripe and green. In Sarawak, in Malaysia, they are dried on mats in the sun, and are raked frequently until the skin shrivels and the berries darken to become black peppercorns. Alternatively, the berries are immersed in boiling water, then drained well before being dried in kilns.

White peppercorns are ripe berries that have had their husks removed. The berries are picked when they are reddish-orange, then soaked in running water for several days. They are then trampled underfoot to loosen the husks and transferred to rattan baskets, where they are washed and the husks and stalks removed by hand to leave the white peppercorns. These are then left to dry on mats in the sun for several weeks. Alternatively, they may be kiln-dried.

Black peppercorns have an earthy aroma and their flavour is hot and pungent. White peppercorns are slightly milder. It is the one spice that is used before, during and after cooking. It not only has its own flavour, but has the ability to enhance the flavour of other ingredients.

Use a peppermill and grind fresh black pepper as it is required. White peppercorns are used where flecks of black might spoil the appearance of a dish.

Buy whole peppercorns and store in an airtight container, where they will keep for a very long time.

GREEN PEPPERCORNS

These are simply unripe berries and are very popular in Thailand. They have a less complex flavour than white or black peppercorns but are still quite fiery.

Green peppercorns can be found on the stem in some Thai supermarkets and are also available dried, pickled or canned. Those that are bottled or canned need to be rinsed well and drained. They can be used whole or crushed, depending on the recipe. Freeze-dried green peppercorns can be ground in a peppermill.

SICHUAN PEPPER/SANCHO

To call this pepper is rather misleading. It actually comes from the prickly ash tree, which is native to the Sichuan province in China, but also grows elsewhere in Asia. Unusually, it is the reddish-brown seed pods themselves, not the seeds they contain, that are used for the spice. They are either added whole to stewed dishes or dried and ground as a seasoning spice.

The prickly ash also grows in Japan, where the ripened pods are called *mizansho* or Japanese peppercorns. When ground, the spice is known as *konazansho*.

Sichuan peppercorns are not as pungent as true pepper but have a warm aroma with a hint of citrus. The full flavour is released when they are dry-fried.

They are immensely popular in Chinese cuisine and are excellent in duck, pork and chicken dishes. The ground peppercorns are used in five-spice powder and Japanese seven-spice powder. Dry-fry the seed pods to heighten their flavour, then use as directed in recipes.

Always buy whole peppercorns, dry-fry then grind. Store in an airtight jar.

WASABI

This is sometimes described as horseradish mustard and it has much in common with both although it is related to neither. Wasabi is a Japanese seasoning, derived from a slow-growing plant that is found near mountain streams. The peeled root reveals vivid green flesh. This is very finely grated, preferably on sharkskin, and then dried or powdered. When mixed to a cream with soy sauce or water, it makes a very hot condiment, which is traditionally served with *sushi* and *sashimi*. Tubes of ready-made paste are also available.

MUSTARD

This is one of the oldest spices known to man and has been cultivated as a crop for thousands of years. Both white (*apounda*) and black (*nigra*) mustard seeds are native to the Mediterranean region, while brown (*juncea*) mustard seeds are native to India.

In Asia, the mustard plant is valued as much for its dark green leaves, which are called mustard greens and are a popular vegetable, as for its seeds. Mustard powders and pastes are not as widely used in Asia as they are in Europe or the US.

Mustard seeds have no aroma in their raw state. When they are roasted, however, they develop a rich, nutty smell. Mustard's hot, peppery taste is only activated when the seeds are crushed and mixed with warm water. Brown mustard seeds, which have largely replaced the black seeds, are not as intensely pungent. White mustard seeds, which are actually a pale honey colour, are slightly larger than the other two varieties and a little milder.

Throughout Asia, mustard seeds are used for pickling and seasoning. The whole seeds are often used in vegetable and dhal dishes, especially in countries such as Malaysia. They are frequently roasted or fried before being used to bring out their flavour. In south India, the seeds are fried in hot ghee or oil, with a few curry leaves for extra flavour. The pan is covered until the seeds splutter and pop. The seeds and oil are then poured, still sizzling, on to hot vegetable dishes, soups, stews or dhal as a flavoursome topping. Mustard oil is occasionally used for frying the seeds.

Mustard powder is used as a condiment. It achieves maximum potency when mixed with warm water. It takes about 15 minutes for the full flavour to develop.

Mustard seeds keep well. Store them in an airtight jar in a cool place.

TAMARIND

This is believed to be a native of East Africa but the tamarind tree is now cultivated in India, South-east Asia and the Caribbean. The brown fruit pods are 15–20cm/6–8in long. Inside, the seeds are surrounded by a sticky brown pulp. It has a high tartaric acid content and is often used as a souring agent.

Tamarind doesn't have much of an aroma, but the flavour is tart and sour without being bitter, and fruity and refreshing. It is used in many curries, chutneys and dhals, and is an essential ingredient of Thai hot-and-sour soups. It is available in a variety of forms. Blocks of compressed tamarind and slices of dried tamarind have been available for a while, but it is now also possible to buy jars of fresh tamarind and cartons of tamarind concentrate and paste.

Compressed tamarind looks rather like dried dates. To use, tear off a piece that is roughly equivalent to 15ml/1 tbsp and soak it in 150ml/¼ pint/⅔ cup warm water for about 10 minutes. Swirl the tamarind around with your fingers so that the pulp is released from the seeds. Strain the juice into a jug (pitcher). Discard the contents of the sieve and use the liquid as required.

Tamarind slices look a little like dried apple slices. To use, place them in a small bowl, then cover with warm water and leave to soak for about 30 minutes. Then squeeze the slices and strain the juice.

To use tamarind concentrate or paste, mix 15ml/1 tbsp of the paste with 60ml/4 tbsp warm water. Stir until it dissolves, then use as required.

Compressed tamarind and slices should be stored in a cool, dry place and will keep well. Jars labelled fresh tamarind, tamarind concentrate or tamarind paste should be stored in the refrigerator once opened and used within 1–2 months.

CURRY POWDERS & PASTES

The word curry evolved from the Tamil word *kari*, literally meaning any food cooked in a sauce. Curry powder is largely a Western invention, but curry pastes can be found on market stalls throughout South-east Asia. A varied selection of both powders and pastes can be found in Western supermarkets, making cooking with spices very simple.

CURRY POWDERS

There is little doubt that curry powder, a ready-made blend of spices, was an early convenience food, prepared for Western merchants, sailors and military men who had served in the East and wished to bring these exotic flavours home. Traditionally, the spices would have been prepared in the kitchen on a daily basis.

Over the decades and centuries these spice and curry mixtures have changed and developed, as have our tastes, so that today supermarket shelves in the West carry a wealth of different spice mixtures from all parts of the globe.

For enthusiastic cooks it is fun and a creative challenge to make up your own curry powder. Keep experimenting until you find the right balance of spices. Of course, it is perfectly possible to mix ground spices, but starting with whole spices will give better results.

Using Spices in Curry Powders

Many whole spices benefit from being dry-fried before grinding. This ensures that no surface moisture remains and heightens and develops the flavour. To dry fry, use a heavy pan, and shake it constantly so the spices do not scorch. Purists dry-fry spices separately, but they can be heated together as long as you watch them very closely.

Coriander seeds These are often used as the base of curry powders, especially those from southern India and Singapore. Shake the pan to keep the seeds on the move, and remove them from the heat when they give off a mild, sweet, orangey perfume.

Dried chillies These can be roasted in a cool oven, but it is better to sear them in a heavy pan. Place the pan of chillies over a medium heat for 2–3 minutes, until the chillies soften and puff up. Do not let them burn, or the flavour will be ruined.

Cumin seeds These should be dry-fried in a pan, and will be ready for grinding when the seeds give out a nutty smell.

Black peppercorns These need gentle dry-frying, just to heighten the flavour.

Fenugreek This should be dry-fried briefly or it will become bitter. It is ready to grind when it turns a brownish yellow colour.

Curry leaves These can be dry-fried over a low to medium heat when fresh. Grind or pound them, using a mortar and pestle, then mix with the other spices. This works well if you are making a curry powder or paste that is to be used immediately, but if it is to be kept, make up the powder, then add the whole leaves just before you are ready to use it. Remove the leaves before serving the curry. Avoid using dried curry leaves, as they will have lost most of their flavour.

MAKING SIMPLE CURRY POWDER

This Malaysian spice mixture is good for poultry, especially chicken, and robust fish curries. It makes about 60ml/4 tbsp curry powder.

1 Remove the seeds from 2 dried red chillies using the point of a knife; discard any stems.

2 Put the chillies, 6 cloves, 1 cinnamon stick, 5ml/1 tsp coriander seeds, 5ml/1 tsp fennel seeds and 10ml/2 tsp Sichuan peppercorns in a heavy frying pan. Dry-fry the spices, tossing them, until they give off a rich, spicy aroma.

3 Grind the spices to a smooth powder in a mortar, using a pestle. Alternatively, use a spice grinder, or an electric coffee grinder reserved for blending spices.

4 Add 2.5ml/½ tsp grated nutmeg, 5ml/ 1 tsp ground star anise and 5ml/1 tsp ground turmeric. Use at once or store in an airtight jar away from strong light.

Cook's Tips
• *If you prefer a very hot and punchy spice mixture, then add the chilli seeds and dry-fry with the other spices.*
• *Ensure that you wash your hands, and the chopping board and other utensils, very thoroughly after preparing chillies.*

CURRY PASTES

On market stalls throughout South-east Asia are mounds of pounded wet spices: lemon grass, chilli, ginger, garlic, galangal, shallots and tamarind. After purchasing meat, chicken or fish all the cook has to do is to call on the spice seller. He or she will ask a few questions: "What sort of curry is it to be? Will it be hot or mild? How many servings?" Having ascertained the answers, the appropriate quantities of each spice will be scooped on to a banana leaf and folded into a neat cone, ready to be taken home.

In the West, we may not be able to buy our spices in such colourful surroundings, but supermarkets stock some very good ready-made pastes, or you can make your own. By experimenting, you will find the balance of flavours you like, and can then make up one or more of your favourite mixtures in bulk.

If you grind wet spices a lot, you may wish to invest in a traditional, large Asian mortar with a rough, pitted or ridged bowl. The coarse, uneven surface helps to hold the ingredients in the bowl while they are being pounded, rather than flying out.

Alternatively, for speed and ease, you can use a food processor or blender instead of a mortar and pestle. Store any surplus curry paste in sealed plastic tubs in the freezer. They will keep well for several months.

In Asia fats and oils are used both for cooking and flavouring foods. Animal fat or lard and certain oils are used for cooking and play a particularly important role because so much of the food in Asia is fried. Highly flavoured oils such as sesame oil and chilli oil are popularly used for dipping sauces and dressings, and to flavour dishes such as soups and stir-fries.

COOKING FATS AND OILS

Historically, animal fat or lard was the medium for frying (and remains so in China). Nowadays, however, vegetable oils are valued because they can be heated to much higher temperatures without smoking – something that is essential for stir-frying, where a high degree of heat is absolutely essential. Similarly, deep-fried foods require a high temperature in order to achieve the desired crispness.

Oil can be extracted from sources as diverse as radishes and poppies. Rape seed (canola) oil was a popular cooking medium in China until the Portuguese introduced peanuts during the sixteenth century. It was not immediately appreciated that the new crop could be a source of oil, but by the nineteenth century groundnut (peanut) oil was firmly established throughout Asia, a

position it still holds despite competition from corn oil. In Japan, sesame oil was used, but Japanese cooks soon appreciated that cooking with a mixture of sesame oil and peanut oil gave better results, especially when deep-frying *tempura* or similar dishes, because the mixed oil could be heated to higher temperatures without smoking, giving very crisp results.

Coconut and palm oil are very popular cooking oils in South-east Asia. Malaysia is one of the world's largest producers of palm oil. However, both coconut oil and palm oil are becoming less popular than they once were, because they are high in unhealthy saturated fats.

Both coconut oil and palm oil are semi solid in colder conditions but become liquid on heating and are excellent for deep-frying. When heated, coconut oil is clear and is virtually tasteless. It keeps well because the high levels of saturated fatty acids make it resistant to rancidity. Palm oil is yellowish in colour and has a mild pleasant flavour. It does not keep well.

Fats and oils all have their own distinct aroma and flavour; some are quite strong, others fairly mild. Both lamb and beef fat, for instance are more strongly flavoured than lard (pork fat) or chicken fat, while peanut oil and rape seed oil have more taste than soya, cottonseed or sunflower oils, though they are still mild in comparison to meat fats and give a much "lighter" result.

FLAVOURING COOKING OILS

Although many Asian recipes depend on fats and oils for their success, it is not considered appropriate for the flavour of the fat to dominate the dish. A technique frequently used to neutralize the flavour of an oil is to season it.

The method is very simple. While the oil is being heated, small pieces of aromatic ingredients such as fresh ginger or garlic are added. When these have flavoured the oil, they are removed from the pan. The technique prevents the finished dish from tasting oily.

In the South-east Asia, fats and oils are mainly used as a cooking medium, but are sometimes ingredients in their own right. In some Chinese dishes, for instance, pure lard is often stirred in shortly before serving.

In normal conditions, fats and oils exposed to the air gradually become rancid due to oxidation. Cooking oil should be stored in a cool, dark place. Oil that has been heated several times in a deep-fryer may acquire an unpleasant flavour and will need to be discarded frequently. Chinese cooks often heat the oil with fresh ginger after every use to obviate this.

SESAME OIL

In Asia, the type of sesame oil used for flavouring is quite different from that used for cooking in India and the Middle East. In both China and Japan, the preferred oil for flavouring is a rich-tasting oil made from processed roasted sesame seeds. Sesame oil made from roasted seeds has a wonderfully nutty aroma and taste. It is much stronger than either walnut oil or olive oil.

Because processed sesame oil smokes easily when heated, it is not really suitable for frying. It is used for salads and dipping sauces, and a few drops are often added to soups or stir-fries shortly before serving. Heating helps to intensify the aroma of processed sesame oil, but it should never be cooked for too long or the taste will be spoiled. Blended sesame oil, which is used for cooking, has a milder flavour and is much paler in colour.

Always store sesame oil in a cool, dark place, because it will lose its strong aroma if exposed to heat and strong light. It becomes rancid much sooner than ordinary cooking oils, so buy in small quantities.

CHILLI OIL

This is made by infusing chopped dried red chillies, chopped red onions, garlic and salt in hot vegetable oil for several hours. There is also an "XO chilli oil", which is flavoured with dried scallops.

Chilli oil has a pleasant aroma with a fiery taste that is much stronger than the flavour of either chilli bean paste or chilli sauce. It is always used as a dipping sauce, never for cooking. In some South-east Asian countries it is used as a dressing, and it is drizzled on top of the Burmese fish soup, *mohinga*. In Thai cooking it is added to stir-fried prawns just before serving.

Store chilli oil in a cool and dark place. It keeps for many months stored in a screw-top jar in the refrigerator.

MAKING CHILLI OIL

Chilli oil is easy to make at home; simply put about 20 seeded and chopped dried chillies in a heatproof container. Heat 250ml/8fl oz/1 cup groundnut (peanut) or corn oil until it just reaches smoking point, then leave to cool for 5 minutes. Carefully pour the oil into the heatproof container and leave to stand for 1–2 hours. Strain the oil, then use as required.

This flavouring ingredient plays an important role in Chinese and Asian cooking and is used in various subtle ways to bring out the tastes of other ingredients. The most widely used vinegar is rice vinegar, of which there are several varieties, but there are also several other types such as coconut vinegar, pon vinegar and *sushi* vinegar.

RICE VINEGAR

Either fermented from rice or distilled from rice grains, rice vinegar is used extensively in Asian cooking. The former is dark amber in colour and is referred to in China as red or black vinegar; the latter is clear, so is called white vinegar. The raw ingredients used for making rice vinegar consist of glutinous rice, long grain rice, wheat, barley, and rice husks. It is fermented twice and matured for up to 6–7 months. Japan has a brown rice vinegar known as *gaen mae su*, which is dark and heady. This vinegar has been likened to balsamic vinegar.

Red or black vinegar has a pleasant fragrant aroma with a mild, sweetish flavour. The distilled white vinegar is much stronger. It smells vinegary and tastes quite tangy and tart. Japanese brown rice vinegar has a distinctive sweet-and-sour flavour.

Vinegar has always played a vital role in Chinese cooking, and in some parts of the country, particularly in the north, it is added to almost every dish, although sometimes in tiny amounts. Rice vinegar is an important ingredient in sweet-and-sour sauce and Sichuan hot-and-sour sauce.

Rice vinegar also features in Thai cucumber sauce and in dipping sauces, such as the Vietnamese vinegar and garlic fish sauce. It is also widely used in preserving and pickling. Thai cooks add rice vinegar to several dishes, like hot-and-sour soup. In Japan, rice vinegar is used for *sushi* rice.

In Asian cooking, vinegar is generally the last item to be stirred into a dish. Do not use too much; in sweet-and-sour sauce the key ingredients should be in perfect balance, the sour having a slight edge on the sweet.

Rice vinegar keeps well if it is not exposed to heat or strong light.

COCONUT VINEGAR

This is made from the nectar of coconut flower sheaths. It is amber coloured and is highly regarded in the Philippines.

PON VINEGAR

This Japanese vinegar is made from the juice of a citrus fruit that resemble limes.

USING SUSHI VINEGAR

Sushi *rice is moistened and flavoured with hot rice vinegar, sugar and salt. The cooked rice is spread out in a shallow dish and the hot vinegar mixture is added. The rice is turned to coat the grains, and fanned so it cools quickly and develops an attractive sheen. It is then covered until it cools completely before being moulded.*

These play an essential role in Chinese and Asian cuisines. There are numerous different sauces and pastes that can be used variously as condiments or an ingredient, or both. Sambals, which are particularly popular in Indonesia, are chilli-based spicy relishes and sauces that are served with dishes as a condiment or an accompaniment.

SAUCES

A wide and varied selection of sauces can be found in the Chinese and Asian kitchen. They are usually highly flavoured and may be added to dishes to bring out the flavours of other ingredients or used as a dip.

SOY SAUCE

Made from fermented soya beans, this is one of Asia's most important contributions to the global kitchen. It is used worldwide, as a condiment and an ingredient.

To make soy sauce, soya beans are first cleaned, soaked until soft and then steamed before being mixed with a yeast culture and wheat flour. The mixture is then fermented for up to two years before being filtered and bottled. There is no short cut to making soy sauce of high quality. Cheaper products tend to have an inferior flavour.

There are three main types of Chinese soy sauce on the market. **Light soy sauce** is the initial extraction. It has the most delicate flavour and is light brown in colour with a beany fragrance. **Dark soy sauce** is left to mature further, and has caramel added to it, so it is slightly sweeter and darker with a powerful aroma. **Regular soy sauce** is a blend of the two.

There are several different types of Japanese soy sauce too: **usukuchi soy sauce** is light in colour and tastes less salty than the Chinese light soy. **Tamari** is dark and thick with a strong flavour, and is even less salty than the light type. **Shoyu** is a full-flavoured sauce that is aged for up to two years. In between, there is the very popular **Kikkoman**, which is a brand name for the equivalent of the Chinese regular soy sauce. It is ideal as a dipping sauce but is not so good for use in cooking.

The Indonesian **kecap manis** is thick and black, with a strong, powerful aroma, but a surprisingly sweet taste. The light variety, **kecap asin**, is quite thin and weak, and is sometimes described as white soy sauce. Indonesian cooks also use the medium-bodied **kecap sedang**.

As a rule, light soy sauce is used for fish and shellfish, white meats, vegetables and soups, while the darker sauce is ideal for red meats, stews, barbecues and gravy. Use the regular variety as a dip, or blend three parts light sauce with two parts dark. The same goes for marinades.

When soy sauce is used for cooking, it should be stirred in towards the end of the cooking time to avoid dulling the colour of the food, and so that the flavour of the principal ingredient is not overwhelmed. This applies to soups, stews, stir-fries and quick-braised dishes, but not to slow-braised dishes, where the ingredients are simmered for a long time in a sauce that includes only a small amount of soy sauce. When soy sauce is used in a dressing for a salad or similar cold dish, the dressing should be added just before serving.

Sealed bottles of naturally fermented soy sauce can be stored for a year or two but, once opened, its flavour and aroma will deteriorate fairly rapidly. Try to use it up as fast as you can, certainly before the use-by date on the label. Check the label, too, for advice on storage. Some bottles do not contain any preservatives and must be kept in the refrigerator once opened.

FISH SAUCE

This is an essential seasoning for both Thai and Vietnamese cooking. In Vietnam (*nuoc cham*) it is often made using shrimps, but in Thailand (*nam pla*), the sauce is more often made using salted, fermented fish.

All types of fish sauce have a pungent flavour and aroma and are very salty. Thai *nam pla* has a slightly stronger flavour and aroma than the Vietnamese or Chinese versions. The colour of fish sauce can vary considerably; lighter-coloured sauces are thought to be better than darker.

Fish sauce is used extensively throughout Asia as a seasoning in all kinds of savoury dishes. It is also used to make a dipping sauce, when it is blended with extra flavourings such as finely chopped garlic and chillies, and sugar and lime juice.

Fish sauce generally comes in either glass or plastic bottles. Once opened it should be kept in a cool, dark place where it will keep for up to a year.

OYSTER SAUCE

This thick, dark brown, soy-based sauce is a Cantonese speciality. It is flavoured with oyster juice, salt and caramel, and is thickened with cornflour (cornstarch). It has a much thicker consistency than soy sauce and fish sauce, but is lighter in colour.

Oyster sauce has a fragrant aroma, and a delicate flavour that, surprisingly, doesn't taste of fish at all. It is a highly versatile flavouring and can be used in a wide variety of dishes. It imparts a certain richness to dishes without overpowering their natural flavour and is especially good with fairly bland foods, such as chicken and tofu, but also marries well with more strongly flavoured ingredients such as beef and fish and shellfish. It can be used as a garnish and is often sprinkled over cooked dishes such as rice and noodles.

The bottled sauce is generally only used as a cooking ingredient, and never served as a dip or sauce at the table. Oyster sauce is best added to dishes towards the end of the cooking time as prolonged cooking may impair the colour of other ingredients.

There are a number of different brands of this sauce, and the more expensive versions are usually far superior, and have a much richer flavour than cheaper varieties. It is readily available from supermarkets and Asian stores. Once opened, the bottle should be stored in the refrigerator where the sauce will keep for a very long time, although it is best to use it before the use-by date printed on the label.

HOISIN SAUCE

Another Cantonese speciality, hoisin is also known as barbecue sauce. Its Chinese name literally means sea-flavour, which reflects on how delicious it is, rather than indicating what its ingredients are. Hoisin sauce does not contain so much as a trace of seafood, unlike oyster sauce and fish sauce.

The main components of this popular sauce are fermented beans, sugar, vinegar, salt, chilli, garlic and sesame oil, but there is no standard formula, so the aroma and flavour of different brands can vary greatly. A good quality hoisin sauce should have a fragrant aroma with a rich, warm, sweet yet slightly salty flavour.

Hoisin sauce is quite versatile and makes a valuable contribution to the kitchen. Mainly intended as a marinade, it can be used at the table as a dipping sauce, but should not accompany Peking duck as is the practice in some restaurants. When used as a marinade, hoisin sauce does not need to be combined with other ingredients but is spooned straight over spare ribs, chicken or other similar foods.

Hoisin sauce usually comes in glass jars or cans. Once opened, jars should be stored in the refrigerator, where the sauce will keep for several months. Canned hoisin should be decanted into a non-metallic container before being stored in the refrigerator.

CHILLI SAUCE

The best known Asian chilli sauce comes from China, although the Vietnamese have a very hot version and there is also a thick, spicy chilli sauce made in Thailand.

The Chinese bottled chilli sauce is quite hot and spicy, with a touch of fruitiness, as it is made from fresh red chillies, salt, vinegar and apples or plums. The Thai version includes both hot and sweet chillies, and contains ginger, spices and vinegar.

There is also a thick Chinese sauce, which is made exclusively from chillies and salt. This is usually sold in jars and is much hotter than the bottled sauce.

Bottled chilli sauce is used both for cooking and as a dip, but the thicker sauce is mainly used for cooking as an alternative to chilli bean paste. Always use chilli sauce sparingly as it can be quite fiery, especially to the Western palate.

Once a jar or bottle of chilli sauce has been opened it should be stored in the refrigerator, where it will keep almost indefinitely. Use before the expiry date.

PLUM SAUCE

This is made from plum juice with sugar, salt, vinegar and a thickening agent. It is a sort of sweet-and-sour sauce and is usually associated with Chinese food. Thai cooks are also partial to plum sauce, but they tend to make their own version, using preserved plums and sugar.

There seems to be no standard recipe for the commercially made plum sauce. The various brands all seem to use slightly different seasonings and some even add garlic, ginger or chilli to give it extra tang. Taste before use, as some brands can be quite fiery, while others are mild.

One of the common uses for plum sauce in the West is to serve it with Peking duck. It is also used as a dip for spring rolls and other *dim sum*.

Plum sauce is usually sold in glass jars. Once opened, store in the refrigerator.

PONZU

This is a tangy Japanese sauce made from citrus juice, vinegar and seasonings. It is often mixed with shoyu and spices and added to hotpot dishes. Bottles of ponzu can be bought in Japanese supermarkets. Once opened, store in the refrigerator.

Black bean sauce should not be used cold straight from the jar or bottle but should always be heated first. It is usually blended with other strongly flavoured seasonings such as spring onions (scallions), garlic, ginger and chillies before being added to stews, stir-fries, and braised or steamed dishes. Ready-made black bean sauces seasoned either with garlic or chillies are available too.

Once opened, the jar should be stored in the refrigerator. Black bean sauce keeps very well in this way.

LEMON SAUCE

This is one of those condiments that was especially created for the Western market. It probably originated in Hong Kong, like black bean sauce. It is thick, smooth and velvety and has an immediate appeal for the Western palate.

The sauce has a rather piquant citrus aroma with a spicy and tangy sweet flavour. It is another sauce from the sweet-and-sour stable, but with the difference that it is made from fresh lemon juice and rind. Salt and sugar are added, and starch is used for thickening. Most brands have artificial colouring added to give the sauce a bright yellow colour.

Lemon sauce is used in the Cantonese dish, lemon chicken. Serve with deep-fried food, particularly fish and shellfish.

Once opened, the bottle or jar should be stored in the refrigerator.

BLACK BEAN SAUCE

This is a mixture of puréed salted black beans with soy sauce, sugar and spice, manufactured for the convenience of Western cooks. In China and South-east Asia cooks use only whole fermented beans, and make their own sauce by crushing the beans in the wok while cooking. Fermented black beans have a powerful fragrance and a strong flavour.

YELLOW BEAN SAUCE

Also known as brown bean sauce or ground bean sauce, this popular Chinese sauce is made of crushed fermented soya beans that have been mixed with salt, wheat flour and sugar to make a paste. It is not only useful on its own, but is also the basis of numerous more elaborate sauces. Hoisin sauce, *chu hu* sauce, *Guilin* chilli sauce, Sichuan hot sauce and Peking duck sauce all owe their ancestry to yellow bean sauce.

Regular yellow bean sauce has a delicious beany aroma and delectable flavour. It is not as salty as black bean sauce, and cooks in every region of China add their own unique mixture of spices and seasonings to make individual blends.

Yellow bean sauce is very versatile in the kitchen. It adds extra dimension to most meat, poultry, fish and even some vegetable dishes, whether in stir-fries, braised dishes or roasts. It is also the ideal basis for a marinade, usually combined with other ingredients such as garlic, spring onions and rice wine.

Once a jar of yellow bean sauce has been opened, any unused sauce should be transferred to a lidded plastic container and stored in the refrigerator. Like black bean sauce, it keeps very well.

Pastes

These are widely used in Chinese and Asian cooking, mainly as an ingredient in other dishes. Savoury pastes are often added to stir-fries and braised dishes, while sweet pastes are often used to fill steamed buns and cakes, or spread on pancakes.

Chilli Bean Paste

This is made with a type of broad (fava) bean. It is also called chilli bean sauce, hot bean sauce or Sichuan sauce. There are several chilli bean pastes, ranging from mild to hot, but all have a beany aroma and rich flavour. It is used in Sichuan cooking to add flavour to stir-fries and braised dishes. Heat before use. Never serve as a dipping sauce.

Once opened, store chilli bean paste in the refrigerator, where it will keep well.

Red Bean Paste

This thick, smooth paste is made from red kidney beans or aduki beans and sweetened with rock sugar. The paste comes in small cans and is available from Asian stores.

It has a mild fragrance with a subtle flavour. Other flavourings such as essence of sesame seeds or ground cassia are sometimes blended in. Red bean paste is used to fill cakes and steamed buns. It is also spread on pancakes, which are then fried.

Once opened, transfer to a plastic tub and store in the refrigerator. It keeps well.

Miso

This is the collective name for several types of soya bean paste, made from steamed soya beans fermented with various natural yeasts. The pastes come in different colours, textures and flavours. Red or *mugi miso* is more strongly flavoured than the sweeter white *kome miso*. *Hacho miso* is dark with a strong flavour. Miso is best known as a flavouring for Japanese miso soup.

Sesame Paste

The sesame paste used in Asian cooking is not the same as tahini, which is made from raw sesame seeds. Sesame paste is made from roasted seeds. You can use peanut butter with a little sesame oil stirred in to approximate the correct flavour.

Shrimp Paste

Also known as *blachan* and *terasi*, this is an essential ingredient throughout South-east Asia. It is made from tiny shrimps that have been salted, dried, pounded and then left to ferment until the aroma is very pungent. The colour ranges from oyster pink to purplish brown. It is sold in block form or packed in tiny tubs or jars.

When the paste is cooked, its very strong odour vanishes and gives the dish a depth and pungency. It is used to flavour rice dishes, is stirred into satay sauces and gives depth to salad dressings, dipping sauces, curries and braised dishes. Burmese cooks use it to add flavour to *balachaung*, a spicy dried shrimp mixture forked into rice.

Store the block form in a screwtop jar in a cool place. It will keep for several months. Keep jars of paste in the refrigerator.

Preparing Shrimp Paste

This can be added straight to fried dishes but, for sambals, dressings and salads, it should be heated to temper its flavour.

To heat, cut off a small piece of paste. Mould it into a 1cm/1/2-inch cube and press on to the end of a metal skewer. Holding the end of the skewer in an oven glove, rotate the paste over a low to medium gas flame or under an electric grill (broiler) until the outside begins to look dry, but not burnt. Alternatively, wrap the paste in a piece of foil and dry fry for 5 minutes, turning occasionally.

SAMBALS

This is the collective terms for spicy relishes, sauces and accompaniments that are based on chillies. They are particularly popular in Indonesia, where they may be served either as accompaniment or as a main dish in their own right. *Sambal goreng*, for instance, is a spicy chilli sauce, which may include a wide variety of foods such as tiny meat balls, cubes of fish, wedges of hard-boiled eggs or vegetables.

In Malaysia, Singapore and Indonesia *sambal blachan* (chilli and shrimp paste sambal) is a favourite. It is extremely hot – especially when the seeds have been left in the chillies. *Sambal oelek* is similar, but a little brown sugar is added to the chopped chillies to bring out the flavours. It is sometimes labelled "chopped chilli", and 1 tsp/5ml is equivalent to a small chilli. Keep in the refrigerator after opening.

At a typical Thai meal there may be one or two sambals plus *nam prik*, which complements raw, steamed, fried or boiled vegetables and is often simply stirred into a bowl of plain boiled or steamed Thai rice. Another popular sambal is made from fish sauce, lemon juice, shallots and chillies; a blend that enhances all kinds of fish and shellfish dishes.

In Vietnam *nuoc cham*, a piquant sambal made from, chillies, garlic, sugar, lime juice or rice vinegar, and fish sauce, is used as a seasoning in the same way that salt and pepper are used in the West.

Sambals and sauces are usually served in small bowls or saucers. At a family meal pieces of cooked meat, fish or vegetables may be dipped into a communal bowl but on special occasions small individual dishes are used for each person.

Once opened, sambals should always be stored in a glass jar in the refrigerator with clear film (plastic wrap) under the lid.

MAKING SAMALS

Sambals are quick and easy to prepare and make wonderful accompaniments. Mix together the ingredients just before serving, using a food processor or blender for wet ingredients and a mortar and pestle for dry ones.

To make 30ml/2 tbsp sambal blachan, *Remove the seeds from 2–3 fresh red chillies. Place in a mortar, add salt and pound to a paste using a pestle. Prepare a 1cm/1/2in cube of shrimp paste (see Preparing Shrimp Paste), add to the chillies and pound to mix well. Add the juice of 1/2 lemon or lime to taste. Serve as an accompaniment to rice meals.*

To make 350g/12oz sambal oelek, *cut 450g/1lb fresh red chillies in half; scrape out the seeds. Plunge into boiling water and cook for 5–8 minutes. Drain, then process in a food processor or blender until finely chopped. Spoon into a glass jar, stir in 10ml/2 tsp salt and cover with clear film (plastic wrap) before screwing on the lid. Store in the refrigerator for up to six weeks. Serve in small dishes as an accompaniment, or use it in recipes. Use a stainless steel or plastic spoon to measure out the sauce. It is fiercely hot, and it will irritate the skin.*

To make 150ml/1/4 pint/2/3 cup sambal kecap, *remove the seeds from 1 fresh red chilli, then chop. Mix the chopped chilli, 2 crushed garlic cloves, 60ml/4 tbsp dark soy sauce and 20ml/4 tsp lemon juice or 15ml/1 tbsp tamarind juice in a small bowl with 30ml/2 tbsp hot water. Stir in 30ml/2 tbsp deep-fried onion slices and leave to stand for about 30 minutes. Serve as a dip for beef or chicken satays or with deep-fried chicken.*

BEERS, WINES & SPIRITS

China and South-east Asia produce a number of alcoholic drinks made from locally grown ingredients. Wine has been made in China for thousands of years; by the time of the Shang Dynasty (c. 1600–1100 BC), a dark wine was being brewed from millet. Nowadays, beer is more popular in Asia, although wine still continues to be an important drink.

BEERS

Brewing was introduced into China and Japan towards the end of the nineteenth century. Today, beer is popular in Asia, and almost every country in the region has breweries. The style of beer most favoured by Asian drinkers is a bottom-fermented brew in the style of Pilsener (Pils).

CHINESE BEERS

The best known Chinese beer is **Tsingtao**, a light, dry Pilsener-type beer that is brewed from the sweet spring water of Laoshan, using Chinese barley and hops. It has a refreshing and delicate taste, and enjoys a huge popularity abroad. The Tsingtao brewery was established in 1903 by the German colony there. After World War II a number of breweries were established all over China, but Tsingtao Brewery remains the largest and most productive.

Other brands that can occasionally be seen in the West are **Beijing Beer, Shanghai Beer, Snowflake** and **Yu Chuan Beer**. These all are Pilsener-type lagers, each with their own individual flavour.

JAPANESE BEERS

The huge beer industry of Japan also owes its origins to foreign investment. In 1869, the American firm of Wiegrand and Copeland started a brewery at Yokohama. It passed to Japanese management, taking the name Kirin, in 1888.

Today, the Kirin Brewery Company has became one of the biggest brewers in the world. **Kirin Beer** is exported to almost every country in the world. Its chief rival is **Asahi Beer**, which has rapidly increased its export market in recent years. Other strong contenders are **Sapporo Beer**, which also challenges Kirin's claim of being the oldest brewer; and the newcomer **Suntory Beer**, which only started brewing in 1963.

SOUTH-EAST ASIAN BEERS

Singapore's **Tiger Beer** came into being by accident. The breweries were established after Heineken failed to reach an agreement with the Dutch Colonial Government to set up breweries in Java in 1929.

From Thailand, the biggest selling lager is **Singha** brewed by Boon Rawd Brewery. The name *singha* refers to an elegant but fearsome lion-like creature of local mythology. The Philippines is the home of one of the world's major brewing groups – **San Miguel**. This group has three breweries in the Philippines, one in Hong Kong, and one in Papua New Guinea. Dutch colonial links are still evident in Indonesia, where **Heineken** eventually did establish an associate company in Java to produce a Pilsener-style beer. Elsewhere in Asia, popular beers include the Vietnamese "**33**"; **Taiwan Beer** from Taiwan; and **OB** and **Crown** from Korea, but these are seldom seen in the West.

WINES

The Chinese tend to be indiscriminate when it comes to alcoholic beverages. They often fail to distinguish between low-alcohol table wine and distilled spirits. In everyday usage, the Chinese character *jiu* or *chiew* means any alcoholic beverage.

CHINESE WINES

China produces hundreds of different varieties of rice wine, but only a few of these are exported. Chinese rice wine is generally known as **huang jiu** (yellow wine), because of its golden amber colour. The best known and best quality rice wine is **Shao Xing**, named after the district where it is made.

There are several varieties of Shao Xing wines, ranging in colour from golden amber to dark brown, and in the percentage of alcohol by volume from 14 to 16 per cent. The aroma is quite distinctive, smelling subtly fragrant and smoky. Shao Xing should be drunk warm, and always with food. It is also used in cooking, and is added to the food towards the end of the cooking time so that the aroma is retained. Beware of Shao Xing/Hsing wine made in Taiwan, which pales, literally, by comparison. Read the small print on the label; if it says "made in ROC (Republic of China)" it is a fake.

China also produces some good grape wines. Several of these are exported to the West, including **Dynasty**, **Great Wall** and **Huadong**. The whites are superior to the red cabernet sauvignon.

JAPANESE WINES

Sake is the national drink of Japan but only a few types are available in the West. It is almost colourless and slightly sweet and has an alcohol content of about 15 per cent. It should be drunk with food, and is usually served warm, except **Ginjo**, a fine, dry wine that is always served chilled.

The traditional way of serving sake is in a porcelain jug (pitcher), which is immersed in hot water until the wine has warmed. It is then poured into small cups. The host lifts a cup in both hands and passes it to his guest with a courteous bow. The guest also bows and downs the warm wine in one.

Mirin is a sweet rice wine with a low alcohol content that is used in cooking. It is added towards the end to retain subtle flavour. Mirin is now available in the West, but dry sherry can be used instead.

Grape wines are also produced in Japan, but the output is quite small. The three big names are **Suntory**, **Mercian** and **Mann's**. All these companies produce both white and red wines, but very little is exported.

SPIRITS

These are distilled from locally grown produce such as rice, fruit and sugar cane and tend to be very potent. Some are flavoured to create sweet liqueurs.

CHINESE SPIRITS

The Chinese name for distilled spirit – *bai jiu* – means white wine and stems from the fact that it is colourless, as opposed to yellow rice wine. Most Chinese spirits have an alcohol content of over 50 per cent. They are distilled from a variety of grains, the commonest being sorghum, a cross between rice and millet. Some spirits are blended with herbs for use as medicinal tonics.

Mou-Tai is probably China's top spirit, and it is used for toasts at celebrations and state banquets. It is distilled from two grains, wheat and sorghum.

Traditionally, good rice wines came from southern China, while the best spirits were produced in the north. Although the distillery in Mou-Tai was established in 1529, the spirit was relatively indifferent until 1704, when a salt merchant from

Shanxi in north China visited the area and was so enchanted by the beauty of the village that he decided to settle down there. Seeking new employment, he discovered the local spirit and set about trying to improve it, employing the techniques of distilling the famous Fen Chiew from his native northern province. Mou-tai was the result.

Fen Chiew is available in the West. It comes from the village of Shanxi province in north China, and is distilled from millet and sorghum. It has a history of well over fifteen hundred years, and has afforded inspiration for many of China's greatest poets. This spirit also forms the basis for the famous **Chu Yeh Ching** (bamboo leaf green), a medicinal liqueur that is blended with herbs. It tastes quite refreshing despite being 47 per cent alcohol by volume.

Other popular Chinese spirits are **Wu Liang Ye** from Sichuan; **Mei Kuei Lu**; **Wu Chia Pi**; and **Dong Chiew**. All of these are quite heady, being over 50 per cent proof.

China also produces Western-style spirits such as brandy, whisky, vodka, rum and gin, but all mainly for home consumption.

JAPANESE SPIRITS

Shochu is distilled from sake. It is 25 per cent alcohol by volume and is usually diluted with warm water. Japan also produces a really good quality whisky. The first distillery was established in 1923. The model for Japan's whiskies is single malt Scotch, but there are equally successful spirits made in the idiom of blended Scotch.

Suntory is the biggest and best-known brand name whisky. Several Suntory labels are marketed worldwide, including **Royal, The Whisky, Excellence, Special Reserve, Old, Kakubin, Gold Label, Gold 1000, White Label, Red Label, Torys Extra** and **Rawhide**, which has a flavour of bourbon. Suntory's greatest rivals in terms of whisky production are Nikka distilleries (**G & G, Super Nikka, Black Nikka** and **Hi Nikka**); Kirin Seagram (**Robert Brown** and **Dunbar**); and Sanraku Ocean (**White Label**). There are other distillers, the best known being **Godo Shusei**.

Suntory also makes good brandy. The leading brands are **Imperial, XO, VSOP, VSO** and **VO**. Liqueurs include **Midori**, a melon-flavoured liqueur; **Ocha**, a green tea liqueur; and the **Crème de Kobai**, a pale pink liqueur made from Japanese plums.

OTHER ASIAN SPIRITS

*Taiwan produces many of the mainland Chinese drinks as well as the Japanese-inspired **Shokushu** rice spirit. In Korea, look out for **Ginseng Ju**, which has a large ginseng root in every bottle. In the East Indies, the island states in the South China Sea, the local **arrack** or **raki** is distilled from either coconut palm juice or sugar cane molasses. A common practice is to add rice to the fermenting base juice to boost the final alcohol content. The result is a potent drink similar to rum.*

CHINA & HONG KONG

More than a quarter of the world's population cooks Chinese food at home, and it has become popular the world over. There is a wealth of different styles of Chinese cooking, which traditionally are classified into four main groups according to their locations. The Eastern Region is represented by Shanghai. The characteristics of the cooking of this region are richness of flavour and exquisiteness of appearance. The Southern Region includes the diverse Canton school. Canton was an important trading port and this is reflected in the many foreign influences that have been included in the local cuisine. This is the best-known style of Chinese cooking in the West. The Western Region is represented by spicy Sichuan-style cooking, which is richly flavoured. Finally, the Northern Region gives us Peking-style dishes. This region is China's culinary capital and has assimilated all the best styles from around the whole country.

One of China's most popular soups, this is famed for its clever balance of flavours. The "hot" is provided by ground white or black pepper and the "sour" comes from the inclusion of rice vinegar. Similar soups are to be found throughout Asia, with regional variations, some relying on chillies and lime juice to provide the essential flavour contrast that gives them their character.

SERVES 6

INGREDIENTS
4–6 Chinese dried mushrooms
2–3 small pieces of wood ear, and a few golden needles (lily buds) (optional)
115g/4oz pork fillet, cut into fine strips
45ml/3 tbsp cornflour (cornstarch)
150ml/¼ pint/⅔ cup water
15–30ml/1–2 tbsp sunflower oil
1 small onion, finely chopped
1.5 litres/2½ pints/6¼ cups good quality beef or chicken stock, or 2 × 300g/11oz cans consommé made up to the full quantity with water
150g/5oz drained fresh firm tofu, diced
60ml/4 tbsp rice vinegar
15ml/1 tbsp light soy sauce
1 egg, beaten
5ml/1 tsp sesame oil
salt and ground white or black pepper
2–3 spring onions (scallions), shredded, to garnish

COOK'S TIP
Do not use condensed consommé in this dish or the taste will be too overpowering. Home-made stock is the best option, as some commercial stocks and those made from stock (bouillon) cubes tend to contain too much salt.

Place the dried mushrooms in a bowl, with the pieces of wood ear and the golden needles, if using. Add sufficient warm water to cover and leave to soak for about 30 minutes. Drain the mushrooms, reserving the soaking water.

Cut off and discard the mushroom stems and slice the caps finely. Trim away any tough stem from the wood ears, then chop them finely. Using kitchen string, tie the golden needles into a bundle.

Lightly dust the strips of pork fillet with some of the cornflour, coating the pieces on all sides. Then mix the remaining cornflour to a smooth paste with the measured water.

Heat the oil in a wok or large pan and fry the onion until soft. Increase the heat and fry the pork until it changes colour. Add the stock or consommé, mushrooms, soaking water, and wood ears and golden needles, if using. Bring to the boil, then simmer for 15 minutes.

Discard the golden needles, lower the heat and stir in the cornflour paste to thicken. Add the tofu, vinegar, soy sauce, and salt and pepper.

Bring the soup to just below boiling point, then drizzle in the beaten egg by letting it drop from a whisk (or to be authentic, the fingertips) so that it forms threads in the soup. Stir in the sesame oil and serve at once, garnished with spring onion shreds.

CRISPY WONTON SOUP

The freshly cooked wontons are supposed to sizzle and "sing" in the hot soup as they are taken to the table. They provide a delightful textural contast to the clear vegetable soup base, and may be eaten either using chopsticks or the traditional Chinese porcelain spoon.

SERVES 6

INGREDIENTS
2 wood ears, soaked for 30 minutes in warm water to cover
1.2 litres/2 pints/5 cups home-made chicken stock
2.5cm/1in piece fresh root ginger, peeled and grated
4 spring onions (scallions), chopped
2 rich-green inner spring greens (collards) leaves, finely shredded
50g/2oz drained canned bamboo shoots, sliced
25ml/1½ tbsp dark soy sauce
2.5ml/½ tsp sesame oil
salt and ground black pepper

FOR THE FILLED WONTONS
5ml/1 tsp sesame oil
½ small onion, finely chopped
10 drained canned water chestnuts, finely chopped
115g/4oz finely minced (ground) pork
24 wonton wrappers
groundnut (peanut) oil, for deep-frying

COOK'S TIP
*The wontons can be filled up to two hours ahead.
Place them in a single layer on a baking sheet dusted
with cornflour (cornstarch) to prevent them from
sticking, and leave in a cool place.*

Make the filled wontons. Heat the sesame oil in a small pan, add the onion, water chestnuts and pork and fry, stirring occasionally, until the meat has changed colour and is no longer pink. Tip the mixture into a bowl, season to taste with salt and ground black pepper, and set aside to cool.

Place the wonton wrappers under a slightly dampened dishtowel so that they do not dry out while you are working. Next, dampen the edges of a wonton wrapper with a little cold water. Place about 5ml/1 tsp of the filling in the centre of the wrapper. Gather the edges up like a purse and twist the top to seal, or roll up as you would a baby spring roll. Continue working in the same way until you have made 24 wontons.

Make the soup. Drain the wood ears, trim away any rough stems, then slice thinly. Bring the stock to the boil, add the ginger and the spring onions and simmer for 3 minutes. Add the sliced wood ears, shredded spring greens, bamboo shoots and soy sauce. Simmer for 10 minutes, then stir in the sesame oil. Season to taste with salt and pepper, then cover the pan and keep hot.

Heat the oil in a wok to 190°C/375°F and fry the wontons, in batches if necessary, for 3–4 minutes, or until they are crisp and golden brown all over. Ladle the soup into six warmed soup bowls and share the wontons among them. Serve immediately.

It is said that these famous snacks were traditionally served with tea when visitors came to call after the Chinese New Year. As this was in the springtime, they came to be known as spring rolls. You can buy spring roll wrappers from Asian stores.

Makes 12

INGREDIENTS
12 spring roll wrappers, thawed if frozen
30ml/2 tbsp plain (all-purpose) flour mixed to a paste with water
sunflower oil, for deep-frying

FOR THE FILLING
6 Chinese dried mushrooms, soaked for 30 minutes in warm water
150g/5oz fresh firm tofu
30ml/2 tbsp sunflower oil
225g/8oz finely minced (ground) pork
225g/8oz peeled cooked prawns (shrimp), roughly chopped
2.5ml/½ tsp cornflour (cornstarch), mixed to a paste with 15ml/1 tbsp light soy sauce
75g/3oz each shredded bamboo shoot or grated carrot, sliced water chestnuts and beansprouts
6 spring onions (scallions) or 1 young leek, finely chopped
a little sesame oil
salt and ground black pepper

FOR THE DIPPING SAUCE
100ml/3½fl oz/scant ½ cup light soy sauce
15ml/1 tbsp chilli sauce or finely chopped fresh red chilli
a little sesame oil
rice vinegar, to taste

COOK'S TIP
If frozen, thaw spring roll wrappers at room temperature, open the parcel and separate with a metal spatula. Cover with a damp cloth while you are working to prevent them from drying out.

Make the filling. Drain the Chinese dried mushrooms. Cut off and discard the tough stems and slice the caps finely. Cut the tofu into slices of a similar size to the mushrooms.

Heat the oil in a wok and stir-fry the pork for 2–3 minutes, or until the colour changes. Add the prawns, cornflour paste and bamboo shoot or carrot. Stir in the water chestnuts.

Increase the heat, add the beansprouts and spring onions or leek and toss for 1 minute. Stir in the mushrooms and tofu. Off the heat, season, then stir in the sesame oil. Cool quickly on a large platter.

Separate the spring roll wrappers (see Cook's Tip). Place a wrapper on the work surface with one corner nearest you. Spoon some of the filling near the centre of the wrapper and fold the nearest corner over the filling. Smear a little of the flour paste on the free sides, turn the sides to the middle and roll up. Repeat this procedure with the remaining wrappers and filling.

Deep-fry the spring rolls in batches in oil heated to 190°C/375°F until they are crisp and golden. Drain on kitchen paper and serve at once with the dipping sauce, made by mixing all the ingredients in a bowl.

CRISPY SPRING ROLLS

These small and dainty vegetarian spring rolls are ideal served as appetizers, or make delicious cocktail snacks to be eaten in the hand. For a non-vegetarian version, just replace the mushrooms with the same amount of minced (ground) chicken or pork, and the carrots with chopped prawns or shrimps.

MAKES 40 ROLLS

INGREDIENTS
115g/4oz tender leeks or spring onions (scallions)
115g/4oz carrots
115g/4oz bamboo shoots, sliced
115g/4oz white mushrooms
45–60ml/3–4 tbsp vegetable oil
225g/8oz fresh beansprouts
5ml/1 tsp salt
5ml/1 tsp soft light brown sugar
15ml/1 tbsp light soy sauce
15ml/1 tbsp Chinese rice wine or dry sherry
20 frozen spring roll skins, defrosted
15ml/1 tbsp cornflour (cornstarch) paste
flour, for dusting
oil, for deep-frying

COOK'S TIP
To make cornflour paste, mix 10ml/2 tsp cornflour with 12.5ml/2½ tsp cold water until smooth.

Cut all the vegetables into thin shreds, roughly the same size and shape as the fresh beansprouts.

Heat the oil in a wok and stir-fry the vegetables and the beansprouts for about 1 minute. Add the salt, sugar, soy sauce and rice wine or sherry and continue stirring for 1½–2 minutes. Remove from the wok and drain the excess liquid, then set aside to cool.

3 To make the spring rolls, cut each spring roll skin in half diagonally, then place about 15ml/1 tbsp of the vegetable mixture one-third of the way down on the skin, with the triangle pointing away from you. Lift the lower flap over the filling and roll once.

4 Fold in both ends and roll once more, then brush the upper edge with a little cornflour paste, and roll into a neat package. Lightly dust a tray with flour and place the spring rolls on the tray with the flap-side down.

5 To cook, heat the oil in a wok or deep-fryer until hot, then reduce the heat to low. Deep-fry the spring rolls in batches (about 8–10 at a time) for 2–3 minutes or until golden and crispy, then remove and drain. Serve the spring rolls hot with a dipping sauce such as soy sauce or Spicy Salt and Pepper.

Ready-made fresh or frozen wonton skins are available from Asian stores. If you buy frozen ones, let them thaw at room temperature, then separate using a metal spatula. Any unused wrappers can be re-frozen.

INGREDIENTS
16–20 ready-made wonton skins
vegetable oil, for deep-frying

FOR THE SAUCE
15ml/1 tbsp vegetable oil
30ml/2 tbsp soft light brown sugar
45ml/3 tbsp rice vinegar
15ml/1 tbsp light soy sauce
15ml/1 tbsp tomato ketchup
45–60ml/3–4 tbsp stock or water
10ml/2 tsp cornflour (cornstarch) mixed to a paste with a little cold water

Pinch the centre of each wonton skin in your fingertips and twist it around to form an attractive floral shape.

Heat the oil for deep-frying to 190°C/375°F. Deep-fry the floral wonton skins a few at a time for 1–2 minutes, or until golden brown and crisp. Remove from the oil using a slotted spoon and drain on kitchen paper.

To make the sauce, heat the oil in a wok or large pan, add the sugar, vinegar, soy sauce, tomato ketchup and stock or water.

Stir in the cornflour paste and cook for 1–2 minutes, stirring until smooth. Pour it over the wonton skins and serve immediately.

These succulent shellfish beg to be eaten with the fingers, so provide finger bowls or hot cloths for your guests. Fried salt is also known as "Cantonese salt" or simply "salt and pepper mix". It is widely used as a table condiment.

SERVES 3–4

INGREDIENTS
15–18 large raw prawns (shrimp), in the shell, about 450g/1lb
vegetable oil, for deep-frying
3 shallots or 1 small onion, very finely chopped
2 garlic cloves, crushed
1cm/½in piece fresh root ginger, peeled and very finely grated
1–2 fresh red chillies, seeded and finely sliced
2.5ml/½ tsp sugar, or to taste
3–4 spring onions (scallions), shredded, to garnish

FOR THE FRIED SALT
10ml/2 tsp salt
5ml/1 tsp Sichuan peppercorns

Make the fried salt by dry-frying the salt and peppercorns in a heavy frying pan over a medium heat until the peppercorns begin to release their aroma. Cool the mixture, then tip into a mortar and crush with a pestle.

Remove the heads and legs from the prawns and discard. Leave the body shells and the tails in place. Pat dry with kitchen paper. Heat the oil for deep-frying to 190°C/375°F. Fry the prawns for 1 minute, then lift them out and drain on kitchen paper. Spoon 30ml/2 tbsp of the hot oil into a large frying pan.

Heat the oil in the frying pan. Add the fried salt, with the shallots or onion, garlic, ginger, chillies and sugar. Toss together for 1 minute, then add the prawns and toss them over the heat for 1 minute more until they are coated. Serve at once, garnished with the shredded spring onions.

Pork Dumplings

These dumplings make an excellent appetizer when they are shallow-fried, and can also be served on their own as a snack, if steamed, or as a complete meal when poached. The recipe makes a large quantity – perfect for a party. However, the dumplings freeze well, so if you don't eat them all, wrap them in plastic bags in batches of 10 or 20. Defrost at room temperature before cooking.

MAKES ABOUT 80–90 DUMPLINGS

INGREDIENTS
450g/1lb/4 cups plain (all-purpose) flour
about 450ml/³/₄ pint/2 cups water
flour, for dusting
45ml/3 tbsp sunflower oil, for frying (optional)
lettuce leaves, for steaming (optional)

FOR THE FILLING
450g/1lb Chinese leaves (Chinese cabbage) or white cabbage
450g/1lb minced (ground) pork
15ml/1 tbsp finely chopped spring onions (scallions)
5ml/1 tsp finely chopped fresh root ginger
10ml/2 tsp salt
5ml/1 tsp soft light brown sugar
30ml/2 tbsp light soy sauce
15ml/1 tbsp Chinese rice wine or dry sherry
10ml/2 tsp sesame oil

FOR THE DIPPING SAUCE
30ml/2 tbsp red chilli oil
15ml/1 tbsp light soy sauce
5ml/1 tsp finely chopped garlic
15ml/1 tbsp finely chopped spring onions (scallions)

1 Sift the flour into a bowl, then slowly pour in the water and mix to a firm dough. Knead until smooth and soft, then cover with a damp cloth and set aside for 25–30 minutes.

2 To make the filling, blanch the Chinese leaves or cabbage until soft. Drain and finely chop. Mix the cabbage with the remaining ingredients.

3 Lightly dust a work surface with flour. Knead and roll the dough into a long sausage about 2.5cm/1in in diameter. Cut the sausage into 80–90 small pieces and flatten each piece with the palm of your hand.

4 Using a rolling pin, roll out each piece into a thin pancake about 6cm/2½in in diameter. Place about 22.5ml/1½ tbsp of the filling in the centre of each pancake and fold into a half-moon-shaped pouch. Pinch the edges firmly so that the dumpling is tightly sealed.

5 Meanwhile, make the dipping sauce. Place all the ingredients in a small bowl and stir well to combine. Set aside while you cook the dumplings.

6 To shallow-fry the dumplings, heat the oil in a wok or frying pan. Arrange the dumplings, about 10 at a time, in rows in the oil and fry over a medium heat for 2–3 minutes until golden brown.

7 To steam, place 10 dumplings on a bed of lettuce leaves on each rack of a bamboo steamer and steam for 10–12 minutes over a high heat. Serve the dumplings hot with the dipping sauce.

These treats are just one example of dim sum, featherlight steamed buns with a range of tasty fillings. They are now a popular snack the world over.

Makes 16

INGREDIENTS

FOR THE BASIC DOUGH
15ml/1 tbsp sugar
about 300ml/½ pint/1¼ cups warm water
25ml/1½ tbsp dried easy-blend (rapid-rise) yeast
450g/1lb/4 cups strong white (bread) flour
5ml/1 tsp salt
15g/½oz/1 tbsp lard or white cooking fat

FOR THE FILLING
30ml/2 tbsp vegetable oil
1 garlic clove, crushed
225g/8oz roast pork, very finely chopped
2 spring onions (scallions), chopped
10ml/2 tsp yellow bean sauce, crushed
10ml/2 tsp sugar
5ml/1 tsp cornflour (cornstarch) mixed to a paste with water

To make the dough, dissolve the sugar in half the water. Add the yeast; leave for 15 minutes. Sift together the flour and salt; rub in the fat. Stir in the yeast and enough water to make a soft dough. Turn out on to a lightly floured surface and knead for 10 minutes. Leave in a covered oiled bowl until doubled in size.

To make the filling, heat the oil and fry the garlic until golden. Add the next four ingredients. Stir in the cornflour paste; cook until thickened. Leave to cool.

Knock back the dough. Knead for 2 minutes; divide into 16 pieces and roll into 7.5–10cm/ 3–4in rounds. Place a spoonful of filling in the centre of each, gather up the sides and twist to seal. Tie with string. Set the buns on baking parchment in a steamer. Leave until doubled in size. Steam for 30–35 minutes. Serve hot.

These attractive little rolls are traditionally served with Mongolian firepot, providing
a delightful contrast in texture to the meat and vegetables cooked in the stock.
Despite their intricate appearance, they are very easy to make – simply using a
chopstick and your fingers.

INGREDIENTS
1 quantity basic dough (opposite) made using only 5ml/1 tsp sugar
15ml/1 tbsp sesame oil

Divide the risen and knocked back dough into two equal portions. Roll each into a rectangle measuring 30 × 20cm/12 × 8in. Brush the surface of one with sesame oil and lay the other on top. Roll up like a Swiss roll. Cut into 16 pieces.

Take each dough roll in turn and press down firmly on the rolled side with a chopstick. Place the rolls on the work surface, coiled side uppermost.

Pinch together the sides of each roll, then pull the ends underneath and seal. The dough should separate into petals. Place the rolls on baking parchment in a steamer and leave to double in size. Steam over rapidly boiling water for 30–35 minutes. Serve hot.

COOK'S TIP
When lining the steamer, fold the paper several
times, then cut small holes like a doily. This lets the
steam circulate, yet prevents the steamed flower rolls
from sticking to the steamer.

TEA EGGS

These marbled eggs have an antique porcelain appearance. Tea eggs can be served as a snack with congee, a popular Chinese soft rice dish. They also make perfect picnic fare; shell them just before eating so that they stay moist.

MAKES 6

INGREDIENTS
6 eggs
30ml/2 tbsp dark soy sauce
5ml/1 tsp salt
½ star anise
2 teabags

1 Add the eggs to a pan of cold water. Heat to simmering point and boil the eggs for 20 minutes.

2 Drain the eggs and pour enough fresh cold water into the pan to cover. Set the eggs aside. When they are cold, gently roll the eggs to craze the shells without breaking them.

3 Stir the soy sauce, salt and star anise into the pan of water. Add the teabags and eggs. Bring to the boil, cover and simmer for 1½–2 hours. Top up the water to keep the eggs covered.

4 Allow the eggs to cool in the liquid overnight, then shell carefully. Quarter and serve as part of a meal.

COOK'S TIPS
• *The soy sauce and tea not only colours the eggs but adds a subtle flavour. Use dark soy sauce, which has a stronger flavour than light soy sauce.*
• *Make sure that the eggs simmer very gently and watch them carefully so that the soy sauce liquid doesn't evaporate too much. Keep topping up the liquid with recently boiled water from the kettle so that the eggs are always covered.*

EGG FOO YUNG

Hearty and full of flavour, this can be cooked either as one large omelette or as individual omelettes. Either way, it is a good way to use up leftovers such as cooked ham, fish, shellfish, chicken, pork or vegetables. Serve it cut into pieces.

SERVES 3–4

INGREDIENTS

6 Chinese dried mushrooms soaked for 30 minutes in warm water
50g/2oz/1 cup beansprouts
6 drained canned water chestnuts, finely chopped
50g/2oz baby spinach leaves, washed
60ml/4 tbsp sunflower oil
50g/2oz roast pork, cut into thin strips
4 eggs
2.5ml/½ tsp sugar
5ml/1 tsp rice wine or medium-dry sherry
salt and ground black pepper
fresh coriander (cilantro) sprigs, to garnish

1 Drain the mushrooms, cut off and discard the stems; slice the caps finely and mix them with the remaining vegetables. Heat half the oil in a large heavy frying pan. Add the roast pork and the vegetables and toss the mixture over the heat for 1 minute.

2 Beat the eggs in a bowl. Add the pork and vegetable mixture and mix together until well combined.

3 Wipe the frying pan and heat the remaining oil. Pour in the egg mixture and tilt the pan so that it covers the base. When the omelette has set on the underside, sprinkle the top with salt, pepper and sugar.

4 Invert a plate over the pan, turn both over, and slide it back into the pan to cook on the other side. Drizzle with rice wine or sherry and serve immediately, garnished with sprigs of coriander.

Surprisingly, the very popular "seaweed" served in Chinese restaurants is, in fact, very finely shredded ordinary spring greens (collards) that have been deep-fried. Ground fried fish makes a very tasty garnish and is available from Asian stores.

INGREDIENTS
450g/1lb spring greens (collards)
vegetable oil, for deep-frying
2.5ml/½ tsp salt
5ml/1 tsp caster (superfine) sugar
15ml/1 tbsp ground fried fish, to garnish (optional)

Cut off the hard stalks in the centre of each spring green leaf. Pile the leaves on top of each other, and roll into a tight sausage shape. Using a sharp knife, cut the leaves into fine shreds. Spread them out to dry on a clean dishtowel or several sheets of kitchen paper.

Heat the vegetable oil in a wok or deep-fryer to 190°C/375°F. Deep-fry the shredded greens in batches, stirring to separate them.

Remove the greens with a slotted spoon as soon as they are crisp, but before they turn brown. Drain well on kitchen paper. Sprinkle the salt and sugar evenly all over the "seaweed". Mix well, garnish with ground fish, if using, and serve.

VARIATION
Other fresh green leaves can also be cooked and served in this way. Try using Chinese leaves (Chinese cabbage) or spinach instead of spring greens.

This straightforward yet versatile vegetarian dish can be served hot, warm or cold, as the occasion demands. Topped with a sprinkling of toasted sesame seeds, it is easy to prepare and tastes absolutely delicious.

INGREDIENTS
2 aubergines (eggplant), total weight about 600g/1lb 6oz, cut into
    large chunks
15ml/1 tbsp salt
5ml/1 tsp chilli powder, or to taste
75–90ml/5–6 tbsp sunflower oil
15ml/1 tbsp rice wine or medium-dry sherry
100ml/3½fl oz/scant ½ cup water
75ml/5 tbsp chilli bean sauce
salt and ground black pepper
toasted sesame seeds, to garnish

Place the aubergine chunks on a plate, sprinkle them with the salt and leave to stand for 15–20 minutes. Rinse well, drain and dry thoroughly on kitchen paper. Toss the aubergine cubes in the chilli powder.

Heat a wok and add the oil. When the oil is hot, add the salted aubergine chunks, with the rice wine or sherry. Stir constantly until the aubergine chunks start to turn a little brown. Stir in the water, cover the wok and steam for about 3 minutes.

Add the chilli bean sauce to the aubergines and cook for 2 minutes. Season with salt and ground black pepper to taste, then spoon on to a serving dish, scatter with sesame seeds and serve.

KAN SHAO GREEN BEANS

A particular style of cooking from Sichuan, kan shao *means "dry-cooked" – in other words using no stock or water. The slim green beans available all the year round from supermarkets are ideal for use in this quick and tasty recipe.*

SERVES 6

INGREDIENTS
175ml/6fl oz/¾ cup sunflower oil
450/1lb fresh green beans, topped, tailed and halved
5 × 1cm/2 × ½in piece fresh root ginger, peeled and cut into matchsticks
5ml/1 tsp sugar
10ml/2 tsp light soy sauce
salt and ground black pepper

1 Heat the oil in a wok. When the oil is just beginning to smoke, carefully add the beans and stir-fry for 1–2 minutes until just tender.

2 Lift out the green beans on to a plate lined with kitchen paper. Using a ladle carefully remove all but 30ml/2 tbsp of the oil from the wok.

3 Reheat the remaining oil, add the ginger and stir-fry for a minute or two to flavour the oil.

4 Return the green beans to the wok, stir in the sugar, soy sauce and salt and pepper, and toss together quickly to ensure the beans are well coated. Serve the beans at once.

VARIATION
This simple recipe works just as well with other fresh green vegetables such as okra, mangetouts and baby asparagus spears.

Chinese Mushrooms
& Bamboo Shoots

Another name for this dish is "Twin Winter Vegetables", because both bamboo shoots and mushrooms are at their best during the winter season. For that reason, try using canned winter bamboo shoots.

SERVES 4

INGREDIENTS
50g/2oz dried Chinese mushrooms (shiitake)
285g/10oz winter bamboo shoots
45ml/3 tbsp vegetable oil
1 spring onion (scallion), cut into short sections
30ml/2 tbsp light soy sauce or oyster sauce
15ml/1 tbsp Chinese rice wine or dry sherry
2.5ml/½ tsp soft light brown sugar
7.5ml/1½ tsp cornflour (cornstarch) mixed to a paste with a little water
a few drops of sesame oil

1 Soak the mushrooms in cold water for at least 3 hours, then squeeze dry and discard any hard stalks, reserving the water. Cut the mushrooms in half, or quarters if they are large – keep them whole if small.

2 Rinse and drain the bamboo shoots, then cut them into small, wedge-shaped pieces roughly equal in size.

3 Heat the oil in a preheated wok and stir-fry the mushrooms and bamboo shoots for about 1 minute. Add the spring onion and seasonings with about 30–45ml/2–3 tbsp of the mushroom water. Bring to the boil and cook for another minute or so, then stir in the cornflour paste, cook for about 15 seconds, stirring, until thickened, then sprinkle with a little sesame oil and serve.

Fragrant Harbour is the Chinese name for Hong Kong, the crossroads for so many styles of cooking. Fried rice is ever popular as yet another way of using up little bits of this and that to make a veritable feast. Cook the rice the day before if possible.

INGREDIENTS
225g/8oz/generous 1 cup long grain rice
about 90ml/6 tbsp vegetable oil
2 eggs, beaten
4 Chinese dried mushrooms, soaked for 30 minutes in warm water
8 shallots or 2 small onions, sliced
115g/4oz peeled cooked prawns (shrimp), thawed if frozen
3 garlic cloves, crushed
115g/4oz cooked pork, cut into thin strips
115g/4oz Chinese sausage
30ml/2 tbsp light soy sauce
115g/4oz/1 cup frozen peas, thawed
2 spring onions (scallions), shredded
1–2 fresh or dried red chillies, seeded (optional)
salt and ground black pepper
fresh coriander (cilantro) leaves, to garnish

Bring a large pan of lightly salted water to the boil. Add the long grain rice and cook for 12–15 minutes until just tender. Drain and leave to go cold. Ideally use the next day.

Heat about 15ml/1 tbsp of the oil in a large frying pan over a medium heat, pour in the beaten eggs and allow to set without stirring. Slide the omelette on to a plate, roll it up and cut into fine strips. Set aside.

Drain the mushrooms, cut off and discard the stems and slice the caps finely. Heat a wok, add 15ml/1 tbsp of the remaining oil and, when hot, add the shallots or onions and stir-fry until crisp and golden brown. Remove with a slotted spoon and set aside.

Add the prawns and garlic to the wok, with a little more oil if needed, and fry for 1 minute, then remove the prawns and garlic and set aside. Add 15ml/1 tbsp more oil to the wok.

Stir-fry the shredded pork and mushrooms for 2 minutes; lift out and reserve. Steam the Chinese sausage in a colander for 5 minutes, or until it plumps up. Trim and slice at an angle.

Wipe the wok, reheat with the remaining oil and stir-fry the rice, adding more oil if needed so the grains are coated. Stir in the soy sauce, salt and pepper, plus half the cooked ingredients.

Add the peas and half the spring onions and toss over the heat until the peas are cooked. Pile the fried rice on a heated platter and arrange the remaining cooked ingredients on top, with the remaining spring onions. Add the chilli, if using, and the coriander leaves, to garnish.

COOK'S TIP
There are many theories on the best way to cook rice. This gives excellent results every time: Put 225g/8oz/generous 1 cup long grain rice in a sieve and rinse thoroughly in cold water. Place in a large bowl, add salt to taste and pour in just under 600ml/1 pint/2½ cups boiling water. Cover with microwave film, leaving a small gap and cook in a 675 watt microwave on full power for 10 minutes. Leave to stand for 5 minutes more. Cool, then stir with a chopstick.

SICHUAN SPICY TOFU

This universally popular dish originated in Sichuan in the nineteenth century. The meat used in the recipe can be omitted to create a purely vegetarian dish. Tofu has little taste of its own, but absorbs the rich flavours of this dish very well.

SERVES 4

INGREDIENTS
3 packets of firm tofu
1 leek
45ml/3 tbsp vegetable oil
115g/4oz minced (ground) beef
15ml/1 tbsp black bean sauce
15ml/1 tbsp light soy sauce
5ml/1 tsp chilli bean sauce
15ml/1 tbsp Chinese rice wine or dry sherry
about 45–60ml/3–4 tbsp stock or water
7.5ml/1½ tsp cornflour (cornstarch) mixed to a paste with a little water
ground Sichuan peppercorns, to taste
a few drops of sesame oil

1 Cut the tofu into 1cm/½in cubes; blanch the cubes in a pan of boiling water for 2–3 minutes to harden. Remove and drain. Cut the leek crossways into short sections.

2 Heat the oil in a wok, add the beef and stir-fry until the colour changes, then add the leek and black bean sauce. Add the tofu cubes with the soy sauce, chilli bean sauce and rice wine or sherry. Stir gently for 1 minute.

3 Add the stock or water, bring the mixture to the boil and then cook for about 2–3 minutes.

4 Add the cornflour paste and cook, stirring, for about 15 seconds until thickened, season with the ground Sichuan pepper and sprinkle with the sesame oil. Serve at once.

SPICY SHREDDED BEEF

In this recipe it is essential that the beef is cut into very fine strips. This is easier to achieve if the piece of beef is placed in the freezer for 30 minutes until it is very firm before being sliced with a sharp knife.

SERVES 2

INGREDIENTS
225g/8oz rump (round) steak or fillet of beef
15ml/1 tbsp each light and dark soy sauce
15ml/1 tbsp rice wine or medium-dry sherry
5ml/1 tsp soft dark brown sugar or golden granulated sugar
90ml/6 tbsp vegetable oil
1 large onion, thinly sliced
2.5cm/1in piece fresh root ginger, peeled and grated
1–2 carrots, cut into matchsticks
2–3 fresh or dried chillies, halved, seeded (optional) and chopped
salt and ground black pepper
fresh chives, to garnish

1 With a sharp knife, slice the beef very thinly, then cut each slice into fine strips or shreds of an equal size. Mix together the light and dark soy sauces with the rice wine or sherry and sugar in a bowl. Add the strips of beef and stir well to ensure they are evenly coated with the marinade.

2 Heat a wok and add half the oil. When it is hot, stir-fry the onion and ginger for 3–4 minutes, then transfer to a plate. Add the carrot, stir-fry for 3–4 minutes until slightly softened, then transfer to a plate and keep warm.

3 Heat the remaining oil in the wok, then add the beef, with the marinade, followed by the chillies. Cook over high heat for 2 minutes, stirring all the time.

4 Return the fried onion and ginger to the wok and stir-fry for 1 minute more. Season to taste, cover and cook for 30 seconds. Spoon the meat into warmed bowls and add the carrots. Garnish with fresh chives and serve immediately.

Chow mein is hugely popular with the thrifty Chinese who believe in turning leftovers into tasty dishes. For this delicious dish, boiled noodles are fried to form a crispy crust, which is topped with a savoury sauce containing whatever tastes good and needs eating up.

Serves 2–3

INGREDIENTS
225g/8oz lean beef steak or pork fillet
225g/8oz can bamboo shoots, drained
1 leek, trimmed
25g/1oz Chinese dried mushrooms, soaked for 30 minutes in 120ml/4fl oz/½ cup
  warm water
150g/5oz Chinese leaves (Chinese cabbage)
450g/1lb cooked egg noodles (255g/8oz dried), drained well
90ml/6 tbsp vegetable oil
30ml/2 tbsp dark soy sauce
15ml/1 tbsp cornflour (cornstarch)
15ml/1 tbsp rice wine or medium-dry sherry
5ml/1 tsp sesame oil
5ml/1 tsp caster (superfine) sugar
salt and ground black pepper

Slice the beef or pork, bamboo shoots and leek into matchsticks. Drain the mushrooms, reserving 90ml/6 tbsp of the soaking water. Cut off and discard the stems, then slice the caps finely. Cut the Chinese leaves into 2.5cm/1in diamond-shape pieces and sprinkle with salt. Pat the noodles dry with kitchen paper.

Heat a third of the oil in a large wok or frying pan and fry the noodles. After turning them over once, press the noodles evenly against the base of the pan with a wooden spatula until they form a flat, even cake. Cook over a medium heat for about 4 minutes, or until the noodles at the bottom have become crisp.

Turn the noodle cake over with a spatula or fish slice or invert on to a large plate and slide back into the wok. Cook for 3 minutes more, then slide on to a heated plate. Keep warm.

Heat 30ml/2 tbsp of the remaining oil in the wok. Add the strips of leek, then the meat strips and stir-fry for 10–15 seconds. Sprinkle over half the soy sauce and then add the bamboo shoots and mushrooms, with salt and pepper to taste. Toss over the heat for 1 minute, then transfer this mixture to a plate and set aside.

Heat the remaining oil in the wok and stir-fry the Chinese leaves for 1 minute. Return the meat and vegetable mixture to the wok and sauté with the leaves for 30 seconds, stirring constantly.

Mix the cornflour with the reserved mushroom water. Stir into the wok along with the rice wine or sherry, sesame oil, sugar and remaining soy sauce. Cook for 15 seconds to thicken. Divide the noodles among 2–3 serving dishes and pile the meat and vegetables on top.

MONGOLIAN FIREPOT

This mode of cooking was introduced to China by the Mongol hordes who invaded in the thirteenth century. It calls for participation on the part of the guests, who cook the assembled ingredients at the table, dipping the meats in a variety of sauces.

SERVES 6–8

INGREDIENTS
900g/2lb boned leg of lamb, preferably bought thinly sliced
225g/8oz lamb's liver and/or kidneys
900ml/1½ pints/3¾ cups lamb stock (see Cook's Tip)
900ml/1½ pints/3¾ cups chicken stock
1cm/½in piece fresh root ginger, peeled and thinly sliced
45ml/3 tbsp rice wine or medium-dry sherry
½ head Chinese leaves (Chinese cabbage), rinsed and shredded
a few young spinach leaves
250g/9oz firm tofu, diced (optional)
115g/4oz cellophane noodles
salt and ground black pepper

FOR THE DIPPING SAUCE
50ml/2fl oz/¼ cup red wine vinegar
7.5ml/½ tbsp dark soy sauce
1cm/½in piece fresh root ginger, peeled and finely shredded
1 spring onion (scallion), finely shredded

TO SERVE
steamed flower rolls
bowls of tomato sauce, sweet chilli sauce, mustard oil and sesame oil
dry-fried coriander seeds, crushed

1 When buying the lamb, ask your butcher to slice it thinly on a slicing machine, if possible. If you have had to buy the lamb in the piece, however, put it in the freezer for about an hour, so that it is easier to slice thinly.

2 Trim the liver and remove the skin and core from the kidneys, if using. Place them in the freezer to firm up before slicing. If you managed to buy sliced lamb, keep it in the refrigerator until needed.

3   Mix the stocks together in a large pan. Add the sliced ginger and rice wine or sherry, and salt and pepper. Heat to simmering point; simmer for 15 minutes.

4   Slice all the meats thinly and arrange them attractively on a large platter. Place the shredded Chinese leaves, spinach leaves and the diced tofu on a separate platter. Soak the noodles in warm or hot water, following the instructions on the packet.

5   Make the dipping sauce by mixing all the ingredients in a small bowl. The other sauces and the crushed coriander seeds should be spooned into separate small dishes and placed on a tray. Have ready a basket of freshly steamed flower rolls.

6   Fill the moat of the hot-pot with the simmering stock. Alternatively, fill a fondue pot and place it over a burner. Each guest selects a portion of meat from the platter and cooks it in the hot stock, using chopsticks or a fondue fork. The meat is then dipped in one of the sauces and coated with the coriander seeds (if liked) before being eaten with a steamed flower roll.

7   When all or most of the meat has been eaten, top up the stock if necessary, then add the vegetables, tofu and drained noodles. Cook for a minute or two, until the noodles are tender and the vegetables retain a little crispness. Serve the soup in warmed bowls, with any remaining steamed flower rolls.

COOK'S TIP

When buying the lamb, ask the butcher for the bones and make your own stock. Rinse the bones and place them in a large pan with water to cover. Bring to the boil and skim the surface well. Add 1 peeled onion, 2 peeled carrots, 1cm/½in piece of peeled and bruised ginger, 5ml/1 tsp salt and ground black pepper to taste. Bring back to the boil, then simmer for about an hour until the stock is full of flavour. Strain, leave to cool, then skim and use.

Mu Shu Pork with Eggs & Wood Ears

Mu Shu is the Chinese name for a bright yellow flower. Traditionally, this dish is served as a filling wrapped in thin pancakes, but it can also be served on its own simply with plain boiled rice.

SERVES 4

INGREDIENTS
15g/½oz dried wood ears
175–225g/6–8oz pork fillet
225g/8oz Chinese leaves (Chinese cabbage)
115g/4oz bamboo shoots, drained
2 spring onions (scallions)
3 eggs
5ml/1 tsp salt
60ml/4 tbsp vegetable oil
15ml/1 tbsp light soy sauce
15ml/1 tbsp Chinese rice wine or dry sherry
a few drops of sesame oil

Soak the wood ears in cold water for 25–30 minutes, rinse and discard the hard stalks, if any. Drain, then thinly shred.

Cut the pork into matchstick-size shreds. Thinly shred the Chinese leaves, bamboo shoots and spring onions.

Beat the eggs with a pinch of the salt and lightly scramble in a little of the warm oil until set, but not too dry. Remove from the heat.

Heat the remaining oil in the wok and stir-fry the pork for about 1 minute, or until the colour changes. Add the vegetables and stir-fry for 1 minute.

Add the remaining salt, soy sauce and rice wine or sherry. Stir for 1 more minute before adding the scrambled eggs. Break up the scrambled eggs and blend well. Sprinkle with sesame oil and serve.

These larger-than-usual pork meatballs are first fried until golden brown, then simmered in stock. They are traditionally served with a fringe of lightly cooked greens such as pak choi (bok choy) to represent the lion's mane.

INGREDIENTS
450g/1lb lean pork, minced (ground) finely with a little fat
4–6 drained canned water chestnuts, finely chopped
5ml/1 tsp finely chopped fresh root ginger
1 small onion, finely chopped
30ml/2 tbsp dark soy sauce
beaten egg, to bind
30ml/2 tbsp cornflour (cornstarch), seasoned with salt and ground black pepper
30ml/2 tbsp groundnut (peanut) oil
300ml/½ pint/1¼ cups chicken stock
2.5ml/½ tsp sugar
115g/4oz pak choi (bok choy), stalks trimmed and the leaves rinsed
salt and ground black pepper

Mix the pork, water chestnuts, ginger and onion with 15ml/1 tbsp of the soy sauce in a bowl. Add salt and pepper to taste, stir in enough beaten egg to bind, then form into eight or nine balls. Toss a little of the cornflour into the bowl and make a paste with the remaining cornflour and water.

Heat the oil in a large frying pan and brown the meatballs all over. Using a slotted spoon, transfer the meatballs to a wok or deep frying pan.

Add the stock, sugar and the remaining soy sauce to the oil that is left in the pan. Heat gently, stirring to incorporate the sediment on the base of the pan. Pour over the meatballs, cover and simmer for 20–25 minutes. Increase the heat and add the pak choi. Cook for 2–3 minutes, or until the leaves are wilted.

Lift out the greens and arrange on a serving platter. Top with the meatballs and keep hot. Stir the cornflour paste into the sauce. Bring to the boil, stirring, until it thickens. Pour over the meatballs and serve at once.

Deep-fried Spare Ribs with Spicy Salt & Pepper

Ideally, each spare rib should be chopped into 3–4 bitesize pieces. You will need a heavy cleaver to do this but if this is not possible, then serve the ribs whole.

Serves 4–6

Ingredients
10–12 spare ribs, about 675g/1½lb in total
about 30–45ml/2–3 tbsp plain (all-purpose) flour
vegetable oil, for deep-frying

For the marinade
1 garlic clove, crushed and finely chopped
15ml/1 tbsp soft light brown sugar
15ml/1 tbsp light soy sauce
15ml/1 tbsp dark soy sauce
30ml/2 tbsp Chinese rice wine or dry sherry
2.5ml/½ tsp chilli sauce
a few drops of sesame oil

1 Chop each rib into 3–4 pieces, then mix with all the marinade ingredients, and leave to marinate for at least 3 hours.

2 Coat the ribs with flour and deep-fry in medium-hot oil for 4–5 minutes, stirring to separate. Remove and drain.

3 Heat the oil to high and deep-fry the ribs again for 1 minute, or until dark brown. Remove and drain, then serve with spicy salt and pepper (see Cook's Tip).

Cook's Tip
To make spicy salt and pepper, mix 15ml/1 tbsp salt with 10ml/2 tsp ground Sichuan peppercorns and 5ml/1 tsp five-spice powder. Heat, stirring, in a preheated dry pan for 2 minutes over a low heat.

CONGEE WITH CHINESE SAUSAGE

Congee – soft rice – is comfort food. Gentle on the stomach, it is frequently eaten for breakfast or served to invalids. Throughout Asia, people will frequently have just a cup of tea on rising; later they will settle down to a bowl of congee or its regional equivalent. Congee is also popular with tea eggs.

SERVES 2–3

INGREDIENTS
115g/4oz/generous ½ cup long grain rice
25g/1oz/3 tbsp glutinous rice
1.2 litres/2 pints/5 cups water
about 2.5ml/½ tsp salt
5ml/1 tsp sesame oil
thin slice of fresh root ginger, peeled and bruised
2 Chinese sausages
1 egg, lightly beaten (optional)
2.5ml/½ tsp light soy sauce
roasted peanuts, chopped, and thin shreds of spring onion (scallion), to garnish

1 Wash both rices thoroughly. Drain and place in a large pan. Add the water, bring to the boil and immediately reduce to the lowest heat, using a heat diffuser if you have one.

2 Cook gently for 1¼–1½ hours, stirring from time to time. If the congee thickens too much, stir in a little boiling water. It should have the consistency of creamy pouring porridge.

3 About 15 minutes before serving, add salt to taste and the sesame oil, together with the slice of ginger.

4 Steam the Chinese sausages for about 10 minutes, then slice and stir into the congee. Cook for 5 minutes.

5 Just before serving, remove the ginger and stir in the lightly beaten egg, if using. Serve hot, garnished with the peanuts and spring onions and topped with a drizzle of soy sauce.

What a descriptive name for this special dish from Sichuan. Use toasted sesame paste to give the sauce an authentic flavour, although crunchy peanut butter can be used instead. Bang bang chicken is perfect for parties and ideal for a buffet.

INGREDIENTS
3 skinless boneless chicken breast portions, about 450g/1lb in total
1 garlic clove, crushed
2.5ml/½ tsp black peppercorns
1 small onion, halved
1 large cucumber, peeled, seeded and cut into thin strips
salt and ground black pepper

FOR THE SAUCE
45ml/3 tbsp toasted sesame paste
15ml/1 tbsp light soy sauce
15ml/1 tbsp white wine vinegar
2 spring onions (scallions), finely chopped
2 garlic cloves, crushed
5 × 1cm/2 × ½in piece fresh root ginger, peeled and cut into matchsticks
15ml/1 tbsp Sichuan peppercorns, dry-fried and crushed
5ml/1 tsp soft light brown sugar

FOR THE CHILLI OIL
60ml/4 tbsp groundnut (peanut) oil
5ml/1 tsp chilli powder

> ### COOK'S TIP
> *Crunchy peanut butter can be used instead of the sesame paste, if preferred. Mix it with 30ml/ 2 tbsp sesame oil and proceed as in Step 2.*

Place the chicken in a pan. Just cover with water, add the garlic, peppercorns and onion, and bring to the boil. Skim the surface, stir in salt and pepper to taste, then cover the pan. Cook for 25 minutes, or until the chicken is just tender. Drain, reserving the stock.

Make the sauce by mixing the toasted sesame paste with 45ml/3 tbsp of the chicken stock, saving the rest for soup. Add the soy sauce, white wine vinegar, spring onions, garlic, fresh root ginger and crushed peppercorns to the sesame mixture. Stir in the sugar.

Make the chilli oil by gently heating the oil and chilli powder together until foaming. Simmer for 2 minutes, cool, then strain off the red-coloured oil and discard the sediment.

Spread out the cucumber batons on a platter. Cut the chicken into pieces of about the same size as the cucumber strips and arrange them on top. Pour over the sauce, drizzle on the chilli oil and serve.

Drunken Chicken

As the chicken is marinated for several days, it is important to use a very fresh bird from a reputable supplier. "Drunken" foods are usually served cold as part of an appetizer, or cut into neat pieces and served as a snack with cocktails.

SERVES 4–6

INGREDIENTS
1 chicken, about 1.4kg/3lb
1cm/½in piece fresh root ginger, peeled and thinly sliced
2 spring onions (scallions), trimmed
1.75 litres/3 pints/7½ cups water, or to cover
15ml/1 tbsp salt
300ml/½ pint/1¼ cups dry sherry
15–30ml/1–2 tbsp brandy (optional)
spring onions (scallions), shredded, and fresh herbs, to garnish

1 Rinse and dry the chicken inside and out. Place the ginger and spring onions in the body cavity. Put the chicken in a large pan or flameproof casserole and just cover with water. Bring to the boil, skim and cook for 15 minutes.

2 Turn off the heat, cover the pan or casserole tightly and leave the chicken in the cooking liquid for 3–4 hours, by which time it will be cooked. Drain well. Pour 300ml/½ pint/1¼ cups of the stock into a bowl. Freeze the remaining stock.

3 Skin the chicken and joint it. Divide each leg into two. Make two more portions from the wings and some of the breast. Cut away the remainder of the breast pieces and divide each breast into two portions.

4 Arrange the chicken in a shallow dish. Rub in salt and cover with clear film (plastic wrap). Leave in a cool place for several hours or overnight in the refrigerator.

5 Later, lift off any fat from the stock. Mix the sherry and brandy, if using, in a jug (pitcher), add the stock and pour over the chicken. Cover again and leave in the refrigerator to marinate for 2 or 3 days, turning occasionally.

6 When ready to serve, cut the chicken through the bone into chunky pieces and arrange on a serving platter garnished with spring onion shreds and herbs.

Sichuan Chicken with Kung Po Sauce

This recipe hails from the Sichuan region of Western China where dishes are highly flavoured and often very spicy. It has become one of the classic recipes in the Chinese repertoire, popular the world over.

SERVES 3

INGREDIENTS

2 skinless boneless chicken breast portions, about 350g/12oz in total
1 egg white
10ml/2 tsp cornflour (cornstarch)
2.5ml/½ tsp salt
30ml/2 tbsp yellow salted beans
15ml/1 tbsp hoisin sauce
5ml/1 tsp soft light brown sugar
15ml/1 tbsp rice wine or medium-dry sherry
15ml/1 tbsp white wine vinegar
4 garlic cloves, crushed
150ml/¼ pint/⅔ cup chicken stock
45ml/3 tbsp groundnut (peanut) oil or sunflower oil
2–3 dried chillies, broken into small pieces
115g/4oz/1 cup roasted cashew nuts
fresh coriander (cilantro), to garnish

1 Cut the chicken into neat pieces. Lightly whisk the egg white in a dish, whisk in the cornflour and salt, then add the chicken and stir until coated.

2 In a separate bowl, mash the beans with a spoon. Stir in the hoisin sauce, brown sugar, rice wine or sherry, vinegar, garlic and stock.

3 Heat a wok, add the oil and then fry the chicken, turning constantly, for about 2 minutes until tender. Drain over a bowl in order to collect the excess oil.

4 Heat the reserved oil and fry the chilli pieces for 1 minute. Return the chicken to the wok and pour in the bean sauce mixture. Bring to the boil and stir in the cashew nuts. Spoon into a heated serving dish and garnish with coriander leaves.

As the Chinese discovered centuries ago, this is quite the best way to eat duck. The preparation is time-consuming, but it can be done in easy stages.

INGREDIENTS
1 duck, about 2.25kg/5¼lb
45ml/3 tbsp clear honey
30ml/2 tbsp water
5ml/1 tsp salt
1 bunch spring onions (scallions), cut into strips
½ cucumber, seeded and cut into matchsticks

FOR THE MANDARIN PANCAKES
275g/10oz/2½ cups strong white bread flour
5ml/1 tsp salt
45ml/3 tbsp groundnut (peanut) or sesame oil
250ml/8fl oz/1 cup boiling water

FOR THE DIPPING SAUCES
120ml/4fl oz/½ cup hoisin sauce
120ml/4fl oz/½ cup plum sauce

Bring a large pan of water to the boil. Place the duck on a trivet in the sink and pour the boiling water over the duck to scald and firm up the skin. Carefully lift it out on the trivet and drain thoroughly. Tie kitchen string firmly around the legs of the bird and suspend it from a butcher's hook from a shelf in a cool place. Place a bowl underneath to catch the drips and leave overnight.

Next day, blend the honey, water and salt and brush half the mixture over the duck skin. Hang for 2–3 hours. Repeat and hang for 3–4 hours.

Make the pancakes. Sift the flour and salt into a bowl or food processor. Add 15ml/1 tbsp of the oil, then gradually add enough of the boiling water to form a soft but not sticky dough. Knead for 2–3 minutes by hand or for 30 seconds in the food processor. Allow to rest for 30 minutes.

Knead the dough, then divide it into 24 pieces and roll each piece to a 15cm/6in round. Brush the rounds with oil, then sandwich the rounds together in pairs.

Brush the surface of two heavy frying pans sparingly with oil. Add one pancake pair to each pan and cook gently for 2–3 minutes until cooked but not coloured. Turn over and cook for 2–3 minutes more.

Slide the double pancakes out of the pan and pull them apart. Stack on a plate, placing a square of baking parchment between each while cooking the remainder. Cool, wrap tightly in foil and set aside.

Preheat the oven to 230°C/450°F/Gas 8. When it reaches that temperature, put the duck on a rack in a roasting pan and place it in the oven. Immediately reduce the temperature to 180°C/350°F/Gas 4 and roast the duck for 1¾ hours without basting. Check that the skin is crisp and, if necessary, increase the oven temperature to the maximum. Roast for 15 minutes more.

Meanwhile, place the spring onion strips in iced water to crisp. Drain. Pat the cucumber pieces dry on kitchen paper. Reheat the prepared pancakes by steaming the foil parcel for 5–10 minutes in a bamboo steamer over a wok or pan of boiling water. Pour the dipping sauces into small dishes.

Carve the duck into 4cm/1½in pieces. At the table, each guest smears some of the sauce on a pancake, tops it with a small amount of crisp duck skin and meat and adds cucumber and spring onion strips before enjoying the rolled-up pancake.

COOK'S TIP
Mandarin pancakes can be cooked ahead and frozen. Separate the cooked pancakes with squares of freezer paper, seal them in a plastic bag and freeze. They can be heated from frozen as described in the recipe.

ANITA WONG'S DUCK

The Chinese are passionately fond of duck and regard it as essential at celebratory meals. To the Chinese, duck denotes marital harmony.

SERVES 4–6

INGREDIENTS
60ml/4 tbsp vegetable oil
2 garlic cloves, chopped
1 duck with giblets, about 2.25kg/5–5¼lb
2.5cm/1in piece fresh root ginger, peeled and thinly sliced
45ml/3 tbsp bean paste
30ml/2 tbsp light soy sauce
15ml/1 tbsp dark soy sauce
15ml/1 tbsp sugar
2.5ml/½ tsp five-spice powder
3 star anise points
450ml/¾ pint/scant 2 cups duck stock (see Cook's Tip)
salt
shredded spring onions (scallions), to garnish

1 Heat the oil in a large pan. Fry the garlic without browning, then add the duck. Turn frequently until the outside is slightly brown. Transfer to a plate.

2 Add the ginger to the pan, then stir in the bean paste. Cook for 1 minute, then add both soy sauces, the sugar and five-spice powder. Return the duck to the pan and fry until the outside is coated. Add the star anise and stock, and season. Cover tightly and simmer for 2–2½ hours. Skim off the excess fat. Leave to cool.

3 Cut the duck into serving portions and pour over the sauce. Garnish with spring onion curls and serve cold.

COOK'S TIP
To make stock, put the duck giblets in a pan with a small onion and a piece of bruised ginger. Cover with 600ml/1 pint/2½ cups water, bring to the boil and then simmer, covered, for 20 minutes.

Duck Breasts with Pineapple & Ginger

Use the boneless duck breasts that are widely available or alternatively do as the Chinese and use a whole bird, saving the legs for another meal and using the carcass to make stock for soup.

SERVES 2–3

INGREDIENTS
2 boneless duck breasts
4 spring onions (scallions), chopped
225g/8oz can pineapple rings in fruit juice
75ml/5 tbsp water
4 pieces drained Chinese stem (preserved) ginger in syrup, plus 45ml/3 tbsp syrup from the jar
30ml/2 tbsp cornflour (cornstarch) mixed to a paste with a little water
¼ each red and green (bell) pepper, seeded and cut into thin strips
salt and ground black pepper
cooked thin egg noodles, baby spinach and green beans, blanched, to serve

1 Skin the duck breasts. Select a shallow bowl that will fit into your steamer and contain the meat side by side. Spread out the spring onions in the bowl, add the duck and cover with baking parchment. Steam for 1 hour, or until tender. Remove the duck breasts and leave to cool slightly.

2 Cut the breasts into thin slices. Place on a plate and moisten them with a little of the cooking juices. Strain the remaining juices into a small pan and set aside. Cover the duck slices with the baking parchment or foil and keep warm.

3 Drain the canned pineapple rings, reserving 75ml/5 tbsp of the juice. Add this to the reserved cooking juices in the pan with the measured water. Add the ginger syrup and cornflour paste. Cook, stirring until thickened. Season.

4 Cut the pineapple and ginger into attractive shapes. Put the cooked noodles, baby spinach and green beans on a plate, add slices of duck and top with the pineapple, ginger and pepper strips. Pour over the sauce and serve.

A fish kettle will come in useful for this recipe. Carp is traditionally used, but any chunky fish that can be cooked whole such as salmon or sea bream can be used. Make sure you have a suitable large platter for serving this spectacular dish.

INGREDIENTS
1–2 carp or similar whole fish, about 1kg/2¼lb in total, cleaned and scaled
2.5cm/1in piece fresh root ginger, peeled and thinly sliced
4 spring onions (scallions), cut into thin strips
2.5ml/½ tsp salt

FOR THE SAUCE
375g/13oz jar chow chow (Chinese sweet mixed pickles)
300ml/½ pint/1¼ cups water
30ml/2 tbsp rice vinegar
25ml/1½ tbsp sugar
25ml/1½ tbsp cornflour (cornstarch)
15ml/1 tbsp light soy sauce
15ml/1 tbsp rice wine or medium-dry sherry
1 small green (bell) pepper, seeded and diced
1 carrot, peeled and cut into matchsticks
1 tomato, peeled, seeded and diced

Rinse the fish and dry with kitchen paper. Create a support for the fish by placing a broad strip of oiled foil on the work surface. Place the fish on the foil. Mix the ginger, spring onions and salt, then tuck the mixture into the body cavity.

Lift the fish on the foil strip and place on the trivet from a fish kettle. Lower the trivet into the fish kettle and tuck the ends of the foil over the fish.

Pour boiling water into the fish kettle to a depth of 2.5cm/1in. Bring to a full rolling boil, then lower the heat and cook the fish until the flesh flakes, topping up the kettle with boiling water as necessary. See Cook's Tip for cooking times.

Meanwhile, prepare the sauce. Tip the chow chow into a sieve placed over a
bowl and reserve the liquid. Cut each of the pickles in half. Pour 250ml/8fl oz/
1 cup of the water into a pan and bring to the boil. Add the vinegar and sugar and
stir until dissolved.

In a small bowl, mix the cornflour to a paste with the remaining water. Stir in
the soy sauce and rice wine or sherry.

Add the mixture to the sauce and bring to the boil, stirring until it thickens and
becomes glossy. Add all the vegetables, the chopped pickles and the pickle
liquid and cook over a gentle heat for 2 minutes.

Using the foil strip as a support, carefully transfer the cooked fish to a platter,
then ease the foil away. Spoon the warm sauce over the fish and serve.

COOK's TIP
*If using one large fish that is too long to fit in a fish
kettle, cut it in half and cook it on a rack placed over
a large roasting pan. Pour in a similar quantity of
boiling water as for the fish kettle, cover the roasting
pan with foil and cook on top of the stove. Allow
about 20 minutes for a 1kg/2¼lb fish; 15–20
minutes for a 675g/1½lb fish. Reassemble the halved
fish before coating it with the sauce.*

SEAFOOD CHOW MEIN

Chow mein is a very versatile dish that can easily be adapted to suit the ingredients you have to hand.

SERVES 4

INGREDIENTS
75g/3oz squid, cleaned
75g/3oz uncooked prawns (shrimp)
3–4 fresh scallops
½ egg white
10ml/2 tsp cornflour (cornstarch) mixed to a paste with a little water
250g/9oz egg noodles
75–90ml/5–6 tbsp vegetable oil
50g/2oz mangetouts (snow peas)
2.5ml/½ tsp salt
2.5ml/½ tsp soft light brown sugar
15ml/1 tbsp Chinese rice wine or dry sherry
30ml/2 tbsp light soy sauce
2 spring onions (scallions), finely shredded
a little stock, if necessary
a few drops of sesame oil

COOK'S TIP
Include the corals (roe) of the scallops in this dish.
They not only provide extra flavour but a different
texture and lovely colour, too.

1 Open up the squid and, using a sharp knife, score the inside in a criss-cross pattern. Cut the squid into pieces each about the size of a postage stamp. Soak the squid in a bowl of just boiled water until all the pieces have curled up. Rinse in cold water and drain.

2 Peel the prawns, removing the tails as well, then carefully cut each prawn in half lengthways.

Cut each scallop into 3–4 slices. Mix the scallops and prawns with the egg white and cornflour paste, making sure that the seafood is coated completely with the mixture.

Cook the noodles in boiling water according to the instructions on the packet, then drain and rinse under cold running water. Mix with about 15ml/1 tbsp of the vegetable oil.

Heat about 30–45ml/2–3 tbsp of the oil in a wok until very hot. Stir-fry the mangetouts and seafood for about 2 minutes, then add the salt, sugar, wine or sherry, half of the soy sauce and about half of the spring onions. Blend well and add a little stock, if necessary. Remove from the heat and keep warm.

Heat the remaining oil in the wok and stir-fry the noodles for 2–3 minutes with the remaining soy sauce. Place in a large serving dish, pour the seafood mixture on top, garnish with the remaining spring onions and sprinkle with sesame oil. Serve hot or cold.

This recipe is far less complicated to make than it looks. Preparing the crab is a little time-consuming but the end result is well worth the effort involved. Use live crabs if you can for the best flavour and texture.

SERVES 4

INGREDIENTS
1 large or 2 medium cooked crabs, about 675g/1½lb in total
30ml/2 tbsp Chinese rice wine or dry sherry
1 egg, lightly beaten
10ml/2 tsp cornflour (cornstarch) mixed to a paste with a little water
45–60ml/3–4 tbsp vegetable oil
15ml/1 tbsp finely chopped fresh ginger root
3–4 spring onions (scallions), cut into short sections
30ml/2 tbsp light soy sauce
5ml/1 tsp soft light brown sugar
about 75ml/5 tbsp stock
a few drops of sesame oil

Cut the crab in half from the underbelly. Break off the claws and crack them with the back of a cleaver. Discard the legs and crack the shell, breaking it into several pieces. Discard the feathery gills and the sac.

Marinate the pieces of crab meat with the wine or sherry, the beaten egg and cornflour paste for 10–15 minutes.

Heat the oil in a preheated wok and stir-fry the crab pieces with the ginger and spring onions for about 2–3 minutes.

Add the soy sauce, sugar and stock, blend well and bring to the boil; braise, covered, for 3–4 minutes. Sprinkle with sesame oil and serve.

In Chinese restaurants, the term baked usually means pot-roasted or pan-baked. Ideally, buy live lobsters and cook them yourself. Ready-cooked ones have usually been boiled for far too long and have lost their delicate flavour and texture.

INGREDIENTS
1 large or 2 medium lobsters, about 800g/1¾lb in total
vegetable oil, for deep-frying
1 garlic clove, finely chopped
5ml/1 tsp finely chopped fresh ginger root
2–3 spring onions (scallions), cut into short sections
30ml/2 tbsp black bean sauce
30ml/2 tbsp Chinese rice wine or dry sherry
100ml/4fl oz/½ cup stock
fresh coriander (cilantro) leaves, to garnish

Starting from the head, cut the lobster in half lengthways. Discard the legs, remove the claws and crack them with the back of a cleaver. Discard the feathery lungs and intestine. Cut each half into 4–5 pieces.

Heat the oil in a wok to 190°C/375°F. Deep-fry the lobster pieces in hot oil for about 2 minutes, or until the shells turn bright orange; remove and drain. Pour off the excess oil leaving about 15ml/1 tbsp in the wok. Add the garlic, ginger, spring onions and black bean sauce.

Add the lobster pieces to the sauce and blend well. Add the rice wine or sherry and stock, bring to the boil and cook, covered, for 2–3 minutes. Serve garnished with coriander leaves.

ICED FRUIT MOUNTAIN

This dramatic display of fruit arranged on a "mountain" of ice cubes is bound to delight. Cut the pieces of fruit larger than for a conventional fruit salad.

SERVES 6–8

INGREDIENTS
1 star fruit
4 kumquats
1 apple and/or 1 Asian pear
2 large oranges, peeled
1 Charentais melon and/or ½ watermelon
6 physalis
225g/8oz seedless black grapes
225g/8oz large strawberries, hulls intact
8 fresh lychees, peeled (optional)
wedges of kaffir lime, to decorate
caster (superfine) sugar, for dipping

1 Slice the star fruit and halve the kumquats. Cut the apple and/or Asian pear into wedges, and the oranges into segments. Use a melon baller for the melon or cut into neat wedges. Chill all the fruit.

2 Prepare the ice cube "mountain". Choose a wide, shallow bowl that, when turned upside down, will fit neatly on a serving platter. Fill the bowl with crushed ice cubes. Put it in the freezer, with the serving platter, for an hour.

3 Remove the serving platter, ice cubes and bowl from the freezer. Invert the serving platter on top of the bowl of ice, then turn platter and bowl over. Lift off the bowl and arrange the pieces of fruit on the "mountain".

4 Decorate the mountain with the kaffir lime wedges, and serve the fruit at once, handing round a bowl of sugar separately for guests with a sweet tooth.

ALMOND CURD JUNKET

Also known as almond float, this is usually made from agar agar or isinglass, though gelatine can also be used.

SERVES 4–6

INGREDIENTS
7g/¼oz agar agar or 25g/1oz powdered gelantine
about 575ml/1 pint/2½ cups water
60ml/4 tbsp granulated or caster (superfine) sugar
300ml/½ pint/1¼ cups milk
5ml/1 tsp almond essence (extract)
fresh or canned mixed fruit salad with syrup, to serve

1 In a small pan, dissolve the agar agar in about half of the water over a gentle heat. This will take at least 10 minutes. If using gelatine, follow the instructions on the packet.

2 In a separate pan, dissolve the sugar in the remaining water over a medium heat. Add the milk and the almond essence, stirring well to combine, but do not allow the mixture to boil.

3 Mix the milk and sugar with the agar agar mixture in a large bowl, or use the prepared gelatine. When cool, place in the refrigerator for 2–3 hours to set.

4 To serve, cut the junket into small cubes and spoon into a serving dish or into individual bowls. Pour the fresh or canned fruit salad, with the syrup, over the junket and serve.

COOK'S TIP
*Agar agar is a gelling agent derived from seaweed. It
is available from health food and Asian stores.*

These scrumptious treats are best prepared for a select number as they require the cook's complete attention. The honey coating crispens delightfully when the apple fritters are dipped in iced water.

SERVES 4–5

INGREDIENTS
4 crisp eating apples
juice of ½ lemon
25g/1oz/¼ cup cornflour (cornstarch)
115g/4oz/1 cup plain (all-purpose) flour
generous pinch of salt
120–150ml/4–5fl oz/½–⅔ cup water
30ml/2 tbsp sunflower oil
2 egg whites
sunflower oil, for deep-frying
toasted sesame seeds, for sprinkling

FOR THE SAUCE
250ml/8fl oz/1 cup clear honey
120ml/4fl oz/½ cup sunflower oil
5ml/1 tsp white wine vinegar

Peel, core and cut the apples into eighths, brush each piece lightly with lemon juice then dust with cornflour. Make the sauce. Heat the honey and oil in a pan, stirring until blended. Remove from the heat and stir in the vinegar.

To make the batter, sift the flour and salt into a bowl, then stir in the water and oil. Whisk the egg whites until stiff; fold into the batter.

Spear each piece of apple in turn on a skewer, dip in the batter and fry in hot oil until golden. Drain on kitchen paper, place in a dish and pour the sauce over. Transfer the fritters to a lightly oiled serving dish. Sprinkle with sesame seeds. Serve at once, offering bowls of iced water for dipping.

These are not too difficult to make, but quite a lot of practice and patience is needed to achieve the perfect result. Today, even restaurants buy frozen ready-made ones from Chinese supermarkets. If you decide to use ready-made pancakes, or are reheating home-made ones, steam them for about 5 minutes, or microwave on full power in a 650 watt oven for 1–2 minutes.

INGREDIENTS
450g/1lb/4 cups plain (all-purpose) flour
about 300ml/½ pint/1¼ cups boiling water
5ml/1 tsp vegetable oil

Sift the flour into a mixing bowl, then pour in the boiling water very gently, stirring as you pour. Mix with the oil and knead the mixture into a firm dough. Cover with a damp dishtowel and set aside for about 30 minutes. Lightly dust a work surface with flour.

Knead the dough for 5–8 minutes or until smooth, then divide it into 3 equal portions. Roll out each portion into a long sausage-shape, cut each into 8–10 pieces and roll each into a ball. Using your palm, press each piece into a flat pancake. With a rolling pin, gently roll each into a 15cm/6in round.

Heat an ungreased frying pan until hot, then reduce the heat to low and place the pancakes, one at a time, in the pan. Remove the pancakes when small brown spots appear on the underside. Keep under a damp dishtowel until all the pancakes are cooked.

COOK'S TIP
Cooked pancakes can be stored in the refrigerator for several days. Layer them between sheets of greaseproof (waxed)paper and wrap tightly in a plastic bag. Reheat before serving.

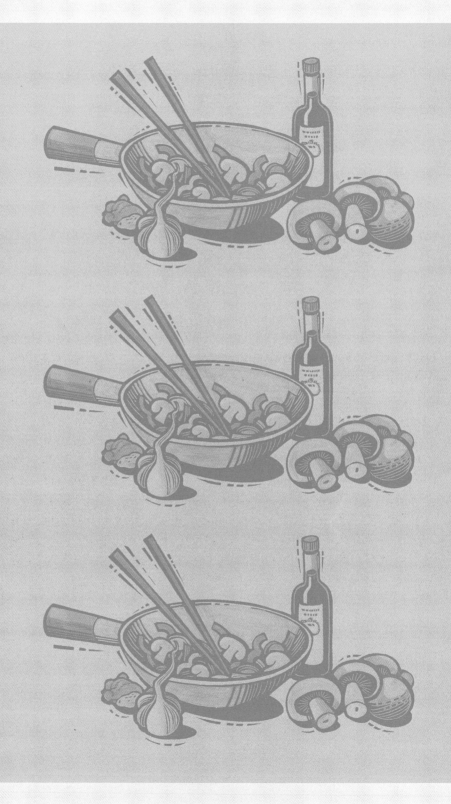

MALAYSIA & SINGAPORE

Because of its large immigrant population, the food of Malaysia is a rich blend of three of the world's most exciting cuisines – Malay, Chinese and Indian. The result is the Malayan melange, a mixture of flavours, some cool and subtle and others very fiery indeed, which are always presented in perfect harmony. Singapore, an important shipping crossroads, has absorbed influences from around the world, and promises sophistication as well as sumptuous flavours. Singapore's Nonya style of cooking, which came about when visiting Chinese merchants married local Muslim women, is famously hot and spicy. The street food stalls of Singapore are well-known to all travellers, and a veritable feast can be had on the street for a minimal outlay, or there are many high-class restaurants from which to choose.

One of the classic foods of the East. The pieces of meat should not be more than a delicate mouthful otherwise they will not absorb the marinade satisfactorily.

INGREDIENTS
4 skinless boneless chicken breast portions
10ml/2 tsp soft light brown sugar

FOR THE MARINADE
5ml/1 tsp cumin seeds
5ml/1 tsp fennel seeds
7.5ml/1½ tsp coriander seeds
6 shallots or small onions, chopped
1 garlic clove, crushed
1 lemon grass stalk, root trimmed
3 macadamia nuts or 6 cashew nuts
2.5ml/½ tsp ground turmeric

FOR THE PEANUT SAUCE
4 shallots or small onions, sliced
2 garlic cloves, crushed
1cm/½in cube shrimp paste (blachan)
6 cashew nuts or almonds
2 lemon grass stalks, trimmed, lower 5cm/2in sliced
45ml/3 tbsp sunflower oil
5–10ml/1–2 tsp chilli powder
400ml/14fl oz can coconut milk
60–75ml/4–5 tbsp tamarind water or 30ml/2 tbsp tamarind concentrate mixed with
   45ml/3 tbsp water
15ml/1 tbsp soft light brown sugar
175g/6oz/½ cup crunchy peanut butter

COOK'S TIP
*Soaking the bamboo skewers for about 30 minutes
in warm water before use ensures that they won't
scorch when placed under the grill (broiler).*

Cut the chicken into thin strips, sprinkle with the sugar and set aside. Make the marinade. Dry-fry the spices, then grind them to a powder. Put the shallots or onions in a mortar or a food processor and add the garlic. Roughly chop the lower 5cm/2in of the lemon grass and add it to the mortar or processor with the nuts, ground spices and turmeric. Grind to a paste and place in a bowl.

Add the chicken pieces and stir well until coated. Cover loosely with clear film (plastic wrap) and leave to marinate in a cool place for at least 4 hours.

Prepare the sauce. Pound or process the shallots or onions with the crushed garlic and shrimp paste. Add the nuts and the lower parts of the lemon grass stalks. Process to a fine purée. Heat the sunflower oil in a wok, then fry the purée for 2–3 minutes. Add the chilli powder and cook for 2 minutes more.

Stir in the coconut milk and bring slowly to the boil. Reduce the heat and stir in the tamarind water and brown sugar. Add the peanut butter and cook over a low heat, stirring gently, until fairly thick. Keep warm. Prepare the barbecue or preheat the grill (broiler).

Thread the chicken on to 16 bamboo skewers. Cook on the barbecue or grill (broil) for 5 minutes, or until golden and tender, brushing with oil occasionally. Serve with the hot peanut sauce.

POPIAH

These are the Straits Chinese or Nonya version of the spring roll. Do not be put off by the number of ingredients; it takes a little time to get everything together but once it is all on the table the cook can retire as guests assemble their own.

MAKES 20–24 PANCAKES

INGREDIENTS
40g/1½oz/⅓ cup cornflour (cornstarch)
215g/7½oz/generous 1¼ cups plain (all-purpose) flour
salt
450ml/¾ pint/scant 2 cups water
6 eggs, beaten
lard or white vegetable fat, for frying

FOR THE COOKED FILLING
30ml/2 tbsp vegetable oil
1 onion, finely chopped
2 garlic cloves, crushed
115g/4oz cooked pork, chopped
115g/4oz crab meat or peeled cooked prawns (shrimp), thawed if frozen
115g/4oz drained canned bamboo shoots, thinly sliced
1 small yam bean, peeled and grated or 12 drained canned water chestnuts,
  finely chopped
15–30ml/1–2 tbsp yellow salted beans
15ml/1 tbsp light soy sauce
ground black pepper

FOR THE FRESH FILLINGS
2 hard-boiled (hard-cooked) eggs, chopped
2 Chinese sausages, steamed and sliced
115g/4oz packet fried tofu, each piece halved
225g/8oz/4 cups beansprouts
115g/4oz crab meat or peeled cooked prawns (shrimp)
½ cucumber, cut into matchsticks
small bunch of spring onions (scallions), finely chopped
20 lettuce leaves, rinsed and dried
fresh coriander (cilantro) sprigs, to garnish (optional)
bottled chopped chillies, bottled chopped garlic and hoisin sauce, to serve

1   Sift the flours and salt into a bowl. Add the measured water and eggs and mix to a smooth batter.

2   Grease a heavy frying pan with lard or cooking fat. Heat the pan, pouring off any excess fat, then pour in just enough batter to cover the base thinly.

3   As soon as it sets, flip and cook the other side. Repeat with the remaining batter to make 20–24 pancakes. Stack the pancakes, with greaseproof (waxed) paper between each to prevent sticking. Wrap in foil; keep warm in a low oven.

4   Make the cooked filling. Heat the oil in a wok, add the onion and garlic and stir-fry for 5 minutes until softened. Add the pork, shellfish, bamboo shoots and yam bean or water chestnuts. Stir-fry over a medium heat for 2–3 minutes.

5   Add the salted yellow beans and soy sauce, and season. Cover and cook gently for 15–20 minutes, adding a little water if needed. Spoon into a serving bowl. Cool.

6   Meanwhile, arrange the fresh fillings, except the coriander, in piles on a large platter or in separate bowls. Spoon the bottled chopped chillies, bottled chopped garlic and hoisin into small bowls.

7   Each person makes up his or her own popiah by spreading a very small amount of chopped chilli, garlic or hoisin sauce on a pancake, adding a lettuce leaf, a little of the cooked filling and a small selection of the fresh ingredients.

8   The ends can be tucked in and the pancake rolled up in typical spring roll fashion, then eaten in the hand. They also look attractive simply rolled with the filling showing. The popiah can also be filled and rolled before guests arrive, in which case, garnish with sprigs of coriander. It is more fun though for everyone to fill and roll their own.

COOK'S TIP
Yam beans are large tubers with a mild sweet texture similar to water chestnuts.

Samosas

These tasty snacks are enjoyed the world over. Throughout Asia, they are sold by street vendors, and eaten at any time of day. Filo pastry can be used instead of the spring roll wrappers.

MAKES ABOUT 20

INGREDIENTS
1 packet 25cm/10in square spring roll wrappers, thawed if frozen
30ml/2 tbsp plain (all-purpose) flour, mixed to a paste with water
vegetable oil, for deep-frying
coriander (cilantro) leaves, to garnish
cucumber, carrot and celery, cut into matchsticks, to serve (optional)

FOR THE FILLING
25g/1oz/2 tbsp ghee or unsalted butter
1 small onion, finely chopped
1cm/½in piece fresh root ginger, peeled and chopped
1 garlic clove, crushed
2.5ml/½ tsp chilli powder
1 large potato, about 225g/8oz, cooked until just tender and finely diced
50g/2oz/½ cup cauliflower florets, lightly cooked and chopped into small pieces
50g/2oz/½ cup frozen peas, thawed
5–10ml/1–2 tsp garam masala
15ml/1 tbsp chopped fresh coriander (cilantro)
squeeze of lemon juice
salt

COOK'S TIP
Prepare samosas in advance if you like. Fry them until they are just cooked through then drain. Before serving, cook in hot oil for a few minutes to brown, then drain.

Make the filling. Heat the ghee or butter in a large wok and fry the onion, ginger and garlic for 5 minutes until softened. Add the chilli powder, cook for 1 minute, then stir in the potato, cauliflower and peas. Sprinkle with garam masala and set aside to cool. Stir in the chopped coriander, lemon juice and salt to taste.

Cut the spring roll wrappers into three strips (or two for larger samosas). Brush the edges with a little of the flour paste. Place a small spoonful of filling about 2cm/¾in in from the edge of one strip. Fold one corner over the filling to make a triangle and continue this folding until the entire strip has been used and a triangular pastry has been formed. Seal any open edges with more flour paste, if necessary adding more water if the paste is very thick.

Heat the oil for deep-frying to 190°C/375°F and fry the samosas, a few at a time, until golden and crisp. Drain well on kitchen paper and serve hot, garnished with coriander leaves and accompanied by cucumber, carrot and celery matchsticks, if you like.

Green Vegetable Salad with Coconut Mint Dip

This dish is traditionally served as an accompaniment to Singapore and Malaysian meat dishes. The coconut mint dip provides a lovely cooling accent.

SERVES 4–6

INGREDIENTS
115g/4oz mangetouts (snow peas), topped and tailed and halved
115g/4oz green beans, trimmed and halved
½ cucumber, peeled, halved and sliced
115g/4oz Chinese leaves (Chinese cabbage), roughly shredded
115g/4oz beansprouts
lettuce leaves, to serve

FOR THE DRESSING
1 garlic clove, crushed
1 small green chilli, seeded and finely chopped
10ml/2 tsp sugar
45ml/3 tbsp coconut cream
75ml/5 tbsp/⅓ cup boiling water
10ml/2 tsp fish sauce
45ml/3 tbsp vegetable oil
juice of 1 lime
30ml/2 tbsp chopped fresh mint

1 Bring a pan of salted water to the boil. Blanch the mangetouts, beans and cucumber for 4 minutes. Refresh under cold running water. Drain and set aside.

2 To make the dressing, pound the garlic, chilli and sugar together in a mortar using a pestle. Add the coconut cream, water, fish sauce, vegetable oil, lime juice and mint. Stir to mix well.

3 Pour the dressing into a shallow bowl. Mix together the blanched vegetables, Chinese leaves and beansprouts. Arrange the lettuce leaves in a large salad bowl and top with the salad vegetables. Serve at once.

SAMBAL NANAS

Sambals are the little side dishes served at almost every Malay meal. In poorer societies, a main meal may simply be a bowl of rice and a sambal made from pounded shrimp paste, chillies and some lime juice.

SERVES 8–10 AS AN ACCOMPANIMENT

INGREDIENTS
1 small or ½ large fresh ripe pineapple
½ cucumber, halved lengthways
50g/2oz dried shrimps
1 large fresh red chilli, seeded
1cm/½in cube shrimp paste (blachan), prepared (see Cook's Tip)
juice of 1 large lemon or lime
soft light brown sugar, to taste (optional)
salt

Cut off both ends of the pineapple. Stand it upright on a board, then slice off the skin from top to bottom, cutting out the spines. Slice the pineapple, removing the central core. Cut into thin slices and set aside.

Trim the ends from the cucumber and slice thinly. Sprinkle with salt and set aside. Place the dried shrimps in a food processor and chop fairly finely. Add the chilli, prepared shrimp paste and citrus juice and process to a paste.

Rinse the cucumber, drain and dry on kitchen paper. Mix with the pineapple and chill. Just before serving, mix in the spice mixture with sugar to taste.

COOK'S TIP
The pungent shrimp paste, which is also known as blachan, is available in Asian stores. Since it can taste a bit strong in an uncooked sambal, dry-fry the paste before combining with the other ingredients. Wrap the paste in foil and heat in a frying pan over a low heat for 5 minutes, turning from time to time.

Indian Mee Goreng

This is a truly international dish combining Indian, Chinese and Western ingredients. It makes a delicious treat for lunch or supper.

SERVES 4–6

INGREDIENTS
450g/1lb fresh yellow egg noodles
115g/4oz fried tofu or 150g/5oz firm tofu
60–90ml/4–6 tbsp vegetable oil
2 eggs
30ml/2 tbsp water
1 onion, sliced
1 garlic clove, crushed
15ml/1 tbsp light soy sauce
30–45ml/2–3 tbsp tomato ketchup
15ml/1 tbsp chilli sauce (or to taste)
1 large cooked potato, diced
4 spring onions (scallions), shredded
1–2 fresh green chillies, seeded and finely sliced (optional)
salt and ground black pepper

Bring a large pan of water to the boil; cook the noodles for 2 minutes. Drain and rinse under cold water. Drain again and set aside.

If using fried tofu, cut each cube in half, refresh it in a pan of boiling water, then drain well. Heat 30ml/2 tbsp of the oil in a large frying pan. If using plain tofu, cut into cubes and fry until brown, then lift out with a slotted spoon.

Beat the eggs with the water and seasoning. Cook in the frying pan without stirring until set. Flip over and cook the other side. Roll up and slice thinly.

Heat the remaining oil in a wok and fry the onion and garlic for 2–3 minutes. Add the drained noodles, soy sauce, ketchup and chilli sauce. Toss well over a medium heat for 2 minutes, then add the potato. Reserve a few spring onions and stir the rest into the noodles with the chilli, if using, and the tofu. When hot, stir in the omelette. Serve on a hot platter garnished with the reserved spring onion.

Sizzling Steak

This was originally a speciality of the Coliseum Restaurant in the Batu Road in Kuala Lumpur. The steaks were brought to the table on individual hot metal platters, each set on a thick wooden board.

SERVES 2

INGREDIENTS
2 rump (round) or sirloin steaks, about 450g/1lb in total
15–30ml/1–2 tbsp vegetable oil
shredded spring onion (scallion), to garnish

FOR THE MARINADE AND SAUCE
15ml/1 tbsp brandy
15ml/1 tbsp rich brown or barbeque sauce
30ml/2 tbsp groundnut (peanut) oil or sunflower oil
a few drops of sesame oil
2 garlic cloves, halved or crushed
150ml/¼ pint/⅔ cup beef stock
30ml/2 tbsp tomato ketchup
15ml/1 tbsp oyster sauce
15ml/1 tbsp Worcestershire sauce
salt and sugar

Place the steaks in a bowl. Mix the brandy, brown sauce, the oils and garlic in a jug (pitcher) then pour over the steaks. Cover loosely with clear film (plastic wrap) and leave for 1 hour, turning once. Drain the meat, reserving the marinade.

Heat the oil in a heavy, ridged griddle pan and fry the steaks for 3–5 minutes on each side, depending on how well done you like them. Transfer to a plate and keep warm while preparing the sauce.

Pour the marinade into the frying pan, discarding any large pieces of garlic. Stir in the stock, ketchup, oyster sauce and Worcestershire sauce, with salt and sugar to taste. Boil rapidly to reduce by half.

Serve each cooked steak on a very hot plate, pouring the sauce over each portion just before serving. Garnish with the shredded spring onion.

STEAMBOAT

This dish is named after the utensil in which it is cooked – a type of fondue with a funnel and a moat. Electric steamboats or fondue pots can be used instead.

SERVES 8

INGREDIENTS

8 Chinese dried mushrooms, soaked for 30 minutes in warm water to cover
1.5 litres/2½ pints/6¼ cups well-flavoured chicken stock, home-made if possible
10ml/2 tsp rice wine or medium-dry sherry
10ml/2 tsp sesame oil
225g/8oz each lean pork and rump (round) steak, thinly sliced
1 skinless boneless chicken breast portion, thickly sliced
2 chicken livers, trimmed and sliced
225g/8oz raw prawns (shrimp), peeled
450g/1lb white fish fillets, skinned and cubed
200g/7oz fish balls
115g/4oz fried tofu, each piece halved
leafy green vegetables, such as lettuce, Chinese leaves (Chinese cabbage) and spinach, cut into 15cm/6in lengths
225g/8oz Chinese rice vermicelli
8 eggs
selection of sauces, including soy sauce with sesame seeds; soy sauce with crushed ginger; chilli sauce; plum sauce and hot mustard
½ bunch spring onions (scallions), chopped
salt and ground white pepper

COOK'S TIP
Fish balls can be found in Chinese and Asian stores.
They may be fresh or frozen.

Drain the mushrooms, reserving the soaking liquid. Cut off and discard the stems; slice the caps finely.

Pour the stock into a large pan, with the rice wine or sherry, sesame oil and reserved mushroom liquid. Bring the mixture to the boil, then season. Reduce the heat and simmer gently while you prepare the remaining ingredients.

3 Put the meat, fish, tofu, green vegetables and mushrooms in bowls on the table. Soak the vermicelli in hot water for about 5 minutes, drain and place in eight soup bowls on a side table. Crack an egg for each diner in a small bowl; place on the side table. Put the sauces in bowls beside each diner.

4 Add the chopped spring onions to the pan of stock, bring it to a full boil and fuel the steamboat. Pour the stock into the moat and seat your guests at once. Each guest lowers a few chosen morsels into the boiling stock, using chopsticks or fondue forks, leaves them for a minute or two, then removes them with a small wire mesh ladle, a fondue fork or chopsticks.

5 When all the meat, fish, tofu and vegetables have been cooked, the stock will be concentrated and wonderfully enriched. Add a little boiling water if necessary. Bring the soup bowls containing the soaked noodles to the table, pour in the soup and slide an egg into each, stirring until it cooks and forms threads.

CHICKEN RENDANG

This makes a marvellous dish for a buffet. The garnish of fresh chives and deep-fried anchovies adds to its appearance and the overall flavour of the dish. Serve it simply with prawn (shrimp) crackers or with plain boiled rice.

SERVES 4

INGREDIENTS
1 chicken, about 1.4kg/3lb
5ml/1 tsp sugar
75g/3oz/1 cup desiccated (dry unsweetened shredded) coconut
4 small red or white onions, roughly chopped
2 garlic cloves, chopped
2.5cm/1in piece fresh root ginger, peeled and sliced
1–2 lemon grass stalks, root trimmed
2.5cm/1in piece fresh galangal, peeled and sliced
75ml/5 tbsp groundnut (peanut) oil or vegetable oil
10–15ml/2–3 tsp chilli powder, or to taste
400ml/14fl oz can coconut milk
10ml/2 tsp salt
fresh chives and deep-fried anchovies, to garnish

COOK'S TIP
Prawn crackers are widely available in Asian stores. There are two different types: Chinese ones are not much bigger than a thumbnail, while Indonesian prawn crackers are much larger. Both crackers are grey in their uncooked state but puff up to four or five times their original size and become very pale.

Joint the chicken into eight pieces and remove the skin, sprinkle with the sugar and leave to stand for 1 hour.

Dry-fry the coconut in a wok or large frying pan over a medium to low heat, turning all the time until it is crisp and evenly golden. Transfer the fried coconut to a food processor and process until it forms an oily paste. Spoon the coconut paste into a bowl and set aside.

Add the onions, garlic and ginger to the processor. Cut off the lower 5cm/2in of the lemon grass, chop and add to the processor with the galangal. Process to a fine paste.

Heat the oil in a wok or large pan and fry the onion and garlic mixture for a few minutes. Reduce the heat, stir in the chilli powder and continue cooking for 2–3 minutes, stirring constantly. Add 120ml/4fl oz/½ cup of the coconut milk and add salt to taste.

As soon as the mixture bubbles, add the chicken pieces, turning them until they are well coated with the spice mixture. Pour in the remaining coconut milk, stirring constantly to prevent the sauce curdling. Bruise the top of the lemon grass stalks and add to the wok or pan. Cover and cook gently for 40–45 minutes until the chicken is tender.

Just before serving stir in the coconut paste. Bring to just below boiling point, then simmer for 5 minutes. Transfer to a serving bowl, garnish with fresh chives and deep-fried anchovies and serve at once with prawn crackers or plain boiled rice.

SPICY CLAY-POT CHICKEN

Clay-pot cooking stems from the practice of burying a glazed pot in the embers of an open fire. The gentle heat surrounds the base and keeps the liquid inside at a slow simmer, similar to the modern-day casserole.

SERVES 4–6

INGREDIENTS
1 chicken, about 1.5kg/3½lb
45ml/3 tbsp grated fresh coconut
30ml/2 tbsp vegetable oil
2 shallots or 1 small onion, finely chopped
2 garlic cloves, crushed
5cm/2in piece lemon grass
2.5cm/1in piece galangal or fresh root ginger, peeled and thinly sliced
2 small green chillies, seeded and finely chopped
1cm/½in cube shrimp paste (blachan), or 15ml/1 tbsp fish sauce
400g/14fl oz can coconut milk
300ml/½ pint/1¼ cups chicken stock
2 lime leaves (optional)
15ml/1 tbsp sugar
15ml/1 tbsp rice or white wine vinegar
2 ripe tomatoes, to garnish
30ml/2 tbsp chopped fresh coriander (cilantro), to garnish
boiled rice, to serve

COOK'S TIP
Avoid using an unglazed clay pot for this recipe as the spicy sauce will taint the clay. Use a deep-glazed ovenproof dish, or a Chinese sand pot.

To joint the chicken, remove the legs and wings with a large, sharp knife. Skin the pieces and divide the drumsticks from the thighs. Then, using a pair of kitchen scissors, remove the lower part of the chicken leaving the breast piece. Remove as many of the bones as you can, to make the dish easier to eat. Cut the breast piece into four and set aside.

2   Dry-fry the coconut in a large wok until evenly brown. Add the vegetable oil, shallots or onion, garlic, lemon grass, galangal or ginger, chillies and shrimp paste or fish sauce. Fry briefly to release the flavours. Preheat the oven to 180°C/350°F/Gas 4. Add the chicken joints to the wok and brown evenly with the spices for 2–3 minutes.

3   Strain the coconut milk, and add the thin part to the wok with the chicken stock, lime leaves if using, sugar and vinegar. Transfer to a glazed clay pot, cover and bake for 50–55 minutes, or until the chicken is tender. Stir in the thick part of the coconut milk and return to the oven for 5–10 minutes to simmer and thicken.

4   Place the tomatoes in a bowl and cover with boiling water, leave for 30 seconds to loosen the skins, then peel. Halve the tomatoes, remove the seeds and cut into large dice. Add the tomatoes to the finished dish, scatter with the chopped coriander and serve with a bowl of boiled rice.

Sesame Baked Fish with Ginger Marinade

This aromatic, spicy fish dish makes an excellent dinner party main dish.
In the summer it can be cooked on a barbecue rather than in the oven.

SERVES 4

INGREDIENTS
2 red snapper, about 350g/12oz each
3–4 banana leaves, or foil
1 lime and 2 red chilli flowers, to garnish

FOR THE MARINADE
30ml/2 tbsp vegetable oil
10ml/2 tsp sesame oil
30ml/2 tbsp sesame seeds
2.5cm/1in piece fresh root ginger, peeled and thinly sliced
2 garlic cloves, crushed
2 small red chillies, seeded and finely chopped
4 shallots or 1 onion, halved and sliced
30ml/2 tbsp water
1cm/½in cube shrimp paste (blachan), or 15ml/1 tbsp fish sauce
10ml/2 tsp sugar
2.5ml/½ tsp very coarsely ground black pepper
juice of 2 limes

COOK'S TIP
Use other fish if snapper is not available: try sea
bream, tilapia or even 4 small trout. If you prefer
not to use whole fish, this recipe is also good with
monkfish tails.

Clean the fish inside and out under cold running water. Pat dry with kitchen paper. Slash both sides of each fish deeply two or three times with a knife to enable the marinade to penetrate effectively.

To make the marinade, heat the vegetable and sesame oils in a wok, add the sesame seeds and fry until golden. Add the ginger, garlic, chillies and shallots or onion, and soften over a gentle heat without burning. Add the water, shrimp paste or fish sauce, sugar, pepper and lime juice, simmer for 2–3 minutes, then remove the wok from the heat and allow to cool.

If using banana leaves, remove the central stem and discard. Soften the leaves by dipping them in boiling water. To keep them supple, rub all over with vegetable oil. Spread the marinade over the fish, wrap in the banana leaf and fasten with a bamboo skewer, or wrap the fish in foil. Leave the fish in a cool place for up to 3 hours to allow the flavours to mingle.

Preheat the oven to 180°C/350°F/Gas 4 or prepare a barbecue and allow the embers to settle to a steady glow. Place the wrapped fish on a wire rack or baking sheet and cook for 35–40 minutes.

FISH MOOLIE

This very popular Malay fish curry in a coconut sauce is truly delicious. Choose a firm-textured fish so that the pieces stay intact during the brief cooking process. Halibut and cod work just as well as monkfish.

SERVES 4

INGREDIENTS
500g/1¼lb monkfish or other firm-textured fish fillets, skinned and cut into
  2.5cm/1in cubes
2.5ml/½ tsp salt
50g/2oz/⅔ cup desiccated (dry unsweetened shredded) coconut
6 shallots or small onions, roughly chopped
6 blanched almonds
2–3 garlic cloves, roughly chopped
2.5cm/1in piece fresh root ginger, peeled and sliced
2 lemon grass stalks, roots trimmed
10ml/2 tsp ground turmeric
45ml/3 tbsp vegetable oil
2 × 400ml/14fl oz cans coconut milk
1–3 fresh chillies, seeded and sliced
salt and ground black pepper
fresh chives, to garnish
boiled rice, to serve

COOK'S TIP
Dry-frying is a feature of Malay cooking. When dry-frying the coconut, don't have the heat too high and keep it constantly on the move so that it becomes crisp and of a uniform golden colour.

1 Spread out the pieces of fish in a shallow dish and sprinkle them with the salt. Dry-fry the coconut in a wok or large frying pan over a medium to low heat, turning all the time until it is crisp and golden (see Cook's Tip).

2 Transfer the coconut to a food processor and process to an oily paste. Spoon into a bowl and set aside.

3 Add the shallots or onions, almonds, garlic and ginger to the food processor. Cut off the lower 5cm/2in of the lemon grass stalks, chop them roughly and add to the processor. Process the mixture to a paste.

4 Add the turmeric to the mixture in the processor and process briefly to mix. Bruise the remaining lemon grass and set the stalks aside.

5 Heat the oil in a wok. Add the onion mixture and cook for a few minutes without browning. Stir in the coconut milk and bring to the boil, stirring constantly to prevent curdling.

6 Add the cubes of fish, most of the sliced chilli and the bruised lemon grass stalks. Cook for 3–4 minutes. Stir in the coconut paste (moistened with some of the sauce if necessary) and cook for a further 2–3 minutes, being careful not to overcook the fish. Taste and adjust the seasoning if necessary.

7 Remove the lemon grass. Transfer the moolie to a hot serving dish and sprinkle with the remaining slices of chilli. Garnish with chopped and whole chives and serve with boiled rice.

Laksa Lemak

This spicy soup is not a dish you can throw together in 20 minutes, but it is marvellous party food. Guests spoon noodles into wide soup bowls, add accompaniments of their choice, top up with soup and then take a few prawn (shrimp) crackers to nibble.

SERVES 6

INGREDIENTS
675g/1½lb small clams
2 × 400ml/14fl oz cans coconut milk
50g/2oz ikan bilis (dried anchovies)
900ml/1½ pints/3¾ cups water
115g/4oz shallots, finely chopped
4 garlic cloves, chopped
6 macadamia nuts or blanched almonds, chopped
3 lemon grass stalks, roots trimmed
90ml/6 tbsp sunflower oil
1cm/½in cube shrimp paste (blachan)
25g/1oz/¼ cup mild curry powder
a few curry leaves
2–3 aubergines (eggplant), about 675g/1¼lb in total, trimmed
675g/1½lb raw peeled prawns (shrimp)
10ml/2 tsp sugar
1 head Chinese leaves (Chinese cabbage), thinly sliced
115g/4oz/2 cups beansprouts, rinsed
2 spring onions (scallions), finely chopped
50g/2oz crispy fried onions
115g/4oz fried tofu
675g/1½lb mixed noodles (laksa, mee and beehoon) or one type only
prawn (shrimp) crackers, to serve

Scrub the clams then place in a large pan with 1cm/½in water. Bring to the boil, cover and steam for 3–4 minutes until all the clams have opened. Drain and discard any unopened clams. Make up the coconut milk to 1.2 litres/2 pints/5 cups with water. Put the ikan bilis in a pan and add the water. Bring to the boil and simmer for 20 minutes.

2 Meanwhile, put the shallots, garlic and nuts into a mortar. Cut off the lower 5cm/2in of two of the lemon grass stalks, chop finely and add to the mortar. Pound the mixture to a paste.

3 Heat the oil in a large heavy pan, add the shallot paste and fry until the mixture gives off a rich aroma. Bruise the remaining lemon grass stalks and add to the pan. Toss over the heat to release its flavour. Mix the shrimp paste and curry powder to a paste with a little of the coconut milk, add to the pan and toss the mixture over a low heat for 1 minute, stirring all the time. Stir in the remaining coconut milk. Add the curry leaves and leave the mixture to simmer while you prepare the accompaniments.

4 Strain the stock into a pan. Discard the ikan bilis, bring the stock to the boil, then add the aubergines. Cook for about 10 minutes, or until tender and the skins can be peeled off easily. Lift out of the stock, peel and cut into thick strips.

Arrange the aubergines on a serving platter. Sprinkle the prawns with sugar, add to the stock and cook for 2–4 minutes until they turn pink. Remove and place next to the aubergines. Add the Chinese leaves, beansprouts, spring onions and crispy fried onions to the platter, along with the clams.

Gradually stir the remaining stock into the pan of soup and bring to the boil. Rinse the fried tofu in boiling water, then leave for a few minutes to cool slightly and squeeze to remove excess oil. Cut each piece in half and add to the soup. Lower the heat to a very gentle simmer.

Cook the noodles according to the instructions on the packet, drain and pile in a dish. Remove the curry leaves and lemon grass from the soup. Place the noodles, soup and the platter of shellfish and vegetables on the table, along with a bowl of prawn crackers. Guests can then help themselves.

VARIATION
You could substitute mussels for clams if preferred.
Scrub them thoroughly before cooking then, like
clams, discard any that remain closed.

Sotong Sambal

In this spectacular looking dish, little squid are stuffed with a ginger-flavoured fish stuffing and then cooked in a chilli-hot onion and coconut sauce. Boiled rice makes an ideal accompaniment.

SERVES 2

INGREDIENTS
8 small squid, each about 10cm/4in long, about 350g/12oz in total
lime juice (optional)
salt
boiled rice, to serve

FOR THE STUFFING
175g/6oz white fish fillets, such as sole or plaice, skinned
2.5cm/1in piece fresh root ginger, peeled and finely sliced
2 spring onions (scallions), finely chopped
50g/2oz peeled cooked prawns (shrimp), roughly chopped

FOR THE SAMBAL SAUCE
4 macadamia nuts or blanched almonds
1cm/½in piece fresh galangal, peeled, or 5ml/1 tsp drained bottled galangal
2 lemon grass stalks, roots trimmed
1cm/½in cube shrimp paste (blachan)
4 fresh red chillies, or to taste, seeded and roughly chopped
175g/6oz small onions, roughly chopped
60–90ml/4–6 tbsp vegetable oil
400ml/14fl oz can coconut milk

COOK'S TIP
Squid is readily available these days, and it now comes cleaned, which is a definite bonus. Wash thoroughly before use especially inside the body pocket to make sure that all the quill has been removed.

1 Clean the squid, leaving them whole. Set aside with the tentacles. Make the stuffing. Put the white fish, ginger and spring onions in a large mortar. Add a little salt and pound to a paste with a pestle. Alternatively, use a food processor.

2 Transfer the fish mixture to a bowl and stir in the chopped prawns, mixing well to combine evenly.

3 Divide the filling among the squid, using a spoon or a piping bag fitted with a plain nozzle. Tuck the tentacles into the stuffing and secure the top of each squid with a cocktail stick (toothpick).

4 Make the sauce. Put the macadamia nuts or almonds and galangal in a food processor. Cut off the lower 5cm/2in from the lemon grass stalks, chop them roughly and add them to the processor with the shrimp paste, chillies and onions. Process to a paste.

5 Heat the oil in a wok and fry the mixture to bring out the full flavours. Bruise the remaining lemon grass and add it to the wok with the coconut milk. Stir constantly until the sauce comes to the boil, then lower the heat and simmer the sauce for 5 minutes.

6 Arrange the squid in the sauce, and cook for 15–20 minutes until tender. Taste the sauce and season with salt and lime juice, if you like. Serve with boiled rice.

Hot Chilli Crab
with Ginger & Lime

This highly flavoured dish requires the minimum of accompaniments. Serve simply with a bowl of cooling chopped cucumber and hot slices of toast.

SERVES 4–6

INGREDIENTS
2 medium cooked crabs
2.5cm/1in piece fresh root ginger, peeled and chopped
2 garlic cloves, crushed
1–2 small red chillies, seeded and finely chopped
15ml/1 tbsp sugar
30ml/2 tbsp vegetable oil
60ml/4 tbsp tomato ketchup
150ml/¼ pint/⅔ cup water
juice of 2 limes
30ml/2 tbsp chopped fresh coriander (cilantro), to garnish

1 To prepare the crab, twist off the legs and claws. Crack open the thickest part of the shell with a hammer or the back of a heavy knife.

2 Prise off the underside leg section. Remove the stomach sac and the grey gills. Cut the section into four and the upper shell into six pieces.

3 Pound the ginger, garlic, chillies and sugar in a mortar using a pestle. Heat the oil in a large wok, add the pounded spices and fry gently for 1–2 minutes. Add the ketchup, water and lime juice and simmer briefly.

4 Add the pieces of crab and heat through for 3–4 minutes. Transfer to a serving bowl and scatter with the chopped coriander.

COOK'S TIP
Provide hot towels at the end of the meal. Dampen flannels (wash cloths) with water, wrap in a plastic bag and microwave at full power for 2 minutes.

MALAYSIAN COCONUT ICE CREAM

This ice cream is delectable and very easy to make in an ice-cream maker, especially if you use the type with a bowl that is placed in the freezer to chill before the ice-cream mixture is added. The ice cream is then churned by a motorized lid with a paddle.

SERVES 6

INGREDIENTS
400ml/14fl oz can coconut milk, chilled
400ml/14fl oz can condensed milk, chilled
2.5ml/½ tsp salt

FOR THE GULA MELAKA SAUCE
150g/5oz/¾ cup palm sugar or muscovado (molasses) sugar
150ml/¼ pint/⅔ cup water
1cm/½in slice fresh root ginger, bruised
1 pandan leaf (if available)
coconut shells (optional) and thinly pared strips of coconut, to serve

Pour the coconut milk and condensed milk into a bowl. Gently whisk together with the salt. Pour the mixture into the frozen freezer bowl of an ice-cream maker (or follow the appliance instructions) and churn until the mixture has thickened. (This will take 30–40 minutes.)

Transfer the mixture to a lidded plastic container, cover and freeze until the consistency is right for scooping. If you do not have an ice-cream maker, pour the mixture into a shallow container and freeze on the coldest setting.

When ice crystals form around the sides of the ice cream, beat the mixture, then return it to the freezer. Do this at least twice.

Make the sauce. Mix the sugar, water and ginger in a pan. Stir over a medium heat until the sugar has dissolved, then bring to the boil. Add the pandan leaf, if using, tying it into a knot first. Lower the heat and simmer for 3–4 minutes. Set aside until required.

Serve the ice cream in coconut shells or in a bowl. Sprinkle with the strips of coconut and serve with the gula melaka sauce, which can be hot, warm or cold.

COCONUT CHIPS

These are a wonderfully tasty nibble to serve with drinks. The chips can be sliced ahead of time and frozen (without salt) on open trays. When frozen, simply shake into plastic containers or bags. You can then take out as few or as many as you wish for the party.

SERVES 8

INGREDIENTS
1 fresh coconut
salt

1 Preheat the oven to 160°C/325°F/Gas 3. Drain the coconut juice by piercing the coconut eyes with a sharp instrument.

2 Lay the coconut on a board and hit the centre sharply with a hammer. The shell should break cleanly in two.

3 Use a round-bladed knife to ease the flesh away from the hard outer shell. Taste a piece of the flesh just to make sure it is fresh. Peel away the brown skin with a vegetable peeler, if you like.

4 Slice the flesh into wafer-thin shavings, using a food processor, mandoline or sharp knife. Scatter these evenly over one or two baking sheets and sprinkle with salt. Bake for 25–30 minutes, or until crisp, turning them from time to time. Cool and serve. Any leftovers can be stored in an airtight container.

COOK'S TIP
This is the kind of recipe where the slicing blade on a food processor comes into its own. It is worth preparing two or three coconuts at a time, and freezing surplus chips. The chips can be cooked from frozen, but will need to be spread out well on the baking sheets, before being salted. Allow a little longer for frozen chips to cook.

SINGAPORE SLING

This gin-based cocktail is enjoyed in bars all around the world. Recipes vary considerably, some using orange or pineapple juice to create a longer, refreshing drink, but they all use a standard measure that equates to a little less than 30ml/2 tbsp.

SERVES 1

INGREDIENTS
ice
2 measures gin
1 measure cherry brandy
1 measure lemon juice
soda water, to taste
1 slice orange
1 slice lemon
1 Maraschino cherry and 1 mint sprig, to decorate

1   Wrap the ice in a clean dishtowel, and crush with a rolling pin or the underside of a large, heavy pan.

2   Half-fill a cocktail shaker with ice. Add the gin, cherry brandy and lemon juice, and shake well.

3   Strain the mixture into a tall glass over ice cubes. Top up with soda water. Add the slices of orange and lemon and decorate with the cherry and mint sprig.

THAILAND
& BURMA

The expertise of many Thai cooks is recognized widely. Their curries are hot and spicy yet subtly flavoured too, and there are many different dishes to try, such as Ginger, Chicken and Coconut Soup, which is highly aromatic and intensely flavoured, crunchy Thai Spring Rolls and Green Papaya Salad. Beef features quite highly on the menu, and piquant Thai Beef Salad makes a substantial main course. Fish is widely used, and in skilled hands even the humble fishcake becomes quite delicious. Burma has a more robust but equally interesting cuisine, and is famous for one of the world's most delicious fish soups, Mohingha, which is widely sold by street vendors but can also be made successfully at home.

Ginger, Chicken & Coconut Soup

This aromatic soup is enriched with coconut milk and intensely flavoured with galangal, lemon grass and kaffir lime leaves.

SERVES 4–6

INGREDIENTS

4 lemon grass stalks, roots trimmed
2 × 400ml/14fl oz cans coconut milk
475ml/16fl oz/2 cups chicken stock
2.5cm/1in piece galangal, peeled and thinly sliced
10 black peppercorns, crushed
10 kaffir lime leaves, torn
300g/11oz skinless boneless chicken breast portions, cut into thin strips
115g/4oz/1 cup button mushrooms
50g/2oz/½ cup baby corn cobs, quartered lengthways
60ml/4 tbsp lime juice
45ml/3 tbsp fish sauce
chopped fresh red chillies, spring onions (scallions) and fresh coriander (cilantro)
  leaves, to garnish

1 Cut off the lower 5cm/2in from each lemon grass stalk and chop it finely. Bruise the remaining pieces of stalk. Bring the coconut milk and chicken stock to the boil in a large pan. Add all the lemon grass, the galangal, black peppercorns and half the kaffir lime leaves, lower the heat and simmer gently for 10 minutes. Strain into a clean pan.

Return the soup to the heat, then add the chicken, mushrooms and corn. Simmer for 5–7 minutes, or until the chicken is cooked.

Stir in the lime juice and fish sauce, then add the remaining lime leaves. Serve hot, garnished with chillies, spring onions and coriander.

HOT & SOUR PRAWN SOUP

This is a classic Thai seafood soup – Tom Yam Kung – and it is probably the most popular and well-known soup from that country.

SERVES 4–6

INGREDIENTS

450g/1lb raw king prawns (jumbo shrimp), thawed if frozen
1 litre/1¾ pints/4 cups chicken stock or water
3 lemon grass stalks, roots trimmed
10 kaffir lime leaves, torn in half
225g/8oz can straw mushrooms, drained
45ml/3 tbsp fish sauce
60ml/4 tbsp lime juice
30ml/2 tbsp chopped spring onion (scallion)
15ml/1 tbsp fresh coriander (cilantro) leaves
4 fresh red chillies, seeded and thinly sliced
salt and ground black pepper

1 Shell the prawns, putting the shells in a colander. Carefully devein the prawns and set them aside.

2 Rinse the shells under cold water, then put in a large pan with the stock or water. Bring to the boil.

3 Bruise the lemon grass stalks and add them to the stock with half the lime leaves. Simmer gently for 5–6 minutes, until the stock is fragrant.

4 Strain the stock, return it to the cleaned pan and reheat. Add the drained mushrooms and the prawns, then cook until the prawns turn pink.

5 Stir in the fish sauce, lime juice, spring onion, coriander, chillies and the remaining lime leaves. Taste and adjust the seasoning if necessary. The soup should be sour, salty, spicy and hot.

THAI SPRING ROLLS

Crunchy spring rolls are as popular in Thailand as they are in China. The Thais fill their version with a delicious garlic, pork and noodle mixture.

MAKES ABOUT 24

INGREDIENTS
24 × 15cm/6in square spring roll wrappers
30ml/2 tbsp plain (all-purpose) flour
vegetable oil, for deep-frying
Thai sweet chilli dipping sauce, to serve (optional)

FOR THE FILLING
4–6 Chinese dried mushrooms, soaked for 30 minutes in warm water
50g/2oz cellophane noodles
30ml/2 tbsp vegetable oil
2 garlic cloves, chopped
2 fresh red chillies, seeded and chopped
225g/8oz minced (ground) pork
50g/2oz peeled cooked prawns (shrimp), thawed if frozen
30ml/2 tbsp fish sauce
5ml/1 tsp sugar
1 carrot, grated
50g/2oz drained canned bamboo shoots, chopped
50g/2oz/1 cup beansprouts
2 spring onions (scallions), finely chopped
15ml/1 tbsp chopped fresh coriander (cilantro)
ground black pepper

Make the filling. Drain the soaked mushrooms. Cut off the mushroom stems and discard, then chop the caps finely. Place the noodles in a large bowl, cover with freshly boiled water and soak for 10 minutes. Drain the noodles and snip them into 5cm/2in lengths.

Heat the oil in a wok, add the garlic and chillies and stir-fry for 30 seconds. Transfer to a plate, add the pork to the wok and cook, stirring, until it has browned. Add the noodles, mushrooms and prawns. Stir in the fish sauce and sugar, then add ground black pepper to taste.

3 Tip the noodle mixture into a bowl and stir in the carrot, bamboo shoots, beansprouts, spring onions and chopped coriander together with the reserved chilli mixture.

4 Unwrap the spring roll wrappers. Cover them with a dampened dishtowel while you are making the rolls, so that they do not dry out. Put the flour in a small bowl and stir in a little water to make a paste. Place a spoonful of filling in the centre of a spring roll wrapper.

5 Turn the bottom edge over to cover the filling, then fold in the left and right sides. Roll up the wrapper almost to the top then brush the top edge with the flour paste and seal. Fill the remaining wrappers in the same way.

6 Heat the oil in a wok or deep-fryer to 190°C/375°F. Fry the spring rolls, a few at a time, until crisp and golden brown. Drain on kitchen paper and keep hot while cooking successive batches. Serve hot with Thai sweet chilli sauce, if you like.

COOK'S TIP
Fish sauce (or nam pla as it is known in Thailand) is made from anchovies that are salted then fermented in wooden barrels. The sauce accentuates the flavour of food, and does not necessarily impart a fishy flavour.

CRISP-FRIED CRAB CLAWS

Crab claws are readily available in the freezer cabinet in many Asian stores and supermarkets. Thaw out thoroughly at room temperature and dry on kitchen paper before dipping in the batter.

SERVES 4

INGREDIENTS
50g/2oz/⅓ cup rice flour
15ml/1 tbsp cornflour (cornstarch)
2.5ml/½ tsp sugar
1 egg
60ml/4 tbsp cold water
1 lemon grass stalk, root trimmed
2 garlic cloves, finely chopped
15ml/1 tbsp chopped fresh coriander (cilantro)
1–2 fresh red chillies, seeded and finely chopped
5ml/1 tsp fish sauce
vegetable oil, for frying
12 half-shelled crab claws
ground black pepper

FOR THE CHILLI VINEGAR DIP
45ml/3 tbsp sugar
120ml/4fl oz/½ cup water
120ml/4fl oz/½ cup red wine vinegar
15ml/1 tbsp fish sauce
2–4 fresh red chillies, seeded and chopped

COOK'S TIP
Look for crabs claws that are of a similar size, so that they cook evenly, and only buy ones with undamaged half-shells.

1 Make the chilli dip. Mix the sugar and water in a pan, stirring until the sugar has dissolved, then bring to the boil. Lower the heat and simmer gently for 5–7 minutes. Stir in the rest of the dip ingredients and set aside.

Combine the rice flour, cornflour and sugar in a bowl. Beat the egg with the cold water, then stir the egg and water mixture into the flour mixture and mix well until it forms a light batter.

Cut off the lower 5cm/2in of the lemon grass stalk and chop it finely. Add the lemon grass to the batter, with the garlic, coriander, red chillies and fish sauce. Stir in ground black pepper to taste.

Heat the oil in a wok or deep-fryer to 190°C/375°F. Pat the crab claws dry using kitchen paper, then dip them into the batter. Drop the battered claws into the hot oil, a few at a time. Fry until golden brown. Drain on kitchen paper and keep hot while cooking successive batches. Pour the dip into a serving bowl and serve with the crab claws.

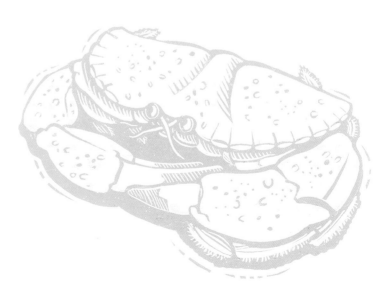

Fishcakes with Cucumber Relish

These wonderful small fish cakes are a very familiar and popular appetizer in Thailand and increasingly throughout South-east Asia. Serve them with chilled Thai beer for a fully authentic experience.

Makes about 12

Ingredients
5 kaffir lime leaves
300g/11oz cod fillet, cut into chunks
30ml/2 tbsp red curry paste
1 egg
30ml/2 tbsp fish sauce
5ml/1 tsp sugar
30ml/2 tbsp cornflour (cornstarch)
15ml/1 tbsp chopped fresh coriander (cilantro)
50g/2oz green beans, finely sliced
vegetable oil, for frying
fresh Chinese mustard cress or coriander (cilantro) leaves, to garnish

For the cucumber relish
60ml/4 tbsp coconut vinegar or rice vinegar
50g/2oz/¼ cup sugar
1 head of pickled garlic
1cm/½in piece fresh root ginger, peeled
1 cucumber, cut into matchsticks
4 shallots, finely sliced

Cook's Tip
Fresh kaffir lime leaves will only keep for a few days, but they can be kept in the freezer for a number of months. Freeze-dried kaffir lime leaves make an acceptable substitute.

Make the cucumber relish. Bring the vinegar and sugar to the boil in a small pan with 60ml/4 tbsp water, stirring until the sugar has dissolved. Remove from the heat and leave to cool.

Separate the pickled garlic into cloves. Chop these finely along with the ginger and place in a bowl. Add the cucumber and shallots, pour over the vinegar mixture and mix together lightly.

Reserve two kaffir lime leaves for garnish and thinly slice the remainder. Put the chunks of fish, curry paste and egg in a food processor and process to a smooth paste. Transfer the mixture to a bowl and stir in the fish sauce, sugar, cornflour, sliced kaffir lime leaves, coriander and green beans. Mix well, then shape the mixture into about twelve 5mm/¼in thick cakes, measuring about 5cm/2in in diameter.

Heat the oil in a wok or deep-fryer to 190°C/375°F. Fry the fish cakes, a few at a time, for about 4–5 minutes until cooked and evenly brown. Lift out the fish cakes and drain them on kitchen paper. Keep each batch hot while frying successive batches. Garnish with the reserved kaffir leaves and serve with the cucumber relish.

THAI FRUIT & VEGETABLE SALAD WITH COCONUT SAUCE

This fruit and vegetable salad is presented with the main course and serves as a cooler to counteract the heat of the chillies included in other dishes.

SERVES 4–6

INGREDIENTS
1 small pineapple
115g/4oz green beans, topped, tailed and halved
1 small mango, peeled and sliced
1 green apple, cored and sliced
6 ramboutans or lychees, peeled and stoned (pitted)
1 red onion, sliced
1 small cucumber, cut into short fingers
115g/4oz beansprouts
2 spring onions (scallions), sliced
1 ripe tomato, quartered

FOR THE COCONUT DIPPING SAUCE
30ml/2 tbsp coconut cream
30ml/2 tbsp sugar
75ml/5 tbsp boiling water
1.5ml/¼ tsp chilli sauce
15ml/1 tbsp fish sauce
juice of 1 lime

1 To make the coconut dipping sauce, put the coconut cream, sugar and water in a screw-top jar. Add the chilli and fish sauces and lime juice and shake.

2 Trim both ends of the pineapple, then cut away the skin. Cut into four down the middle and remove the core. Roughly chop the flesh and set aside.

3 Boil the beans for 3–4 minutes. Refresh under cold running water. To serve, arrange the fruits and vegetables in heaps in a shallow bowl. Serve with the dip.

Green Papaya Salad

This salad appears in many guises in South-east Asia. As green papaya is not easy to get hold of, finely grated carrots, cucumber or green apple can be used instead. Alternatively, use very thinly sliced white cabbage.

Serves 4

Ingredients
1 green papaya
4 garlic cloves, roughly chopped
15ml/1 tbsp chopped shallots
3–4 fresh red chillies, seeded and sliced
2.5ml/½ tsp salt
2–3 snake beans or 6 green beans, cut into 2cm/¾in lengths
2 tomatoes, cut into thin wedges
45ml/3 tbsp fish sauce
15ml/1 tbsp caster (superfine) sugar
juice of 1 lime
30ml/2 tbsp crushed roasted peanuts
sliced fresh red chillies, to garnish

1   Cut the papaya in half lengthways. Scrape out the seeds with a spoon, then peel using a swivel-bladed vegetable peeler or a small sharp knife. Shred the flesh finely using a food processor or grater.

2   Put the garlic, shallots, chillies and salt in a large mortar and grind to a paste with a pestle. Add the shredded papaya, a little at a time, pounding until it becomes slightly limp and soft.

3   Add the sliced beans and wedges of tomato to the mortar and crush them lightly with the pestle.

4   Season the mixture with the fish sauce, sugar and lime juice. Transfer the salad to a serving dish and sprinkle with crushed peanuts and garnish with sliced red chillies. Serve immediately.

THAMIN LETHOK

This is the Burmese way of dealing with leftovers, and very successful it is too. The noodles and rice are arranged on platters with some or all of the accompaniments.

SERVES 6

INGREDIENTS
175g/6oz/scant 1 cup long grain rice
1–2 red chillies, seeded and roughly chopped
1 small onion, roughly chopped
15ml/1 tbsp vegetable oil
350g/12oz potatoes, diced
115g/4oz egg noodles, soaked for 30 minutes in cold water
115g/4oz rice noodles, soaked for at least 10 minutes in cold water
50g/2oz cellophane noodles (or increase either of the above)
225g/8oz spinach leaves
175g/6oz/3 cups beansprouts
25ml/1½ tbsp tamarind pulp or concentrate, soaked in 200ml/7fl oz/
   scant 1 cup warm water, or 6 lemon wedges
salt

FOR THE ACCOMPANIMENTS
1 very small onion, thinly sliced
3 spring onions (scallions), finely shredded
crisp fried onion
50g/2oz cellophane noodles, fried until crisp
25g/1oz/3 tbsp chickpeas, dry-roasted and pounded
3 dried chillies, dry-fried and pounded
fresh coriander (cilantro) leaves

> COOK'S TIP
> *Cook noodles following the instructions on the packet: egg noodles need about 4 minutes and rice noodles are ready when the water boils again.*

Bring a large pan of water to the boil and cook the rice for 12–15 minutes until tender. Drain, tip into a bowl and set aside.

In a mortar, pound the chillies with the onion. Heat the oil in a small frying pan, add the mixture and fry for about 3 minutes. Stir into the cooked rice.

Boil the potatoes in salted water for 8–10 minutes until just tender; drain and set aside. Drain the noodles and cook them in separate pans of salted, boiling water (see Cook's Tip). Drain, refresh under cold water and drain again.

Put the spinach into a large pan with just the water that clings to the leaves after washing. Cover the pan and cook over a medium heat for 2 minutes until the leaves are starting to wilt. Drain well. Cook the beansprouts in the same way. Leave both to get cold.

Arrange the cold flavoured rice, potato cubes, noodles, spinach and beansprouts attractively on a large serving platter. Set out the range of accompaniments. Strain the tamarind juice, if using, into a small jug (pitcher) or put the lemon wedges on a plate. Each guest takes a little of whichever main ingredients they fancy, adds some accompaniments and drizzles over a little tamarind juice or a squeeze of lemon juice to taste.

STUFFED THAI OMELETTES

Serve individual omelettes or make two large omelette parcels to serve four. They are remarkably easy to prepare and provide a tasty lunch or light supper.

SERVES 3–4

INGREDIENTS
30ml/2 tbsp vegetable oil
2 garlic cloves, finely chopped
1 small onion, finely chopped
225g/8oz minced (ground) pork
30ml/2 tbsp fish sauce
5ml/1 tsp sugar
2 tomatoes, peeled and chopped
15ml/1 tbsp chopped fresh coriander (cilantro)
ground black pepper
fresh coriander (cilantro) sprigs, to garnish

FOR THE OMELETTES
6 eggs
15ml/1 tbsp fish sauce
about 30ml/2 tbsp vegetable oil

1 Heat the oil in a wok. Fry the garlic and onion for 3–4 minutes until softened. Add the pork and stir-fry for 7–10 minutes until lightly browned. Stir in the fish sauce, sugar and tomatoes, with pepper to taste. Simmer for 5–8 minutes, until the sauce thickens. Remove from the heat and stir in the chopped fresh coriander.

2 Make the omelettes. Whisk the eggs and fish sauce in a bowl. Heat a little of the oil in a 20cm/8in omelette pan. Add a quarter of the egg mixture. Tilt the pan to spread the egg into a thin, even layer. As soon as it sets, spoon some of the filling over the centre of the omelette. Fold the top and bottom over, then the right and left sides to make a neat, square parcel.

3 Slide the omelette out on to a warm serving dish, folded side down, and keep hot while you make the rest. Serve garnished with sprigs of coriander.

Thai Beef Salad

A hearty main meal salad, this dish combines tender strips of steak with a wonderful piquant chilli and lime dressing.

Serves 4

Ingredients

2 sirloin steaks, each about 225g/8oz
1 lemon grass stalk, root trimmed
1 red onion, finely sliced
½ cucumber, cut into strips
30ml/2 tbsp chopped spring onion (scallion)
juice of 2 limes
15–30ml/1–2 tbsp fish sauce
Chinese mustard cress or salad cress, to garnish

1   Pan-fry or grill (broil) the steaks for 6–8 minutes for medium-rare. Allow to rest and cool for 10–15 minutes. Meanwhile, cut off the lower 5cm/2in from the lemon grass stalk and chop it finely.

2   When the meat is cool, slice it thinly using a very sharp knife and put the slices in a large bowl.

3   Add the sliced red onion, cucumber, lemon grass and chopped spring onion to the meat slices in the bowl.

4   Toss the salad and season with the lime juice and fish sauce. Transfer the salad to a serving bowl or plate and serve at room temperature or chilled, garnished with Chinese mustard cress or salad cress.

Variation
Look out for gui chai *leaves in Thai grocery stores. These look like very thin spring onions and are often used as a substitute for them. They taste very good in this salad.*

MUSSAMAN CURRY

This dish is traditionally made with beef, but chicken, lamb or tofu would work equally well. It has a rich, sweet and spicy flavour, and is best served with plain boiled rice. For the best results, make the Mussaman curry paste yourself. The quantities given below will make more than the required amount but you can keep the leftover paste in a sealed container in the refrigerator for use on another occasion.

SERVES 4–6

INGREDIENTS

600ml/1 pint/2½ cups canned coconut milk
675g/1½lb stewing steak, cut into 2.5cm/1in chunks
250ml/8fl oz/1 cup coconut cream
30ml/2 tbsp fish sauce
15ml/1 tbsp palm sugar
60ml/4 tbsp tamarind juice
6 green cardamom pods
1 cinnamon stick
1 large potato, about 225g/8oz, cut into even-size chunks
1 onion, cut into wedges
50g/2oz/½ cup roasted peanuts

FOR THE MUSSAMAN CURRY PASTE

12 large dried red chillies, seeded
60ml/4 tbsp chopped shallots
5 garlic cloves
1 lemon grass stalk, base only
30ml/2 tbsp chopped galangal
5ml/1 tsp cumin seeds
15ml/1 tbsp coriander seeds
2 cloves
6 black peppercorns
5ml/1 tsp shrimp paste (blachan)
5ml/1 tsp salt
5ml/1 tsp sugar
30ml/2 tbsp vegetable oil

Make the curry paste. You will need 45ml/3 tbsp for use in this recipe. Soak the chillies in hot water for 15 minutes, then chop finely. Place in a large mortar with the shallots, garlic, lemon grass and galangal. Pound to a paste with a pestle. Alternatively, use a food processor.

Put the cumin and coriander seeds, the cloves and peppercorns in a pan and dry-fry over a low heat for 1–2 minutes. Grind to a powder, then add the shrimp paste, salt, sugar and oil. Stir into the shallot mixture to make a paste. Set aside until required.

Bring the coconut milk to a gentle boil in a large pan. Add the beef, lower the heat and simmer for about 40 minutes, or until tender.

Put the coconut cream into a pan and cook for 5–8 minutes, stirring, until it separates. Stir in 45ml/3 tbsp of the Mussaman curry paste and cook over a high heat until fragrant. Add to the cooked beef, and mix well.

Stir in the fish sauce, sugar, tamarind juice, cardamom pods, cinnamon, potato and onion. Simmer for 15–20 minutes, or until the potato is cooked. Add the peanuts and mix well. Cook for 5 minutes and serve.

COOK'S TIP
If you are short of time, you may be able to find ready-made Mussaman curry paste in Asian stores. Once opened, store in the refrigerator and use before the expiry date printed on the jar.

CRISPY FRIED RICE VERMICELLI

Mee Krob, *as this delicious dish is known in Thailand, is usually served at celebration meals. It is a crisp tangle of fried rice vermicelli, tossed in a piquant garlic sauce.*

SERVES 4–6

INGREDIENTS
vegetable oil, for deep-frying
175g/6oz rice vermicelli
15ml/1 tbsp chopped garlic
4–6 small dried red chillies
30ml/2 tbsp chopped shallots
15ml/1 tbsp dried shrimps, rinsed
115g/4oz minced (ground) pork
115g/4oz raw peeled prawns (shrimp), thawed if frozen, chopped
30ml/2 tbsp brown bean sauce
30ml/2 tbsp rice wine vinegar
45ml/3 tbsp fish sauce
75g/3oz palm sugar
30ml/2 tbsp tamarind juice or lime juice
115g/4oz/2 cups beansprouts
salt and ground black pepper

FOR THE GARNISH
2 spring onions (scallions), shredded
30ml/2 tbsp fresh coriander (cilantro) leaves
2-egg omelette, rolled and sliced
2 fresh red chillies, seeded and cut into thin strips

1 Heat the oil in a wok. Cut or break the rice vermicelli into small handfuls about 7.5cm/3in long. Deep fry these for a few seconds in the hot oil until they puff up. Lift out with a slotted spoon and drain on kitchen paper.

2 Ladle off all but 30ml/2 tbsp of the oil, pouring it into a pan. Reheat the oil in the wok and fry the garlic, chillies, shallots and shrimps for about 1 minute.

3 Add the pork and stir-fry for 3–4 minutes, until no longer pink. Add the prawns and fry for 2 minutes. Spoon into a bowl and set aside.

4 Add the brown bean sauce, vinegar, fish sauce and sugar to the wok. Heat gently, stirring in any sediment. Bring to a gentle boil, stir to dissolve the sugar and cook until the mixture is thick and syrupy.

5 Add the tamarind or lime juice to the sauce and adjust the seasoning as necessary. The sauce should be sweet, sour and salty. Lower the heat, then return the pork and prawn mixture to the wok, add the beansprouts and stir them into the sauce.

6 Add the fried rice noodles to the wok and toss gently to coat them with the sauce without breaking them up too much. Transfer the mixture to a large, warm serving platter or individual serving dishes. Garnish with the spring onions, coriander, omelette strips and fresh red chillies, and serve immediately.

COOK'S TIPS

• *Pickled garlic can also be used as one of the garnish ingredients. Thai garlic is smaller than Western garlic; the heads are pickled whole, in sweet-and-sour brine.*
• *Always deep-fry rice vermicelli in small quantities, as it puffs up to two or three times its original volume. It cooks in seconds, so be ready to remove it from the wok using a slotted spoon or wire basket as soon as it has puffed up and before it takes on any colour.*

Chiang Mai is a city in the north-east of Thailand. The city is culturally very close to Laos and famous for its chicken salad, which is sometimes called "Larp". Duck, beef or pork can be used instead of chicken.

SERVES 4–6

INGREDIENTS
450g/1lb minced (ground) chicken
1 lemon grass stalk, root trimmed
3 kaffir lime leaves, finely chopped
4 fresh red chillies, seeded and chopped
60ml/4 tbsp lime juice
30ml/2 tbsp fish sauce
15ml/1 tbsp roasted ground rice (see Cook's Tip)
2 spring onions (scallions), chopped
30ml/2 tbsp fresh coriander (cilantro) leaves
thinly sliced kaffir lime leaves, mixed salad leaves and fresh mint sprigs, to garnish

Heat a large non-stick frying pan without any oil. Add the chicken and moisten with a little water. Stir over a medium heat for 7–10 minutes until cooked through. Cut off the lower 5cm/2in of the lemon grass stalk and chop finely.

Transfer the cooked chicken to a bowl and add the chopped lemon grass, lime leaves, chillies, lime juice, fish sauce, ground rice, spring onions and coriander. Mix together thoroughly to combine.

Spoon the chicken mixture into a salad bowl. Scatter sliced kaffir lime leaves over the top and garnish with salad leaves and sprigs of mint.

COOK'S TIP
Use glutinous rice for the roasted ground rice. Put the rice in a frying pan and dry-roast until it is golden brown. Remove and grind to a powder, using a pestle and mortar or a food processor. When the rice is cold, store it in a glass jar in a cool dry place.

STIR-FRIED CHICKEN WITH BASIL & CHILLI

This quick and easy chicken dish is an excellent introduction to Thai cooking. Thai basil, which is sometimes known as holy basil, has a unique, pungent flavour that is both spicy and sharp. Deep-frying the leaves adds another dimension to this dish.

SERVES 4–6

INGREDIENTS
45ml/3 tbsp vegetable oil
4 garlic cloves, thinly sliced
2–4 fresh red chillies, seeded and finely chopped
450g/1lb skinless boneless chicken breast portions, cut into bite-size pieces
45ml/3 tbsp fish sauce
10ml/2 tsp dark soy sauce
5ml/1 tsp sugar
10–12 Thai basil leaves
vegetable oil, for deep frying
2 fresh red chillies, seeded and finely chopped and about 20 Thai basil
   leaves, to garnish

Heat the oil in a wok or large frying pan. Add the garlic and chillies and stir-fry over a medium heat for 1–2 minutes until the garlic is golden. Add the chicken to the wok or pan and stir-fry until the chicken changes colour.

Stir in the fish sauce, soy sauce and sugar. Continue to stir-fry the mixture for 3–4 minutes or until the chicken is fully cooked with the sauce. Stir in the fresh Thai basil leaves.

Meanwhile, deep-fry the basil leaves for garnishing. First rinse the leaves and pat dry on kitchen paper. Deep-fry the leaves in hot oil for 30–40 seconds until crisp and transluscent. Lift out using a slotted spoon and drain on kitchen paper.

Spoon the stir-fry on to a warm serving platter or individual serving dishes and garnish with deep-fried basil leaves before serving.

RED CHICKEN CURRY
WITH BAMBOO SHOOTS

Bamboo shoots have a lovely crunchy texture. It is quite acceptable to use canned ones, as fresh bamboo is not readily available in the West. Buy canned whole bamboo shoots, which are crisper and of better quality than sliced shoots. Drain then rinse well before using.

SERVES 4–6

INGREDIENTS

1 litre/1¾ pints/4 cups coconut milk
450g/1lb skinless boneless chicken breast portions, cut into bite-size pieces
30ml/2 tbsp fish sauce
15ml/1 tbsp sugar
225g/8oz drained canned bamboo shoots, rinsed and sliced
5 kaffir lime leaves, torn
salt and ground black pepper
chopped fresh red chillies and kaffir lime leaves, to garnish

FOR THE RED CURRY PASTE

5ml/1 tsp coriander seeds
2.5ml/½ tsp cumin seeds
12–15 fresh red chillies, seeded and roughly chopped
4 shallots, thinly sliced
2 garlic cloves, chopped
15ml/1 tbsp chopped galangal or fresh root ginger
2 lemon grass stalks, chopped
3 kaffir lime leaves, chopped
4 fresh coriander roots
10 black peppercorns
a good pinch of ground cinnamon
5ml/1 tsp ground turmeric
2.5ml/½ tsp shrimp paste (blachan)
5ml/1 tsp salt
30ml/2 tbsp vegetable oil

1 Make the curry paste. Dry-fry the coriander and cumin seeds for 1–2 minutes, then put in a mortar or food processor with the remaining ingredients except the oil and pound or process to a paste. Add the oil, a little at a time, and mix well. Transfer to a jar and keep in the refrigerator until ready to use.

2 Pour half the coconut milk into a large heavy pan. Bring to the boil, stirring constantly until it has separated. Stir in 30ml/2 tbsp of the red curry paste and cook for 2–3 minutes, stirring constantly. Leftover curry paste can be kept in the refrigerator for up to 3 months.

3 Add the chicken pieces, fish sauce and sugar to the pan. Stir well, then cook for 5–6 minutes until the chicken changes colour, stirring constantly to prevent the mixture from sticking. Pour in the remaining coconut milk, the bamboo shoots and kaffir lime leaves. Bring back to the boil over a medium heat, stirring constantly, then taste for seasoning.

4 To serve, spoon the curry into a warmed serving dish and garnish with chopped chillies and kaffir lime leaves.

COOK'S TIPS

• *Instead of, or as well as, bamboo shoots, use lightly sautéed oyster mushrooms or canned straw mushrooms, which are available from Asian stores. Stir into the curry just before serving.*

• *It is essential to use chicken breast portions, rather than any other cut, for this curry, as it is cooked very quickly. Look out for diced chicken or strips of chicken (which are often labelled "stir-fry chicken").*

Hot Chilli Duck with Crab & Cashew Nut Sauce

This dish may be served with Thai rice and a dish of Thai dipping sauce. To increase its heat, include some or all of the chilli seeds.

Serves 4–6

Ingredients
1 duck, about 2.7kg/6lb
1.1 litre/2 pints/5 cups water
2 lime leaves
5ml/1 tsp salt
2–3 small red chillies, seeded and finely chopped
25ml/5 tsp sugar
2.5ml/½ tsp salt
30ml/2 tbsp coriander seeds
5ml/1 tsp caraway seeds
115g/4oz raw cashew nuts, chopped
7.5cm/3in piece lemon grass, shredded
2.5cm/1in piece galangal or fresh root ginger, peeled and finely chopped
2 garlic cloves, crushed
4 shallots or 1 onion, finely chopped
2cm/¾in cube shrimp paste (blachan)
25g/1oz coriander root or stem, finely chopped
175g/6oz frozen white crab meat, thawed
50g/2oz creamed coconut or 120ml/4 fl oz/½ cup coconut cream
1 small bunch fresh coriander (cilantro), chopped, to garnish

To cut the duck into manageable portions, first remove the legs. Separate the thighs from the drumsticks and chop each thigh and drumstick into two pieces. Trim away the lower half of the duck with kitchen scissors. Cut the breast piece in half down the middle, then chop each half into four pieces.

Put the pieces of duck into a large pan with the water. Add the lime leaves and salt, bring to the boil and simmer, uncovered, for 35–40 minutes until the meat is tender. remove the duck from the pan and discard the bones. Skim off the fat from the stock, then return the duck to the pan and set aside.

3 To make the curry sauce, grind the red chillies together with the sugar and salt in a mortar using a pestle, or in a food processor. Dry-fry the coriander and caraway seeds and the cashew nuts in a wok for 1–2 minutes to release their flavour. Add the chillies, the lemon grass, galangal or ginger, garlic and shallots or onion and reduce to a smooth paste. Add the shrimp paste and coriander.

4 Add a cup of the duck stock and blend to make a thin paste. Stir the curry paste into the pan with the duck, bring to the boil and simmer, uncovered, for 20–25 minutes.

5 Add the crab meat and creamed coconut or coconut cream, and simmer briefly. Turn out on to a warm serving dish, garnish with chopped coriander, and serve.

Thai Steamed Fish
with Citrus Marinade

Lime and mandarin orange flavour the marinade in this simple yet delicious dish.
Serve with fragrant Thai rice or fine rice noodles.

Serves 4–6

INGREDIENTS

1.3kg/3lb parrot fish, pomfret, plaice or sea bream, gutted with heads on
2 small red chillies, seeded and finely chopped
15ml/1 tbsp sugar
2 garlic cloves, crushed
3 spring onions (scallions), white part only, chopped
2.5cm/1in piece fresh galangal or fresh root ginger, peeled and finely chopped
finely chopped rind and juice of 1 mandarin orange
juice of 1 lime
15ml/1 tbsp tamarind sauce
15ml/1 tbsp fish sauce
30ml/2 tbsp light soy sauce
15ml/1 tbsp vegetable oil
2 limes, quartered, to garnish
4 spring onion (scallion) curls, to garnish

1 Wash the fish thoroughly and slash 3–4 times with a sharp knife on each side to allow the marinade to penetrate deeply. Place the fish in a shallow dish that will fit in the base of a steamer. Alternatively, wrap the fish loosely in foil.

2 Grind the chilli and sugar together using a pestle and mortar or food processor, add the garlic, spring onion, galangal or ginger and the rind of the mandarin orange. Combine well. Add the orange and lime juice, the tamarind, fish and soy sauces, and the vegetable oil, then spread over the fish. Leave to marinate for at least 1 hour.

3 Cook the fish in a covered steamer for 25–30 minutes. Lift the fish on to a serving plate and decorate with wedges of lime and spring onion curls.

CURRIED PRAWNS IN COCONUT MILK

This wonderfully quick and easy dish features prawns in a spicy coconut sauce. It would make a colourful addition to any buffet table.

SERVES 4–6

INGREDIENTS

600ml/1 pint/2½ cups coconut milk
30ml/2 tbsp yellow curry paste (see Cook's Tip)
15ml/1 tbsp fish sauce
2.5ml/½ tsp salt
5ml/1 tsp sugar
450g/1lb raw king prawns (jumbo shrimp) peeled, thawed if frozen
225g/8oz cherry tomatoes
juice of ½ lime
yellow and orange (bell) peppers, seeded and cut into thin strips and fresh chives,
   to garnish

1 Bring half the coconut milk to the boil. Stir in the yellow curry paste, then simmer for 10 minutes. Add the fish sauce, salt, sugar and remaining coconut milk. Simmer for 5 minutes.

2 Add the prawns and tomatoes. Simmer for 5 minutes until the prawns turn pink. Spoon into a serving dish, sprinkle with lime juice and garnish.

COOK'S TIP
To make yellow curry paste, put 6–8 fresh yellow chillies, the chopped base of 1 lemon grass stalk, 4 chopped shallots, 4 chopped garlic cloves, 15ml/1 tbsp chopped fresh root ginger, 5ml/1 tsp coriander seeds, 5ml/1 tsp mustard powder, 5ml/1 tsp salt, 2.5ml/½ tsp ground cinnamon, 15ml/1 tbsp light brown sugar and 30ml/2 tbsp sunflower oil into a food processor. Process to a paste. Keep in a covered jar in the refrigerator.

Ragout of Shellfish with Basil

This delicious shellfish curry is cooked in a wonderfully rich coconut milk sauce flavoured with green curry paste. If you are in a hurry, you can use ready-made green curry paste rather than making your own.

SERVES 4–6

INGREDIENTS
575ml/1 pint/2½ cups fresh mussels in the shell, cleaned
225g/8oz cuttlefish or squid
400ml/14oz can coconut milk
300ml/½ pint/1¼ cups chicken or vegetable stock
350g/12oz monkfish, hoki or red snapper, skinned
150g/5oz raw or cooked large prawn (shrimp) tails, peeled and deveined
4 scallops, sliced (optional)
75g/3oz green beans, trimmed and cooked
50g/2oz canned bamboo shoots, drained
1 ripe tomato, skinned, seeded and roughly chopped
fresh basil leaves, torn, to garnish

FOR THE GREEN CURRY PASTE
10ml/2 tsp coriander seeds
2.5ml/½ tsp caraway or cumin seeds
3–4 green chillies, finely chopped
20ml/4 tsp sugar
10ml/2 tsp salt
7.5cm/3in piece lemon grass
2cm/¾in piece galangal or fresh root ginger, peeled and finely chopped
3 garlic cloves, crushed
4 shallots or 1 onion, finely chopped
2cm/¾in cube shrimp paste
50g/2oz coriander (cilantro) leaves, finely chopped
45ml/3 tbsp finely chopped fresh mint or basil
2.5ml/½ tsp grated nutmeg
30ml/2 tbsp vegetable oil

1   Place the mussels in a stainless steel or enamel pan, add 60ml/4 tbsp water, cover, and cook for 6–8 minutes. Allow to cool. Take three-quarters of the mussels out of their shells, reserving the rest, strain the cooking liquid and set aside.

2   To prepare the cuttlefish or squid, trim off the tentacles beneath the eye. Rinse under cold running water, discarding the gut. Remove the cuttle shell from inside the body and rub off the paper-thin skin. Cut the body open and score in a criss-cross pattern with a sharp knife. Cut into strips and set aside.

3   To make the green curry paste, dry-fry the coriander and caraway or cumin seeds in a wok to release their flavour. Grind the chillies with the sugar and salt using a pestle and mortar or food processor to make a smooth paste. Combine the seeds from the wok with the chillies, add the lemon grass, galangal or ginger, garlic and shallots or onion, then grind smoothly. Add the shrimp paste, coriander, mint or basil, nutmeg and vegetable oil and combine well.

4   Strain the coconut milk into a bowl. Pour the thin part of the milk together with the chicken or vegetable stock into a wok. Reserve the thick part of the coconut milk. Add 60–75ml/4–5 tbsp of the green curry paste, according to taste. You can add more paste later if you need to. Boil rapidly until the liquid has reduced.

5   Add the thick part of the coconut milk, then add the cuttlefish or squid and monkfish, hokey or red snapper. Simmer uncovered for 15–20 minutes. Then add the prawns, scallops and cooked mussels with the beans, bamboo shoots and tomato. Simmer for 2–3 minutes, transfer to a bowl and garnish with the basil.

MOHINGA

Burmese housewives buy this one-course meal from hawkers, who carry a bamboo pole across their shoulders. At one end is a container with a charcoal fire and at the other end are all the ingredients they need to make the meal.

SERVES 8

INGREDIENTS

675g/1½lb huss, cod or mackerel, gutted

3 lemon grass stalks, roots trimmed

2.5cm/1in piece fresh root ginger, peeled

30ml/2 tbsp fish sauce

3 onions, roughly chopped

4 garlic cloves, roughly chopped

2–3 fresh red chillies, seeded and chopped

5ml/1 tsp ground turmeric

75ml/5 tbsp groundnut (peanut) oil, for frying

400ml/14fl oz can coconut milk

25g/1oz/3 tbsp rice flour

25g/1oz/3 tbsp chickpea flour

pieces of banana trunk, or heart, if available, or 540g/1lb 5oz drained canned
   bamboo shoots, sliced

salt and ground black pepper

wedges of hard-boiled (hard-cooked) egg, thinly sliced red onions, finely chopped
   spring onions (scallions), a few deep fried prawns (shrimp) and fried chillies
   (see Cook's Tip), to garnish

fresh rice noodles, to serve

> COOK'S TIP
> To make fried chillies, dry-roast 8–10 dried red chillies in a heavy frying pan, then pound them. Add 30ml/2 tbsp peanut oil and 25g/1oz dried shrimps and pound again.

1 Place the fish in a large pan and pour in cold water to cover. Bruise two lemon grass stalks and half the ginger and add to the pan. Bring to the boil, add the fish sauce and cook for 10 minutes. Lift out the fish and allow to cool while straining the stock into a large bowl. Remove the skin and bones from the fish and break the flesh into small pieces.

2 Cut off the lower 5cm/2in of the remaining lemon grass stalk and discard; roughly chop the lemon grass. Put it in a food processor with the remaining ginger, the onions, garlic, chillies and turmeric. Process to a smooth paste. Heat the oil in a frying pan and fry the paste until it gives off a rich aroma. Remove from the heat and add the fish.

3 Stir the coconut milk into the reserved fish stock, then add enough water to make up to 2.5 litres/4 pints/10 cups and pour into a large pan. In a jug (pitcher), mix the rice flour and chickpea flour to a thin cream with some of the stock. Add this to the coconut mixture and bring to the boil, stirring all the time.

4 Add the banana trunk or heart or bamboo shoots and cook for 10 minutes, or until just tender. Stir in the fish mixture and season. Cook until hot. Guests pour soup over the noodles and add hard-boiled egg, onions, spring onions, prawns and fried chillies as a garnish.

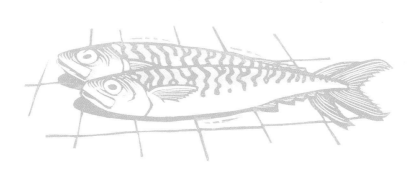

Stewed Pumpkin in Coconut Cream

Stewed fruit is a popular dessert in Thailand. Pumpkins, bananas and melons can all be prepared in this way, and you can even stew sweetcorn kernels or pulses such as mung beans and black beans in coconut milk.

Serves 4–6

INGREDIENTS
1kg/2¼lb kabocha pumpkin
750ml/1¼ pints/3 cups coconut milk
175g/6oz/¾ cup sugar
pinch of salt
toasted pumpkin seeds and fresh mint sprigs, to decorate

1 Cut the pumpkin in half using a large, sharp knife, then cut away and discard the skin. Scoop out the seed cluster and reserve a few seeds. Using a sharp knife, cut the pumpkin flesh into pieces about 5cm/2in long and 2cm/¾in thick.

2 Put the coconut milk, sugar and salt in a pan and bring to the boil. Add the pumpkin and simmer for about 10–15 minutes until it is tender. Serve warm, in individual dishes. Decorate each serving with a few toasted pumpkin seed kernels and mint sprigs.

MANGOES WITH STICKY RICE

The delicate fragrance, sweet and sour flavour and velvety flesh of mango blends especially well with coconut sticky rice. You need to start preparing this dish the day before you intend to serve it.

SERVES 4

INGREDIENTS
115g/4oz/⅔ cup white glutinous rice
175ml/6fl oz/¾ cup thick coconut milk
45ml/3 tbsp sugar
pinch of salt
2 ripe mangoes, peeled and sliced
strips of lime rind, to decorate

1 Rinse the glutinous rice thoroughly in several changes of cold water, then leave to soak overnight in a bowl of fresh cold water.

2 Drain the rice and spread evenly in a steamer lined with muslin (cheesecloth). Cover and steam over simmering water for 20 minutes or until tender.

3 Reserve 45ml/3 tbsp of the top of the coconut milk. Bring the rest to the boil in a pan with the sugar and salt, stirring until the sugar dissolves. Pour into a bowl and set aside to cool.

4 Tip the cooked rice into a bowl and pour over the cooled coconut milk mixture. Stir well, then leave to stand for about 10–15 minutes.

5 Spoon the rice on to individual serving plates. Arrange mango slices on one side and then drizzle with the reserved coconut milk. Decorate with strips of lime rind and serve.

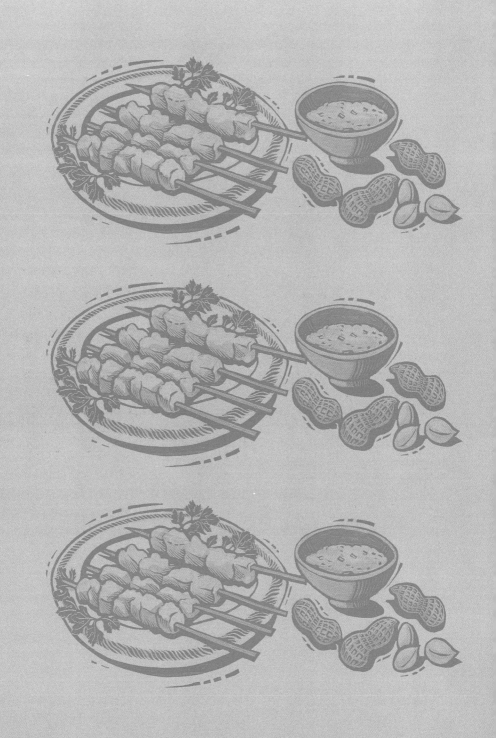

INDONESIA

The lush tropical archipelago of Indonesia is made up of over 13,000 islands. Many and varied cultures have flourished in this area over the centuries from the early Hindu and Buddhist empires through to the rise of Islam. Later on the area became important to Portuguese and British merchants who set up trading posts on some of the larger islands, but it was the Dutch who had the greatest impact, occupying the islands for 250 years. The culinary heritage of Indonesia therefore has diverse origins. There is an abundance of locally grown ingredients available, including rice, chillies, limes and spices, and Indonesian cooks make the best use of the fish and seafood that are caught in the waters surrounding the islands. Lamb, chicken and beef also feature in the local cuisine.

CHICKEN WONTON SOUP WITH PRAWNS

This delicious soup is a more luxurious version of basic Wonton Soup and almost makes a meal in itself. The stuffed wantons are easy to prepare and provide a delicious extra dimension to the soup.

SERVES 4

INGREDIENTS
325g/11oz skinless chicken breast fillet
200g/7oz prawn (shrimp) tails, fresh or cooked
5ml/1 tsp finely chopped fresh root ginger
2 spring onions (scallions), finely chopped
1 egg
10ml/2 tsp oyster sauce (optional)
1 packet wonton skins
15ml/1 tbsp cornflour (cornstarch) paste
850ml/1½ pints/3¾ cups chicken stock
¼ cucumber, peeled and diced
salt and ground black pepper

FOR THE GARNISH
1 spring onion (scallion), roughly shredded
1 tomato, skinned, seeded and diced
4 fresh coriander (cilantro) sprigs

Place the chicken breast, 150g/5oz of the prawn tails, the ginger and spring onions in a food processor and process for 2–3 minutes. Add the egg, oyster sauce and seasoning and process briefly. Set aside.

Place 8 wonton skins at a time on the work surface, moisten the edges with cornflour paste and place 2.5ml/½ tsp of the filling in the centre of each. Fold in half and pinch to seal. Simmer in salted water for 4 minutes, working in batches.

Bring the chicken stock to the boil, add the remaining prawn tails and the cucumber, and simmer for 3–4 minutes. Add the wontons and simmer to warm through. Serve hot garnished with the spring onion, tomato and coriander sprigs.

BALINESE VEGETABLE SOUP

This popular soup is based on beans, but any seasonal vegetables can be added or substituted, according to what is available.

SERVES 8

INGREDIENTS
225g/8oz green beans, trimmed and cut into small pieces
1.2 litres/2 pints/5 cups lightly salted water
1 garlic clove, roughly chopped
2 macadamia nuts or 4 almonds, finely chopped
1cm/½in cube shrimp paste
10–15ml/2–3 tsp coriander seeds, dry-fried
30ml/2 tbsp vegetable oil
1 onion, finely sliced
400ml/14fl oz can coconut milk
2 bay leaves
225g/8oz/4 cups beansprouts
8 thin lemon wedges
30ml/2 tbsp lemon juice
salt and ground black pepper

Cook the green beans in the lightly salted water for 3–4 minutes. Drain, reserving the water. Set the beans aside.

Finely grind the chopped garlic, nuts, shrimp paste and coriander seeds to a paste using a mortar and pestle or in a food processor.

Heat the oil in a wok, and fry the onion for about 5 minutes, or until transparent. Remove with a slotted spoon. Fry the nut paste for 2 minutes without browning. Add the vegetable water. Reserve 60ml/4 tbsp of the top of the coconut milk, add the rest to the wok with the bay leaves. Cook, uncovered, for 15–20 minutes.

Reserve some beans, fried onions and beansprouts for garnish, then stir the rest into the soup. Add the lemon wedges, reserved coconut cream, lemon juice and seasoning; stir well. Serve, garnished, at once.

PRAWN CRACKERS

These are a popular addition to many Asian dishes and are often served before guests come to the table. The Indonesian version are quite large. Some supermarkets and food stores sell crackers ready for cooking.

SERVES 4–6

INGREDIENTS
300ml/½ pint/1¼ cups vegetable oil
50g/2oz uncooked prawn (shrimp) crackers
fine table salt, to taste

1 Line a tray with kitchen paper. Heat the oil in a large wok until it begins to smoke. Lower the heat to maintain a steady temperature.

2 Drop 3–4 prawn crackers into the oil. Remove from the oil before they begin to colour and transfer to the paper-lined tray. Serve sprinkled with salt.

SPICY PEANUT RICE CAKES

Serve these spicy rice cakes with a crisp green salad and hot tomato sambal as a dipping sauce for guests to help themselves.

MAKES 16 PIECES

INGREDIENTS
1 garlic clove, crushed
1cm/½in piece fresh root ginger, peeled and finely chopped
1.5ml/¼ tsp turmeric
5ml/1 tsp sugar
2.5ml/½ tsp salt
5ml/1 tsp chilli sauce
10ml/2 tsp fish or soy sauce
30ml/2 tbsp chopped fresh coriander (cilantro)
juice of ½ lime
115g/4oz long grain rice, cooked
raw peanuts, chopped
150ml/¼ pint/⅔ cup vegetable oil, for deep-frying

FOR THE TOMATO SAMBAL
3 ripe tomatoes
2.5ml/½ tsp salt
5ml/1 tsp chilli sauce
60ml/4 tbsp fish sauce, or soy sauce
15ml/1 tbsp chopped coriander (cilantro) leaves

1 Make the sambal. Place the tomatoes in a bowl, pour over boiling water and leave to stand for 30 seconds. Drain, then peel, halve, discard the seeds and chop finely. Place in a bowl and stir in the salt, chilli sauce, fish or soy sauce, and coriander.

2 Pound the garlic, ginger and turmeric using a mortar and pestle. Add the sugar, salt, sauces, coriander and lime juice. Add three-quarters of the rice and pound until smooth. Stir in the remaining rice. Wet your hands and shape into thumb-size balls. Roll the balls in chopped peanuts. Set aside.

3 Heat the oil in a deep frying pan. Deep-fry 3 cakes at a time until crisp and golden. Drain on kitchen paper. Serve with the sambal.

Beef Satay with Spicy Mango Dip

Satay are enormously popular in Indonesia. Here best quality beef is marinated in a spicy mixture for up to eight hours, creating a flavoursome dish. Serve with a green salad and a bowl of plain rice.

Makes 12 skewers

Ingredients
450g/1lb sirloin steak, 2cm/¾in thick, trimmed
15ml/1 tbsp coriander seeds
4ml/1 tsp cumin seeds
50g/2oz/½ cup raw cashew nuts
15ml/1 tbsp vegetable oil
2 shallots or 1 small onion, finely chopped
1cm/½in piece fresh root ginger, peeled and finely chopped
1 garlic clove, crushed
30ml/2 tbsp tamarind sauce
30ml/2 tbsp dark soy sauce
10ml/2 tsp sugar
5ml/1 tsp rice or white wine vinegar

For the dip
1 ripe mango, peeled and stoned (pitted)
1–2 small red chillies, seeded and finely chopped
15ml/1 tbsp fish sauce
juice of 1 lime
10ml/2 tsp sugar
1.5ml/¼ tsp salt
30ml/2 tbsp chopped fresh coriander (cilantro)

Variations
Try this recipe using lamb, turkey or chicken in place of the beef if you wish. You could also use peanuts in place of the cashew nuts if you prefer a nuttier flavour.

Soak 12 bamboo skewers in cold water for about 5 minutes. Slice the beef into long narrow strips and thread, zig-zag fashion, on to the skewers. Lay on a flat plate and set aside.

For the marinade, dry-fry the coriander and cumin seeds and cashew nuts in a large wok until evenly brown. Tip into a large mortar and crush finely using a pestle. Alternatively, use a food processor. Add the vegetable oil, shallots or onion, ginger, garlic, tamarind and soy sauces, sugar and vinegar to the crushed spice mixture and stir to combine.

Spread the marinade over the beef and leave in a cool place to marinate for up to 8 hours. After marinating, cook the beef under a moderate grill (broiler) or over a barbecue for 6–8 minutes, turning to ensure an even colour.

Meanwhile, make the mango dip. Process the mango flesh with the chillies, fish sauce, lime juice, sugar and salt until smooth, then add the fresh coriander and stir to combine well. Serve with the hot beef satay.

LAMB SATAY

These tasty lamb skewers are traditionally served with dainty diamond-shape pieces of compressed rice, which are surprisingly simple to make. Offer the remaining sauce for dipping, allowing the guests help themselves.

MAKES 25–30 SKEWERS

INGREDIENTS
1kg/2¼lb leg of lamb, boned
3 garlic cloves, crushed
5–10ml/1–2 tsp chilli powder
90ml/6 tbsp dark soy sauce
juice of 1 lemon
salt and ground black pepper
groundnut (peanut) or sunflower oil, for brushing
thinly sliced onion, cucumber wedges (optional), compressed rice shapes
   (see Cook's Tip), to serve

FOR THE SAUCE
6 garlic cloves, crushed
2–3 fresh chillies, seeded and ground to a paste
90ml/6 tbsp dark soy sauce
25ml/1½ tbsp lemon juice
30ml/2 tbsp boiling water

1 Using a sharp knife, cut the lamb into neat 1cm/½in cubes. Remove any pieces of gristle, but do not trim off any of the fat because this keeps the meat moist during cooking and enhances the flavour. Spread out the lamb cubes in a single layer in a shallow dish.

2 Put the garlic, chilli powder, soy sauce and lemon juice in a mortar. Add salt and pepper and grind to a paste using a pestle. Alternatively, process the mixture using a food processor.

3 Pour the marinade over the cubed lamb and mix to coat. Cover and leave in a cool place for at least 1 hour. Soak some wooden or bamboo skewers in water to prevent them from scorching during cooking.

4 Prepare the sauce. Put the crushed garlic into a bowl. Add the fresh chillies, soy sauce, lemon juice and boiling water. Stir well to combine thoroughly.

5 Preheat the grill (broiler). Thread the meat on to the skewers. Brush the skewered meat with oil and grill (broil), turning often. Brush the satay with a little of the sauce and serve hot, with onion, cucumber wedges, if using, rice shapes and the sauce.

COOK'S TIP
Compressed rice shapes are easy to make. Put two 115g/4oz packets of boil-in-the-bag rice in a large pan of salted, boiling water and then simmer for 1¼ hours until the cooked rice fills each bag like a plump cushion. The bags must be covered with water throughout; use a saucer or plate to weigh them down. Let the bags cool completely before slitting them and removing the slabs of cooked rice. With a sharp, wetted knife, cut each rice slab horizontally in half, then into diamond shapes.

PORK & PEANUT WONTONS WITH PLUM SAUCE

These crispy filled wontons are delicious served with egg pancake salad wrappers, a popular salad dish of Indonesia. The wontons can be made eight hours ahead of time.

MAKES 40–50 WONTONS

INGREDIENTS

175g/6oz minced (ground) pork or 175g/6oz fresh pork sausages, skinned
2 spring onions (scallions), finely chopped
30ml/2 tbsp peanut butter
10ml/2 tsp oyster sauce (optional)
1 packet wonton skins
30ml/2 tbsp plain (all-purpose) flour paste
vegetable oil, for deep-frying
salt and ground black pepper

FOR THE PLUM SAUCE
225g/8oz dark plum jam (jelly)
15ml/1 tbsp rice or white wine vinegar
15ml/1 tbsp dark soy sauce
2.5ml/½ tsp chilli sauce

1 Combine the minced pork, spring onions, peanut butter, oyster sauce and seasoning in a bowl and set aside.

2 For the plum sauce, combine the plum jam, vinegar, soy and chilli sauces in a serving bowl and set aside.

3 Place 8 wrappers at a time on a work surface; moisten the edges with a little flour paste. Place about 2.5ml/½ tsp of the filling on each one. (Do not be tempted to overfill the wontons.) Fold and twist to seal.

4 Heat the oil in a wok or deep frying pan to 196°C/385°F. Fry the wontons, 8 at a time, until golden, 1–2 minutes. Drain on kitchen paper and sprinkle with salt. Serve immediately with the plum sauce.

Sweet & Sour Salad

This dish, called Acar Bening, *makes a perfect accompaniment to a variety of spicy dishes and curries, with its clean taste and bright, jewel-like colours.*

Serves 8

Ingredients
1 small cucumber
1 onion, thinly sliced
1 small ripe pineapple or 425g/15oz canned pineapple rings
1 green (bell) pepper, seeded and thinly sliced
3 firm tomatoes, chopped
30ml/2 tbsp golden granulated sugar
45–60ml/3–4 tbsp white wine vinegar
120ml/4fl oz/½ cup water
salt
seeds of 1–2 pomegranates, to garnish

Halve the cucumber lengthways, remove the seeds, slice and spread on a plate with the onion. Sprinkle with salt. After 10 minutes, rinse and dry.

If using a fresh pineapple, peel and core it, removing the eyes, then cut it into bite-size pieces. If using canned pineapple, drain and cut into wedges. Place the pineapple in a bowl with the cucumber, onion, green pepper and tomatoes.

Heat the sugar, vinegar and water in a pan, stirring until the sugar has dissolved. Remove the pan from the heat and leave to cool. When cold, add a little salt to taste and pour over the fruit and vegetables. Cover and chill until required. Serve in small bowls, garnished with pomegranate seeds.

Cook's Tip
To make an Indonesian-style cucumber salad, salt a cucumber as described in the recipe. Make half the dressing and pour it over the cucumber. Add a few chopped spring onions. Cover and chill. Serve scattered with toasted sesame seeds.

FRUIT & RAW VEGETABLE GADO GADO

This classic Indonesian salad combines the sweet and savoury flavours of fresh fruit and vegetable with hot and spicy peanut sauce perfectly. It looks stunning served on a fresh banana leaf; these can be found in Asian stores.

SERVES 6

INGREDIENTS

½ cucumber
2 firm pears or 175g/6oz wedge of yam bean
1–2 eating apples
juice of ½ lemon
mixed salad leaves
6 small tomatoes, cut in wedges
3 slices fresh pineapple, cored and cut in wedges
3 eggs, hard-boiled (hard-cooked) and shelled
175g/6oz egg noodles, cooked, cooled and chopped
deep-fried onions, to garnish

FOR THE PEANUT SAUCE

2–4 fresh red chillies, seeded and ground
300ml/½ pint/1¼ cups coconut milk
350g/12oz/1¼ cups crunchy peanut butter
15ml/1 tbsp dark soy sauce or dark brown sugar
5ml/1 tsp tamarind pulp, soaked in 45ml/3 tbsp warm water
coarsely crushed peanuts
salt

VARIATION
Quail's eggs can be used instead of normal eggs and look particularly attractive in this dish. Hard-boil (hard-cook) for 3 minutes and halve or leave whole.

1 First make the peanut sauce. Put the ground red chillies in a pan. Pour in the coconut milk, then stir in the crunchy peanut butter. Heat gently, stirring, until the mixture is well blended.

2 Simmer gently over a low heat until the sauce thickens, then stir in the soy sauce or sugar. Strain in the tamarind juice, add salt to taste and stir well. Spoon into a bowl and sprinkle with a few coarsely crushed peanuts.

3 To make the salad, core the cucumber and peel the pears or yam bean. Cut them into matchsticks. Finely shred the apples and sprinkle them with the lemon juice. Spread a bed of salad leaves on a flat platter, then pile the fruit and vegetables on top.

4 Slice or quarter the hard-boiled eggs and add to the salad, then add the chopped noodles and deep-fried onions. Serve at once, with the peanut sauce.

Egg Pancake Salad Wrappers

One of Indonesia's favourite snack foods is pancakes. They can be assembled according to taste and dipped in chilli or soy sauce.

Makes 12

Ingredients
2 eggs
2.5ml/½ tsp salt
5ml/1 tsp vegetable oil, plus a little for frying
115g/4oz plain (all-purpose) flour
300ml/½ pint/1¼ cups water
lettuce and beansprout salad, to serve

For the filling
45ml/3 tbsp vegetable oil
1cm/½in piece fresh root ginger, peeled and chopped
1 garlic clove, crushed
1 small red chilli, seeded and finely chopped
15ml/1 tbsp rice or white wine vinegar
10ml/2 tsp sugar
115g/4oz giant white radish, peeled and grated
1 carrot, grated
115g/4oz Chinese leaves (Chinese cabbage) or white cabbage, shredded
2 shallots or 1 small red onion, thinly sliced

Break the eggs into a bowl, add the salt, vegetable oil and flour and stir until smooth. Do not over-mix. Add the water a little at a time and strain into a jug (pitcher). Allow the batter to stand for 15–20 minutes.

Moisten a small non-stick frying pan with oil and heat. Cover the base of the pan with batter and cook for 30 seconds. Turn over and cook briefly. Repeat with the remaining batter. Stack the pancakes on a plate, cover and keep warm.

For the filling, heat the oil in a large wok, add the ginger, garlic and chilli and fry gently. Add the vinegar, sugar, white radish, carrot, Chinese leaves or cabbage and shallots or onion. Cook for 3–4 minutes. Serve with the pancakes and lettuce and beansprout salad.

Nasi Goreng

This famous Indonesian dish is a marvellous way to use up leftovers. The rice must be cold and the grains separate before the other ingredients are added.

Serves 4–6

Ingredients

2 eggs
30ml/2 tbsp water
105ml/7 tbsp oil
2 fresh red chillies, halved and seeded
1cm/½in cube shrimp paste
2 garlic cloves, crushed
1 onion, roughly chopped
225g/8oz pork fillet or fillet of beef, cut into neat strips
115g/4oz peeled cooked prawns (shrimp), thawed if frozen
175–225g/6–8oz cooked chicken, finely chopped
350g/12oz/1¾ cups long grain rice, cooked
30ml/2 tbsp dark soy sauce or 45–60ml/3–4 tbsp tomato ketchup
salt and ground black pepper
deep-fried onions, celery leaves and fresh coriander (cilantro) sprigs, to garnish

Put the eggs in a bowl and beat in the water, with salt and pepper to taste. Using a non-stick frying pan make two or three omelettes using as little oil as possible for greasing. Roll up each omelette and cut in strips when cold. Set aside. Shred one of the chillies and reserve it.

Put the shrimp paste in a food processor, add the remaining chilli, garlic and onion, then process to a fine paste. Heat the remaining oil in a wok and fry the paste, without browning, until it gives off a spicy aroma. Add the pork or beef and toss over the heat, then cook for 2 minutes, stirring constantly.

Add the prawns and stir-fry for 2 minutes. Finally, stir in the chicken, cold rice, dark soy sauce or ketchup and seasoning to taste. Reheat the rice fully, stirring all the time to keep the rice light and fluffy and prevent it from sticking.

Spoon into individual dishes and arrange the omelette strips and reserved chilli on top. Garnish with the onions, celery leaves and coriander and serve.

Spicy Meatballs
with Chilli Sambal

Serve these spicy little patties – Pergedel Djawa – *with egg noodles and chilli sambal.*
This fierce condiment is bottled as Sambal Oelek, *but it is easy to prepare and will*
keep for several weeks in a well-sealed jar in the refrigerator. Use a stainless-steel or
plastic spoon to measure; if sauce drips on your fingers, wash in soapy water at once.

SERVES 4–6

INGREDIENTS
1cm/½in cube shrimp paste
1 large onion, roughly chopped
1–2 fresh red chillies, seeded and chopped
2 garlic cloves, crushed
15ml/1 tbsp coriander seeds
5ml/1 tsp cumin seeds
450g/1lb lean minced (ground) beef
10ml/2 tsp dark soy sauce
5ml/1 tsp dark brown sugar
juice of 1½ lemons
a little beaten egg
vegetable oil, for shallow-frying
salt and ground black pepper
1 green and 2 fresh red chillies, to garnish

FOR THE SAMBAL
450g/1lb fresh red chillies, seeded
10ml/2 tsp salt

1   For the sambal, bring a pan of water to the boil, add the seeded chillies and
    cook for 5–8 minutes. Drain the chillies then grind them in a food processor,
without making the paste too smooth.

2   Scrape the paste into a screw-top glass jar, stir in the salt and cover with
    greaseproof (waxed) paper. Screw on the lid and store in the refrigerator.

3 Make the meatballs. Wrap the shrimp paste in a piece of foil and warm in a frying pan for 5 minutes, turning a few times. Unwrap and put in a food processor. Add the onion, chillies and garlic and process until finely chopped. Set aside. Dry-fry the coriander and cumin seeds for 1 minute to release the aroma. Tip the seeds into a mortar and grind with a pestle.

4 Put the minced beef in a large bowl. Stir in the onion mixture. Add the ground spices, soy sauce, brown sugar, lemon juice and beaten egg and season. Wet your hands and shape the meat mixture into small, even-size balls. Chill for about 10 minutes to firm them up.

5 Heat the oil in a wok or large frying pan and fry the meatballs, in batches, for 4–5 minutes, turning often, until cooked through and browned all over.

6 Drain the meatballs on kitchen paper then pile them into a large serving bowl. Remove the seeds from the green chilli and one of the red chillies, then finely slice and scatter over the meatballs. Garnish with the remaining red chilli. Serve with the chilli sambal handed separately.

COOK'S TIP
When processing the shrimp paste, onion, chillies and garlic, do not process for too long, otherwise the onion will become too wet and spoil the consistency of the meat balls.

Beef Rendang with Deep-fried Onion

In Indonesia, this spicy dish is usually served with the meat quite dry; if you prefer more sauce, simply add more water when stirring in the potatoes. Deep-fried onions, known as Bawang Goreng, *are a traditional garnish and accompany many Indonesian dishes. Asian stores sell them ready-prepared but they are easy to make at home. The small red onions sold in Asian stores are ideal as they contain less water.*

SERVES 6–8

INGREDIENTS

2 onions or 5–6 shallots, chopped
4 garlic cloves, chopped
2.5cm/1in piece fresh galangal, peeled and sliced, or 15ml/1 tbsp galangal paste
2.5cm/1in piece fresh root ginger, peeled and sliced
4–6 fresh red chillies, seeded and roughly chopped
1 lemon grass stalk, lower part only, sliced
2.5cm/1in piece fresh turmeric, peeled and sliced, or 5ml/1 tsp ground turmeric
1kg/2¼lb prime beef in one piece
5ml/1 tsp coriander seeds, dry-fried
5ml/1 tsp cumin seeds, dry-fried
2 kaffir lime leaves, torn
2 × 400ml/14fl oz cans coconut milk
300ml/½ pint/1¼ cups water
30ml/2 tbsp dark soy sauce
5ml/1 tsp tamarind pulp, soaked in 60ml/4 tbsp warm water
8–10 small new potatoes, scrubbed
salt and ground black pepper
sliced fresh red chillies and spring onions (scallions), to garnish

FOR THE DEEP-FRIED ONIONS

450g/1lb onions
vegetable oil, for deep-frying

Prepare the deep-fried onions. Thinly slice the onions with a sharp knife or in a food processor. Spread the slices out in a single layer on kitchen paper and leave them to dry, in an airy place, for 30 minutes–2 hours.

Heat the oil in a deep-fryer or wok to 190°C/375°F. Fry the onions in batches, until crisp and golden, turning all the time. Drain well on kitchen paper, cool and store in an airtight container until required.

For the beef rendang, put the onions or shallots in a food processor. Add the garlic, galangal, ginger, chillies, lemon grass and turmeric. Process to a fine paste. Alternatively, grind in a mortar, using a pestle.

Cut the meat into cubes using a large sharp knife, then place in a bowl. Using a mortar and pestle, grind the dry-fried coriander and cumin seeds, then add to the meat with the onion-chilli paste and kaffir lime leaves; stir well. Cover and leave in a cool place to marinate while you prepare the other ingredients.

Pour the coconut milk and water into a wok, then stir in the spiced meat and soy sauce. Strain the tamarind juice; add to the wok. Stir over a medium heat until the liquid boils, then simmer gently, half-covered, for 1½ hours.

Add the potatoes and simmer for 20–25 minutes, or until meat and potatoes are tender. Add extra water if necessary. Season and serve, garnished with deep-fried onions, chillies and spring onions.

COOK'S TIP
This dish is even better if you can cook it a day or two in advance of serving, which allows the flavours to mellow and blend beautifully. Add the potatoes on reheating and simmer until tender.

Spicy Pork with Lemon Grass and Coconut

This wonderfully fragrant dish is very quick and easy to prepare, yet the results are delicious and highly flavoured. Tangy lemon grass and spicy chilli are perfect partners to rich and creamy coconut milk. Serve this rich stew with plain boiled rice and a dish of fresh and spicy tomato sambal.

SERVES 4–6

INGREDIENTS

700g/1½lb lean pork, loin or fillet
30ml/2 tbsp vegetable oil
4 shallots or 1 onion, chopped
5cm/2in piece lemon grass, finely shredded
1–2 small red chillies, seeded and finely chopped
1cm/½in cube shrimp paste
400ml/14fl oz can coconut milk
300ml/½ pint/1¼ cups chicken stock
5ml/1 tsp sugar
juice of 1 lemon
zest of 1 satsuma, finely shredded
1 small bunch fresh coriander (cilantro), chopped

1 Place the pork in the freezer and leave for about 30 minutes, or until firm. Slice the meat thinly, using a sharp knife, and set aside.

2 Heat the vegetable oil in a large wok, add the shallots or onion, lemon grass, chillies and shrimp paste. Add the thinly sliced pork and stir gently to seal in the meat juices.

3 Add the coconut milk, chicken stock, sugar and lemon juice to the wok, then bring to the boil and simmer for 15–20 minutes, stirring occasionally. Turn the pork out into a serving dish or bowl and sprinkle with the finely shredded satsuma zest and chopped coriander.

Bamie Goreng

This fried noodle dish is infinitely variable. You can add other vegetables such as mushrooms, tiny pieces of chayote, broccoli, leeks or beansprouts.

SERVES 6–8

INGREDIENTS
450g/1lb dried egg noodles
2 eggs
25g/1oz/2 tbsp butter
90ml/6 tbsp vegetable oil
1 skinless boneless chicken breast portion, sliced
115g/4oz pork fillet, sliced
115g/4oz calf's liver, finely sliced (optional)
2 garlic cloves, crushed
115g/4oz peeled cooked prawns (shrimp)
115g/4oz pak choi (bok choy)
2 celery sticks, finely sliced
4 spring onions (scallions), shredded
about 60ml/4 tbsp chicken stock
dark soy sauce and light soy sauce
salt and ground black pepper
deep-fried onions and shredded spring onions (scallions), to garnish (optional)

Bring a pan of lightly salted water to the boil, add the noodles and cook for 3–4 minutes. Drain, rinse under cold water and drain again. Set aside.

Break the eggs into a bowl, beat and season. Heat the butter with 5ml/1 tsp oil in a small pan, add the eggs and stir until scrambled but still moist. Set aside.

Heat the remaining oil in a wok and fry the chicken, pork and liver, if using, with the garlic for 2–3 minutes. Toss in the prawns and vegetables. Add the noodles and toss over the heat until the greens are lightly cooked. Add enough stock to moisten and season with dark and light soy sauce. Add the scrambled eggs and toss to mix. Spoon on to a warmed serving platter, garnish and serve.

GRILLED CASHEW NUT CHICKEN

This dish comes from the beautiful island of Bali where nuts are widely used as a base for sauces and marinades. Serve with a green salad and a chilli dipping sauce.

SERVES 4–6

INGREDIENTS
4 chicken legs
50g/2oz/½ cup raw cashew or macadamia nuts
2 shallots or 1 small onion, finely chopped
2 garlic cloves, crushed
2 small red chillies, chopped
5cm/2in piece lemon grass
15ml/1 tbsp tamarind sauce
30ml/2 tbsp dark soy sauce
15ml/1 tbsp fish sauce (optional)
10ml/2 tsp sugar
2.5ml/½ tsp salt
15ml/1 tbsp rice or white wine vinegar
Chinese leaves (Chinese cabbage), to serve
radish and cucumber slices, to garnish

Using a sharp knife, slash the chicken legs several times through to the bone, chop off the knuckle end and set aside.

To make the marinade, place the cashew or macadamia nuts in a coarse mortar and grind with a pestle. Alternatively, grind in a food processor.

Add the shallots or onion, garlic, chillies and lemon grass and pound or blend. Add the tamarind and soy sauce, fish sauce (if using), sugar, salt and vinegar. Stir well to combine.

Spread the marinade over the chicken pieces and leave in a cool place to marinate for up to 8 hours. Grill (broil) the chicken under a moderate heat or over a barbecue for 15 minutes on each side. Place on a dish lined with Chinese leaves and garnish with the sliced radishes and cucumber. Serve immediately.

FISH WITH CASHEW NUT & GINGER MARINADE

The marinated fish is wrapped in green banana leaves or foil and baked. The packets are brought to the table, releasing a sweet spicy aroma when opened.

SERVES 4

INGREDIENTS

1.1kg/2½lb pomfret, parrot fish or sea bass, scaled and cleaned
150g/5oz/1¼ cups raw cashew nuts
2 shallots or 1 small onion, finely chopped
1cm/½in piece fresh root ginger, peeled and finely chopped
1 garlic clove, crushed
1 small red chilli, seeded and finely chopped
30ml/2 tbsp vegetable oil
15ml/1 tbsp shrimp paste
10ml/2 tsp sugar
2.5ml/½ tsp salt
30ml/2 tbsp tamarind sauce
30ml/2 tbsp tomato ketchup
juice of 2 limes
4 young banana leaves (optional)

Slash the fish 3–4 times on each side with a sharp knife to help it cook through to the bone. Set aside.

Finely grind the cashew nuts, shallots or onion, ginger, garlic and chilli using a mortar and pestle or food processor. Blend in the vegetable oil, shrimp paste, sugar and salt. Add the tamarind sauce, ketchup and lime juice. Cover both sides of the fish with the marinade and leave in a cool place for up to 8 hours.

Preheat the oven to 180°C/350°F/Gas 4. To soften the banana leaves, if using, remove the thick central stem and immerse in boiling water for 1 minute. Brush with vegetable oil. Wrap the fish in a banana leaf fastened with a bamboo skewer, or wrap in foil. Bake for 30–35 minutes.

SPICY SQUID

This aromatically spiced squid dish, Cumi Cumi Smoor, *is simple yet delicious. You can buy ready-cleaned squid from fishmongers and larger supermarkets.*

SERVES 3–4

INGREDIENTS
675g/1½lb squid, cleaned
45ml/3 tbsp groundnut (peanut) oil
1 onion, finely chopped
2 garlic cloves, crushed
1 beefsteak tomato, peeled and chopped
15ml/1 tbsp dark soy sauce
2.5ml/½ tsp grated nutmeg
6 cloves
150ml/¼ pint/⅔ cup water
juice of ½ lemon or lime
salt and ground black pepper
fresh coriander (cilantro) leaves and shredded spring onion (scallion), to garnish
boiled rice, to serve

Rinse and drain the squid, then slice lengthways along one side and open it out flat. Score the inside of the squid in a criss-cross pattern, using the blunt side of a sharp knife, then cut it crossways into long thin strips.

Heat a wok and add 15ml/1 tbsp of the oil. When hot, toss in the squid strips and stir-fry for 2–3 minutes, by which time the squid will have curled into attractive shapes or into firm rings. Lift out and set aside.

Wipe out the wok, add the remaining oil and heat. Stir-fry the onion and garlic until soft and beginning to brown. Stir in the tomato, soy sauce, nutmeg, cloves, water and lemon or lime juice. Bring to the boil, lower the heat and add the squid. Season to taste. Cook gently for a further 3–5 minutes stirring occasionally to prevent sticking.

Divide boiled rice among 3–4 serving plates and spoon the spicy squid on top. Garnish with coriander leaves and shredded spring onions and serve.

Sambal Goreng with Prawns

This spicy sambal is very adaptable. Here it is combined with prawns and green pepper. Store leftover sauce in the refrigerator for up to 3 days.

SERVES 4–6

INGREDIENTS

350g/12oz peeled cooked prawns (shrimp)
1 green (bell) pepper, seeded and thinly sliced
60ml/4 tbsp tamarind juice
pinch of sugar
45ml/3 tbsp coconut milk or cream
lime rind and red onion, to garnish
boiled rice, to serve

FOR THE SAMBAL

2.5cm/1in cube shrimp paste
2 onions, roughly chopped
2 garlic cloves, roughly chopped
2.5cm/1in piece fresh galangal, peeled and sliced
2 fresh red chillies, seeded and sliced
1.5ml/¼ tsp salt
30ml/2 tbsp vegetable oil
45ml/3 tbsp tomato purée (paste)
600ml/1 pint/2½ cups vegetable stock or water

Make the sambal goreng. Grind the shrimp paste with the onions and garlic using a mortar and pestle. Alternatively use a food processor. Add the galangal, chillies and salt. Pound or process or pound to a fine paste.

Heat the oil in a wok and fry the paste for 1–2 minutes until it gives off a rich aroma. Stir in the tomato purée and the stock or water and cook for about 10 minutes. Ladle half the sauce into a bowl and leave to cool.

Add the prawns and green pepper to the wok. Cook for 3–4 minutes, then stir in the tamarind juice, sugar and coconut milk or cream. Spoon into warmed serving bowls and garnish. Serve with boiled rice.

BANANA FRITTERS

Known as Pisang Goreng, *these delicious deep-fried bananas should be cooked at the last minute, so that the batter is crisp and the banana inside is soft and warm.*

SERVES 8

INGREDIENTS
115g/4oz/1 cup self-raising (self-rising) flour
40g/1½oz/¼ cup rice flour
2.5ml/½ tsp salt
200ml/7fl oz/scant 1 cup water
finely grated lime rind (optional)
8 baby bananas
vegetable oil, for deep-frying
strips of lime rind, to decorate
caster (superfine) sugar and lime wedges, to serve

1 Sift together the flours and salt into a bowl. Add just enough water to make a smooth, coating batter. Mix well, then add the lime rind, if using.

2 Heat the oil in a deep-fryer or wok to 190°C/375°F. Meanwhile, peel the bananas. Dip them into the batter two or three times until well coated, then deep-fry until crisp and golden brown. Drain on kitchen paper. Serve hot, dredged with the caster sugar and decorated with strips of lime. Offer the lime wedges for squeezing over the bananas.

BLACK GLUTINOUS RICE PUDDING

This very unusual rice pudding, known as Bubor Pulot Hitam, *is flavoured with bruised fresh root ginger and is quite delicious served with coconut milk or cream. When cooked, black rice still retains its husk and has a lovely nutty texture.*

SERVES 6

INGREDIENTS
115g/4oz/⅔ cup black glutinous rice
475ml/16fl oz/2 cups water
1cm/½in piece fresh root ginger, peeled and bruised
50g/2oz/⅓ cup dark brown sugar
50g/2oz/¼ cup caster (superfine) sugar
300ml/½ pint/1¼ cups coconut milk or coconut cream, to serve

1 Put the black glutinous rice in a sieve (strainer) and rinse well under plenty of cold running water. Drain the rice and place in a large pan, along with the water. Bring the water to the boil and stir it as it heats, to prevent the rice from settling on the base of the pan and sticking. Cover the pan and cook over a very low heat for about 30 minutes.

2 Add the ginger and both types of sugar to the pan. Cook for about 15 minutes more, adding a little more water if necessary, or until the rice is cooked and porridge-like in consistency.

3 Remove the ginger and pour the rice pudding into individual bowls. Serve warm, topped with coconut milk or coconut cream.

COOK'S TIP
Canned coconut milk and cream is easy to make at home. Blend 225g/8oz/2⅔ cups desiccated (dry unsweetened shredded) coconut with 450ml/¾ pint/ 1¾ cups boiling water in a food processor for 30 seconds, then cool slightly. Tip into a muslin-(cheesecloth-)lined sieve and twist the muslin to extract as much liquid as possible.

VIETNAM & THE PHILIPPINES

Vietnam borders China, Laos and Cambodia, in the heart of South-east Asia. It is therefore not surprising that its cuisine shares many of the characteristics of its neighbours' culinary heritages. In the north, nearest China, stir-fries and mildly flavoured curries are very popular; further south there is a strong French influence, and the staple, rice, is joined by baguettes. Pâtés, herb salads, rare beef and casseroles feature alongside more traditional dishes served with the pungent fish sauce, nuoc cham. In the Philippines, dishes such as Puchero, Escabèche and Adobo of Pork and Chicken owe much to their Spanish origins but have their own distinct flavour.

SWEET & SOUR PORK & PRAWN SOUP

This main course soup has a sour, rich flavour. Underripe fruits and vegetables provide a special tartness to the dish, creating a unique taste sensation.

SERVES 4–6

INGREDIENTS

350g/12oz lean pork, diced
225g/8oz raw or cooked prawn (shrimp) tails
30ml/2 tbsp tamarind sauce
juice of 2 limes
1 small green guava, peeled, halved and seeded
1 small, underripe mango, peeled, stoned (pitted) and chopped
1.4 litres/2½ pints/6¼ cups chicken stock
15ml/1 tbsp fish or soy sauce
285g/10oz sweet potato, peeled and cut into even-size pieces
225g/8oz unripe tomatoes, quartered
115g/4oz green beans, topped, tailed and halved
1 star fruit, thickly sliced
75g/3oz green cabbage, shredded
salt
5ml/1 tsp crushed black pepper
2 spring onions (scallions), shredded, to garnish
2 limes, quartered, to garnish

1 Trim any fat off the pork, peel the prawn tails and set aside. Put the tamarind sauce and lime juice into a pan, then add the pork, guava and mango. Pour in the chicken stock. Add the fish or soy sauce and simmer, uncovered, for about 30 minutes.

2 Add the sweet potato, tomatoes, green beans, star fruit, cabbage and the prawns to the pan. Simmer the soup for 10–15 minutes. Adjust the seasoning if necessary, garnish with shredded spring onions and serve.

Pork & Noodle Broth with Prawns

This quick and delicious recipe can be made with other meats. Try using 200g/7oz boneless skinless chicken breast instead of pork fillet, if you prefer.

SERVES 4–6

INGREDIENTS
350g/12oz pork chops or 200g/7oz pork fillet
225g/8oz fresh prawn (shrimp) tails or cooked prawns (shrimp)
150g/5oz thin egg noodles
15ml/1 tbsp vegetable oil
10ml/2 tsp sesame oil
4 shallots or 1 onion, sliced
1cm/½in piece fresh root ginger, finely sliced
1 garlic clove, crushed
5ml/1 tsp granulated sugar
1.4 litres/2½ pints/6¼ cups chicken stock
2 lime leaves
45ml/3 tbsp fish sauce
juice of ½ lime
4 sprigs coriander (cilantro) and 2 spring onions (scallions), green part only, chopped, to garnish

1 If using chops, trim away any fat and bone; freeze for 30 minutes, then slice thinly. If using fresh prawns, peel and devein them. Cook the noodles according to the instructions on the packet. Drain and refresh under cold water. Set aside.

2 Heat the vegetable and sesame oils in a large pan, add the shallots or onion and brown evenly, for 3–4 minutes. Remove from the pan and set aside. Add the ginger, garlic, sugar and chicken stock and bring to a simmer with the lime leaves. Add the fish sauce and lime juice. Add the pork, then simmer for 15 minutes. Add the prawns and noodles and simmer for 3–4 minutes. Serve in soup bowls garnished with coriander and spring onions.

ASPARAGUS & CRAB SOUP

There is a strong French influence on Vietnamese cooking, which is shown here in the use of asparagus. It combines perfectly with crab in this delicious soup, Cahn Cua.

SERVES 4–6

INGREDIENTS
900ml/1½ pints/3¾ cups chicken stock, preferably home-made
350g/12oz asparagus spears, trimmed and halved
30–45ml/2–3 tbsp sunflower oil
6 shallots, chopped
115g/4oz crab meat, fresh or canned, chopped
15ml/1 tbsp cornflour (cornstarch), mixed to a paste with water
30ml/2 tbsp fish sauce
1 egg, lightly beaten
snipped fresh chives, plus extra to garnish
salt and ground black pepper

1 Pour the chicken stock into a large pan and bring to the boil. Add the asparagus and cook for 5–6 minutes until tender. Drain, reserving the stock.

2 Heat the oil in a large wok or frying pan and stir-fry the chopped shallots for 2 minutes, without allowing them to brown. Add the asparagus spears, chopped crab meat and chicken stock.

3 Bring the mixture to the boil and cook for 3 minutes, then remove the wok or pan from the heat and spoon some of the liquid into the cornflour mixture. Return this to the wok or pan and stir until the soup begins to thicken slightly.

4 Stir the fish sauce into the soup, season to taste, then pour in the beaten egg, stirring briskly so that the egg forms threads. Finally, stir the snipped chives into the soup and serve immediately, garnished with chives.

COOK'S TIP
If fresh asparagus isn't available, use a 350g/12oz
can asparagus. Drain and halve the spears.

SAVOURY PORK PIES

These pies, called empanadas, *are native to Galicia in Spain and were brought to the Philippines in the sixteenth century by Spanish merchants.*

MAKES 12 PASTRIES

INGREDIENTS
350g/12oz frozen shortcrust pastry, thawed

FOR THE FILLING
15ml/1 tbsp vegetable oil
1 onion, chopped
1 garlic clove, crushed
5ml/1 tsp dried thyme
115g/4oz minced (ground) pork
5ml/1 tsp paprika
1 hard-boiled (hard-cooked) egg, chopped
1 gherkin, chopped
30ml/2 tbsp chopped fresh parsley
vegetable oil, for deep-frying
salt and ground black pepper

To make the filling, heat the vegetable oil in a frying pan or wok and soften the onion, garlic and thyme without browning, for about 3–4 minutes. Add the pork and paprika then brown evenly for 6–8 minutes.

Season the filling well, turn out into a bowl and cool. When the mixture has cooled completely, add the hard-boiled egg, gherkin and parsley.

Roll out the pastry on a floured work surface and cut out 12 circles, 12.5cm/5in diameter. Place 15ml/1 tbsp of the filling on each circle, moisten the edges with a little water, fold over and seal.

Heat the vegetable oil in a deep-fryer fitted with a basket, to 196°C/385°F. Place 3 pies at a time in the basket and deep-fry until golden brown. Frying should take at least 1 minute or the inside filling will not be heated through. Serve warm in a basket covered with a napkin.

VIETNAMESE RICE PAPER ROLLS

Rice paper wrappers come in small and large rounds and can be bought from Asian supermarkets. They soften when brushed with warm water, but they are very brittle so must be handled with care. Casualties can be used for patching other papers.

SERVES 8

INGREDIENTS

2 litres/3½ pints/8 cups water
1 small onion, sliced
a few fresh coriander (cilantro) stems
30ml/2 tbsp fish sauce
225g/8oz piece belly pork, boned and rind removed
50g/2oz fine rice vermicelli
225g/8oz/4 cups beansprouts, rinsed and drained
8 crisp lettuce leaves, halved
fresh mint and coriander (cilantro) leaves
175g/6oz peeled cooked prawns (shrimp), thawed if frozen
16 large rice papers

FOR THE BLACK BEAN SAUCE

15–30ml/1–2 tbsp groundnut (peanut) oil
2 garlic cloves, crushed
1 fresh red chilli, seeded and sliced
60–75ml/4–5 tbsp canned black salted beans
30ml/2 tbsp fish sauce
5ml/1 tsp rice vinegar
10–15ml/2–3 tsp light brown sugar
15ml/1 tbsp crunchy peanut butter
15ml/1 tbsp sesame seeds, dry-fried
5ml/1 tsp sesame oil
90ml/6 tbsp fish, pork or chicken stock

Mix the water, onion slices, coriander stems and fish sauce in a large pan. Bring to the boil. Add the pork and boil for 20–30 minutes, turning the pork from time to time until it is tender when tested with a skewer. Lift the pork from the pan, leave to cool, then slice into thin strips. (Strain the stock and reserve it for making soup.)

2 Make the sauce. Heat the groundnut oil in a frying pan and fry the garlic and chilli for 1 minute. Stir in all the remaining ingredients, mix well, then transfer to a food processor and process briefly. Pour into a serving bowl and leave to cool.

3 Soak the rice vermicelli in warm water until softened. Drain well, then snip into neat lengths. Bring a pan of water to the boil and add the vermicelli. As soon as the water boils again, after about 1 minute, drain the noodles, rinse them under cold water, then drain them again. Put them in a serving bowl. Put the beansprouts in a separate dish, and arrange the lettuce and mint and coriander leaves on a platter. Put the prawns in a bowl.

4 When almost ready to serve, place the rice papers two at a time on a dishtowel and brush both sides with warm water to soften them.

5 Transfer two rice papers very carefully to each of eight individual serving plates. Each guest places a piece of lettuce on a rice paper wrapper at the end closest to them, topping it with some of the noodles and beansprouts, a few mint or coriander leaves and some strips of pork.

6 They then roll up one turn and place a few prawns on the open part of the wrapper, then continue rolling to make a neat parcel. The roll can be cut in half, if preferred, then it is dipped in the black bean sauce before being eaten. The second wrapper is filled and eaten in the same way.

CHA GIO & NUOC CHAM

These immensely popular crispy spring rolls (cha gio) *are served with a delicious, spicy sauce* (nuoc cham). *Chinese spring roll wrappers are used here instead of the rice papers traditionally used in Vietnam.*

MAKES 15

INGREDIENTS
25g/1oz cellophane noodles soaked for 10 minutes in hot water
6–8 dried wood ears, soaked for 30 minutes in warm water
225g/8oz minced (ground) pork
225g/8oz fresh or canned crab meat
4 spring onions (scallions), trimmed and finely chopped
5ml/1 tsp fish sauce
250g/9oz packet spring roll wrappers
flour and water paste, to seal
vegetable oil, for deep-frying
salt and ground black pepper

FOR THE SAUCE
2 fresh red chillies, seeded and pounded to a paste
2 garlic cloves, crushed
15ml/1 tbsp sugar
45ml/3 tbsp fish sauce
juice of 1 lime or ½ lemon

> ### COOK'S TIP
> *Serve these rolls Vietnamese-style, if you like, by wrapping each roll in a lettuce leaf together with a few sprigs of fresh mint and coriander (cilantro) and a stick of cucumber.*

Make the *nuoc cham* sauce. Mix the chillies, garlic, sugar and fish sauce in a bowl and stir in lime or lemon juice to taste. Set aside. Drain the noodles and snip into 2.5cm/1in lengths, using a pair of scissors. Drain the wood ears, trim away any rough stems and slice finely.

2 Mix the noodles and the wood ears with the pork and set aside. Remove any cartilage from the crab meat and add to the pork mixture with the spring onions and fish sauce. Season to taste, mixing well.

3 Place a spring roll wrapper in front of you, diamond-fashion. Spoon some mixture just below the centre, fold over the nearest point and roll once.

4 Fold in the sides to enclose, then brush the edges with flour paste and roll up to seal. Repeat with the remaining wrappers and filling.

5 Heat the oil in a wok or deep-fryer to 190°C/375°F. Deep-fry the rolls in batches for 8–10 minutes or until they are cooked through. Drain them well on kitchen paper and serve hot. To eat, dip the rolls in the *nuoc cham* sauce

FILIPINO PRAWN FRITTERS

Ukoy are a favourite snack or appetizer in the Philippines. Unusually, they are first shallow-fried, then deep-fried. They are best eaten piping hot fresh from the pan, first dipped in the piquant sauce.

SERVES 2–4

INGREDIENTS
16 raw prawns (shrimp) in the shell
225g/8oz/2 cups plain (all-purpose) flour
5ml/1 tsp baking powder
2.5ml/½ tsp salt
1 egg, beaten
1 small sweet potato
1 garlic clove, crushed
115g/4oz/2 cups beansprouts, soaked in cold water and well drained
vegetable oil, for shallow- and deep-frying
4 spring onions (scallions), chopped

FOR THE DIPPING SAUCE
1 garlic clove, sliced
45ml/3 tbsp rice or wine vinegar
15–30ml/1–2 tbsp water
6–8 small red chillies
salt

1 Make the dipping sauce. Combine the garlic, rice or wine vinegar, water and chillies and season with salt, then divide between two small bowls.

2 Put the whole prawns in a pan with water to cover. Bring to the boil, then simmer for 4–5 minutes or until the prawns are pink and tender. Lift the prawns from the pan with a slotted spoon. Discard the heads and the body shell, but leave the tails intact. Strain and reserve the cooking liquid. Allow to cool.

3 Sift the flour, baking powder and salt into a bowl. Add the beaten egg and about 300ml/½ pint/1¼ cups of the prawn stock, then stir to make a batter that has the consistency of double (heavy) cream.

Peel and grate the sweet potato using the large holes on a grater, and add it to the batter, then stir in the crushed garlic and the drained beansprouts.

Pour the oil for shallow-frying into a large frying pan. It should be about 5mm/¼in deep. Pour more oil into a wok for deep-frying. Heat the oil in the frying pan. Taking a generous spoonful of the batter, drop it carefully into the frying pan so that it forms a fritter, about the size of a large drop scone.

Make more fritters in the same way. As soon as the fritters have set, top each one with a single prawn and a few chopped spring onions. Continue to cook over a medium heat for 1 minute, then remove with a fish slice.

Heat the oil in the wok to 190°C/375°F and deep-fry the prawn fritters in batches until they are crisp and golden brown. Drain the fritters on absorbent kitchen paper and then arrange on a serving plate or platter. Offer a bowl of the sauce for dipping.

COOK'S TIP
Use cooked tiger prawns (jumbo shrimp) if you prefer. In this case, make the batter using fish stock or chicken stock.

Braised Beef in Rich Peanut Sauce

Like many dishes brought to the Philippines by the Spanish, this slow-cooking *Estofado,* renamed *Kari Kari,* *retains much of its original charm. Rice and peanuts* *are used to thicken the juices, yielding a rich glossy sauce.*

SERVES 4–6

INGREDIENTS
900g/2lb stewing (braising) chuck, shin or blade steak
30ml/2 tbsp vegetable oil
15ml/1 tbsp annatto seeds or 5ml/1 tsp paprika and a pinch of turmeric
2 onions, chopped
2 garlic cloves, crushed
285g/10oz celeriac or swede (rutabaga), peeled and roughly chopped
425ml/15fl oz/1¾ cups beef stock
350g/12oz new potatoes, peeled and cut into large dice
15ml/1 tbsp fish or anchovy sauce
30ml/2 tbsp tamarind sauce
10ml/2 tsp sugar
1 bay leaf
1 thyme sprig
45ml/3 tbsp long grain rice
50g/2oz peanuts or 30ml/2 tbsp peanut butter
15ml/1 tbsp white wine vinegar
salt and ground black pepper

1 Cut the beef into 2.5cm/1in cubes and set aside. Heat the vegetable oil in a flameproof casserole, add the annatto seeds if using, and stir to colour the oil dark red. Remove the seeds with a slotted spoon and discard. If you are not using annatto seeds, paprika and turmeric will be added later.

2 Soften the onions, garlic and the celeriac or swede in the oil without letting them colour. Add the beef and seal to keep in the flavour. If you have not used annatto seeds to redden the sauce, stir the paprika and turmeric in with the beef. Add the beef stock, potatoes, fish or anchovy and tamarind sauces, sugar, bay leaf and thyme. Bring to a simmer and cook on top of the stove for 2 hours.

3 Meanwhile cover the rice with cold water and leave to stand for 30 minutes. Spread the peanuts, if using, out on a baking tray and roast under a hot grill (broiler), then rub the skins off in a clean dishtowel. Drain the rice and grind with the peanuts or peanut butter using a mortar and pestle or a food processor.

4 When the beef is tender, add 60ml/4 tbsp of the cooking liquid to the ground rice mixture. Blend smoothly and stir into the casserole. Simmer gently on the stove to thicken, for about 15–20 minutes. To finish, stir in the wine vinegar and season well with the salt and ground pepper. Remove the bay leaf.

Pork Balls with Minted Peanut Sauce

This recipe is equally delicious made with chicken breast meat. Both the pork balls and the sauce can be made ahead of time. Set the balls aside on a tray until you are ready to cook them.

SERVES 4–6

INGREDIENTS

285g/10oz leg of pork, trimmed and diced
1cm/½in piece fresh root ginger, peeled and grated
1 garlic clove, crushed
10ml/2 tsp sesame oil
15ml/1 tbsp medium-dry sherry
15ml/1 tbsp soy sauce
5ml/1 tsp sugar
2.5ml/½ tsp salt
a pinch of white pepper
1 egg white
350g/12oz long grain rice, washed and cooked for 15 minutes
50g/2oz ham, diced
1 Iceberg or Little Gem (Bibb) lettuce, to serve

FOR THE SAUCE

15ml/1 tbsp creamed coconut
75ml/5 tbsp/⅓ cup boiling water
30ml/2 tbsp smooth peanut butter
juice of 1 lime
1 red chilli, seeded and finely chopped
1 garlic clove, crushed
15ml/1 tbsp chopped fresh mint
15ml/1 tbsp chopped fresh coriander (cilantro)
15ml/1 tbsp fish sauce (optional)

To make the pork balls, place the diced pork, ginger and garlic in a food processor and blend for about 2–3 minutes until smooth. Add the sesame oil, sherry, soy sauce and sugar, salt and white pepper and blend again. Blend in the egg white.

Spread the cooked rice and ham in a shallow dish. Using wet hands, shape the pork mixture into thumb-size balls. Roll in the rice to cover and pierce each ball with a bamboo skewer.

To make the sauce, put the creamed coconut in a measuring jug (cup) and cover with the boiling water. Place the peanut butter in a bowl with the lime juice, chilli, garlic, mint and coriander. Combine evenly, then add the creamed coconut and season with the fish sauce, if using.

Place the pork balls in a bamboo steamer, cover and steam over a pan of boiling water for 8–10 minutes. Arrange the lettuce leaves on a large serving platter. Place the pork balls on the leaves and serve with the dipping sauce in small bowls for guests to help themselves.

PUCHERO

This Filipino pot-au-feu has Spanish connections. Sometimes it is served as two courses, first soup, then meat and vegetables with rice, but it can happily be served as is, on rice in a wide soup bowl. Either way it is very satisfying and a siesta afterwards is highly recommended.

SERVES 6–8

INGREDIENTS
225g/8oz/generous 1 cup chickpeas, soaked overnight in water
1 chicken, about 1.5kg/3–3½lb, cut into 8 pieces
350g/12oz belly pork, rinded, or pork fillet, cubed
2 chorizo sausages, thickly sliced
2 onions, chopped
2.5 litres/4 pints/10 cups water
60ml/4 tbsp vegetable oil
2 garlic cloves, crushed
3 large tomatoes, peeled, seeded and chopped
15ml/1 tbsp tomato purée (paste)
1–2 sweet potatoes, cut into 1cm/½in cubes
2 plantains, sliced (optional)
½ head Chinese leaves (Chinese cabbage), shredded
salt and ground black pepper
snipped fresh chives or chopped spring onions (scallions), to garnish
boiled rice, to serve

FOR THE SAUCE
1 large aubergine (eggplant)
3 garlic cloves, crushed
60–90ml/4–6 tbsp wine or cider vinegar

Drain the chickpeas and place in a large pan. Cover with water, bring to the boil and boil rapidly for 10 minutes. Reduce the heat and simmer for 30 minutes until the chickpeas are half tender. Drain.

Put the chicken pieces, pork, sausage and half of the onions in a large pan. Add the chickpeas and pour in the water. Bring to the boil and lower the heat, cover and simmer for 1 hour or until the meat is just tender when tested with a skewer.

3 Meanwhile, make the sauce. Preheat the oven to 200°C/400°F/Gas 6. Prick the aubergine in several places, then place it on a baking sheet and bake for about 30 minutes, or until very soft.

4 When cooled slightly, peel away the aubergine skin and scrape the flesh into a bowl. Mash the flesh with the crushed garlic, season to taste and add enough vinegar to sharpen the sauce, which should be quite piquant. Set aside.

5 Heat the vegetable oil in a frying pan and fry the remaining onion and garlic for 5 minutes, until soft but not brown. Stir in the tomatoes and tomato purée and cook for 2 minutes, then add this mixture to a large pan with the diced sweet potato. Add the plantains, if using. Cook over a gentle heat for about 20 minutes until the sweet potato is thoroughly cooked. Add the Chinese leaves for the last minute or two.

6 Spoon the thick meat soup into a soup tureen, and put the vegetables in a separate serving bowl. Garnish both with chives or spring onions, and serve with boiled rice and the aubergine sauce.

ADOBO OF PORK & CHICKEN

Four ingredients are essential in an adobo, one of the best-loved recipes in the Filipino repertoire. They are vinegar, garlic, peppercorns and bay leaves.

SERVES 4

INGREDIENTS
1 chicken, about 1.5kg/3–3½lb, or 4 chicken quarters
350g/12oz pork leg steaks (with fat)
10ml/2 tsp sugar
60ml/4 tbsp sunflower oil
75ml/5 tbsp wine or cider vinegar
4 plump garlic cloves, crushed
2.5ml/½ tsp black peppercorns, crushed lightly
15ml/1 tbsp light soy sauce
4 bay leaves
2.5ml/½ tsp annatto seeds, soaked in 30ml/2 tbsp boiling water,
  or 2.5ml/½ tsp ground turmeric
salt

FOR THE CHIPS
1–2 large plantains and/or 1 sweet potato
vegetable oil, for deep-frying

Wipe the chicken and cut into eight even-size pieces, or halve the chicken quarters, if using. Cut the pork into neat pieces. Spread out all the meat on a board, sprinkle lightly with sugar and set aside.

Heat the oil in a wok and fry the meat in batches, until golden on both sides. Add the vinegar, garlic, peppercorns, soy sauce and bay leaves; stir well. Strain the annatto seed liquid into the pan or stir in the turmeric. Add salt. Simmer, covered, for 35 minutes. Uncover for 10 minutes more.

For the plaintain chips, heat the oil in a deep-fryer to 195°C/390°F. Peel the plantains or sweet potato (or both), if you like, and slice into rounds or chips. Deep-fry them in batches until cooked but not brown. Drain on kitchen paper. When ready to serve, reheat the oil and fry until crisp. Remove the bay leaves from the adobo and serve with the plantain and/or sweet potato chips.

Hot Chilli Chicken with Ginger

This dish can also be prepared using duck legs. Be sure to remove the jointed parts of the drumsticks and thigh bones to make the meat easier to eat with chopsticks.

SERVES 4–6

INGREDIENTS
3 chicken legs (thighs and drumsticks)
15ml/1 tbsp vegetable oil
2cm/³⁄₄in piece fresh root ginger, peeled and finely chopped
1 garlic clove, crushed
1 small red chilli, seeded and finely chopped
5cm/2in piece lemon grass, shredded
150ml/¹⁄₄ pint/²⁄₃ cup chicken stock
15ml/1 tbsp fish sauce (optional)
10ml/2 tsp sugar
2.5ml/¹⁄₂ tsp salt
juice of ¹⁄₂ lemon
50g/2oz/¹⁄₂ cup raw peanuts
2 spring onions (scallions), shredded
1 zest of mandarin orange or satsuma, shredded
30ml/2 tbsp chopped fresh mint
rice or rice noodles, to serve

With the heel of the knife, chop through the narrow end of the drumsticks. Remove the jointed parts of the drumsticks and thigh bones, and the skin.

Heat the oil in a large wok or frying pan. Add the chicken, ginger, garlic, chilli and lemon grass and cook for 3–4 minutes. Add the chicken stock, fish sauce if using, sugar, salt and lemon juice. Cover and simmer for 30–35 minutes.

Grill (broil) the peanuts until evenly brown, about 2–3 minutes. Turn out on to a dishtowel and rub to loosen the skins.

Serve the chicken scattered with roasted peanuts, spring onions, citrus zest and mint. Serve with rice or rice noodles.

CHICKEN, VEGETABLE & CHILLI SALAD

This salad is known as Goi Tom *in Vietnam. It is full of surprising textures and flavours. Serve as a light lunch dish or for supper with crusty French bread.*

SERVES 4

INGREDIENTS
225g/8oz Chinese leaves (Chinese cabbage)
2 carrots, cut in matchsticks
½ cucumber, cut in matchsticks
2 fresh red chillies, seeded and cut into thin strips
1 small onion, sliced into fine rings
4 gherkins, sliced, plus 45ml/3 tbsp of the liquid
50g/2oz/½ cup peanuts, lightly ground
225g/8oz cooked chicken, finely sliced
1 garlic clove, crushed
5ml/1 tsp sugar
30ml/2 tbsp cider or white vinegar
salt

1 Finely slice the Chinese leaves and set aside with the carrot matchsticks. Spread out the cucumber matchsticks on a board and sprinkle with salt. Set aside for about 15 minutes.

2 Mix together the chillies and onion rings, then add the sliced gherkins and peanuts. Tip the salted cucumber into a colander, rinse well and pat dry.

3 Put all the vegetables into a salad bowl and add the chilli mixture and chicken. Mix the gherkin liquid with the garlic, sugar and vinegar. Pour over the salad, toss lightly and serve.

COOK'S TIP
Add a little more cider or white wine vinegar to the dressing if a sharper taste is preferred.

Honey-glazed Quail with Five-spice Marinade

Chinese supermarkets sell five-spice powder in packets. Provided the blend is not kept for longer than 3 months, the flavour can be good, and provides a useful alternative to making your own.

Serves 4–6

Ingredients
4 quails, cleaned
2 pieces star anise
10ml/2 tsp ground cinnamon
10ml/2 tsp fennel seeds
10ml/2 tsp Sichuan or Chinese pepper
pinch of ground cloves
1 small onion, finely chopped
1 garlic clove, crushed
60ml/4 tbsp clear honey
30ml/2 tbsp dark soy sauce
2 spring onions (scallions), chopped, mixed with the zest of 1 satsuma, shredded,
   to garnish
banana leaves, to serve

1 Remove the backbones from the quails by cutting down either side with a pair of kitchen scissors. Flatten the birds with the palm of your hand and secure each bird using 2 bamboo skewers.

2 Grind the star anise, cinnamon, fennel seeds, pepper and cloves using a mortar and pestle. Add the onion, garlic, honey and soy sauce, and combine well. Place the quails in a flat dish, cover with the marinade and leave for at least 8 hours.

3 Preheat a grill (broiler) or barbecue to a medium heat and cook the quails for 7–8 minutes on each side, basting occasionally with the marinade.

4 Arrange the quails on a bed of banana leaves, garnish with the spring onion and satsuma mixture and serve.

Escabeche

This pickled fish dish is eaten wherever there are – or have been – Spanish settlers.
Here it has been modified to reflect the Chinese influence on Filipino cuisine.

SERVES 6

INGREDIENTS

675–900g/1½–2lb white fish fillets, such as sole or plaice
45–60ml/3–4 tbsp seasoned plain (all-purpose) flour
vegetable oil, for shallow-frying

FOR THE SAUCE

30ml/2 tbsp vegetable oil
2.5cm/1in piece fresh root ginger, peeled and thinly sliced
2–3 garlic cloves, crushed
1 onion, cut into thin rings
½ large green (bell) pepper, seeded and cut in small neat squares
½ large red (bell) pepper, seeded and cut in small neat squares
1 carrot, cut into matchsticks
25ml/1½ tbsp cornflour (cornstarch)
450ml/¾ pint/scant 2 cups water
45–60ml/3–4 tbsp herb or cider vinegar
15ml/1 tbsp light soft brown sugar
5–10ml/1–2 tsp fish sauce
salt and ground black pepper
1 small chilli, seeded and sliced, and spring onions (scallions),
  finely shredded, to garnish (optional)
boiled rice, to serve

COOK'S TIP
Red snapper or small sea bass could be used for this
recipe, in which case ask your fishmonger to cut the
fish into fillets for you.

Wipe the fish fillets and leave them whole, or cut into serving portions, if you like. Pat dry on kitchen paper then dust lightly with the seasoned flour.

Heat oil for shallow-frying in a frying pan and fry the fish in batches until golden and almost cooked. Transfer to an ovenproof dish and keep warm.

Make the sauce in a wok or large frying pan. Heat the oil and fry the ginger, garlic and onion for 5 minutes or until the onion is softened but not browned.

Add the green and red pepper squares and carrot matchsticks to the wok or pan, and stir-fry for about 1 minute.

Put the cornflour in a bowl and add a little of the water to make a paste. Stir in the remaining water, vinegar and sugar. Pour the cornflour mixture over the vegetables in the wok and stir until the sauce boils and thickens a little. Season with fish sauce and salt and ground black pepper.

Add the fried fish to the sauce and reheat briefly without stirring. Transfer to a warmed serving platter and garnish with chilli and spring onions, if liked. Serve immediately with boiled rice.

SINIGANG

Many Filipinos would consider this soured soup-like stew to be their national dish.
It is always served with noodles or rice, and fish – prawns (shrimp) or thin slivers of
fish fillet – is often added for good measure.

SERVES 4–6

INGREDIENTS
15ml/1 tbsp tamarind pulp
150ml/¼ pint/⅔ cup warm water
2 tomatoes
115g/4oz spinach or Chinese kangkong leaves
115g/4oz peeled cooked large prawns (shrimp), thawed if frozen
1.2 litres/2 pints/5 cups fish stock
½ mooli (daikon), peeled and finely diced
115g/4oz green beans, cut into 1cm/½in lengths
225g/8oz piece of cod or haddock fillet, skinned and cut into strips
a little fish sauce
squeeze of lemon juice
salt and ground black pepper
boiled rice or noodles, to serve

1 Put the tamarind pulp in a bowl and pour over the warm water. Set aside while you peel and chop the tomatoes, discarding the seeds. Strip the spinach or kangkong leaves from the stems and tear into small pieces.

2 Remove the heads and shells from the prawns, leaving the tails intact, then set aside until required.

3 Pour the fish stock into a large pan and add the diced mooli. Cook for about 5 minutes, then add the green beans and continue to cook for a further 3–5 minutes.

4 Add the fish strips, tomato and spinach or kangkong leaves. Strain in the tamarind juice and cook for 2 minutes. Stir in the prawns and cook for 1–2 minutes to heat through. Season with salt and pepper and add a little fish sauce and lemon juice to taste. Transfer to individual serving bowls and serve immediately, with boiled rice or noodles.

Exotic Fruit Salad

A variety of fruits can be used for this salad depending on what is available. Look out for mandarin oranges, star fruit, papaya and passion fruit.

INGREDIENTS
85g/3oz/6 tbsp sugar
300ml/½ pint/1¼ cups water
30ml/2 tbsp stem (crystallized) ginger syrup
2 pieces star anise
2.5cm/1in piece cinnamon stick
1 clove
juice of ½ lemon
2 mint sprigs
1 mango, peeled and sliced
2 bananas, sliced
8 lychees, fresh or canned
225g/8oz fresh strawberries, trimmed and halved
2 pieces stem (crystallized) ginger, cut into sticks
1 pineapple

1 Put the sugar into a pan with the water, ginger syrup, star anise, cinnamon, clove, lemon juice and mint. Bring to the boil and simmer for 3 minutes. Strain into a large bowl and leave to cool.

2 Top and tail the mango and remove the outer skin. Stand the mango on one end and remove the flesh in two pieces either side of the flat stone (pit). Slice evenly and add to the syrup. Add the bananas, lychees, strawberries and ginger. Chill until ready to serve.

Cut the pineapple in half down the centre. Cut out the flesh with a small serrated knife to make two boat shapes. Cut the flesh into large chunks and place in the cooled syrup.

Spoon enough of the fruit salad into the pineapple halves to fill them and bring to the table on a large serving dish. There will be enough fruit salad left over to refill the pineapple boats if necessary.

LECHE FLAN

Serve this delicious baked custard with whipped cream or crème fraîche. The use of evaporated milk reflects the fifty years of American presence in the Philippines.

SERVES 8

INGREDIENTS
5 large eggs
30ml/2 tbsp caster (superfine) sugar
few drops vanilla essence (extract)
410g/14½oz can evaporated milk
300ml/½ pint/1¼ cups milk
5ml/1 tsp finely grated lime rind
strips of lime rind, to decorate

FOR THE CARAMEL
225g/8oz/1 cup sugar
120ml/4fl oz/½ cup water

1 Make the caramel. Put the sugar and water in a heavy pan. Stir to dissolve the sugar, then boil without stirring until golden. Quickly pour into eight ramekins, rotating them to coat the sides. Set aside to set.

2 Preheat the oven to 150°C/300°F/Gas 2. Beat the eggs, sugar and vanilla essence in a bowl. Mix the evaporated milk and fresh milk in a pan. Heat to just below boiling point, then pour on to the egg mixture, stirring all the time. Strain the custard mixture into a jug (pitcher), add the grated lime rind and cool. Pour into the caramel-coated ramekins.

Place the ramekins in a roasting pan and pour in enough warm water to come halfway up the sides of the dishes.

Transfer the roasting pan to the oven and cook the custards for 35–45 minutes or until they just shimmer when the ramekins are gently shaken.

Serve the custards in their ramekin dishes or by inverting on to serving plates, in which case break the caramel and use as decoration. The custards can be served warm or cold, decorated with strips of lime rind.

CHURROS

These irresistible fritters, which are often served with hot chocolate or coffee, came to the Philippines with the Spanish merchants who were keen to keep memories of their homeland alive.

MAKES ABOUT 24

INGREDIENTS
450ml/15fl oz/scant 2 cups water
15ml/1 tbsp olive oil
15ml/1 tbsp sugar, plus extra for sprinkling
2.5ml/½ tsp salt
150g/5oz/1¼ cups plain (all-purpose) flour
1 large (US extra large) egg
sunflower oil, for deep-frying
caster (superfine) sugar, for sprinkling

1 Mix the water, oil, sugar and salt in a large pan and bring to the boil. Remove from the heat, and then sift in the flour. Beat well with a wooden spoon until the mixture is smooth.

2 Beat in the egg to make a smooth, glossy mixture with a piping consistency. Spoon into a pastry bag fitted with a large star nozzle.

3 Heat the oil in a wok or deep-fryer to 190°C/375°F. Carefully pipe two loops of the mixture into the hot oil. Cook the loops, two at a time, for 3–4 minutes until they are golden all over but not browned.

4 Lift out the churros with a wire skimmer or slotted spoon and drain them on kitchen paper. Repeat with the remaining mixture Dredge the churros with caster sugar and serve warm.

COOK'S TIP
If you don't have a piping bag, you could fry teaspoons of mixture in the same way. Don't try to fry too many churros at a time as they swell a little during cooking.

COCONUT RICE FRITTERS

These delicious fritters can be served at any time of the day, with a mug of steaming coffee or hot chocolate. They make a wonderful treat.

MAKES 28 FRITTERS

INGREDIENTS
150g/5oz long grain rice, cooked
30ml/2 tbsp coconut milk powder
45ml/3 tbsp sugar
2 egg yolks
juice of ½ lemon
85g/3oz desiccated (dry unsweetened shredded) coconut
oil, for deep-frying
icing (confectioners') sugar, for dusting

1 Place two-thirds of the rice in a mortar and pound with a pestle until smooth and sticky. Alternatively, use a food processor. Turn out into a large bowl, combine with the remaining rice, the coconut milk powder, sugar, egg yolks and lemon juice. Spread the desiccated coconut on to a tray, divide the mixture into thumb-size pieces, roll into balls, then roll in the coconut to coat.

2 Heat the oil in a wok or deep-fryer fitted with a wire basket to 180°C/350°F. Fry the coconut rice balls, 3–4 at a time, for 1–2 minutes until the coconut is evenly brown. Turn out on to a plate and dust with icing sugar. Place a wooden skewer in each fritter and serve with milky coffee or hot chocolate.

Ensaimadas

These sweet bread rolls are a popular snack in the Philippines and come with various fillings, several of them savoury. This version includes cheese.

Makes 10–12

INGREDIENTS
30ml/2 tbsp caster (superfine) sugar, plus extra for sprinkling
150ml/¼ pint/⅔ cup warm water
15ml/1 tbsp dried active yeast
450g/1lb/4 cups strong white bread flour
5ml/1 tsp salt
115g/4oz/½ cup butter, softened, plus 30ml/2 tbsp melted butter for brushing
4 egg yolks
90–120ml/6–8 tbsp warm milk
115g/4oz/1 cup grated Cheddar cheese (or similar well-flavoured hard cheese)

1 Dissolve 5ml/1 tsp of the sugar in the water; sprinkle in the yeast. Stir, then set aside for 10 minutes. Sift the flour and salt into a large bowl.

2 Cream the butter with the remaining sugar in a large bowl until fluffy. Beat in the egg yolks and a little of the flour. Gradually stir in the remaining flour with the yeast mixture and enough milk to form a soft dough. Transfer to an oiled plastic bag and close loosely. Leave in a warm place until doubled in bulk.

3 On a floured surface, knock back the dough, then roll it out into a rectangle. Brush the surface with half the melted butter, scatter with the cheese, then roll up Swiss-roll style. Knead again; divide into 10–12 pieces.

4 Roll each piece of dough into a thin rope, about 38cm/15in long. On greased baking sheets, coil each rope into a loose spiral. Tuck the ends under. Leave to rise, in a warm place, for 45 minutes. Preheat the oven to 220°C/425°F/Gas 7.

5 Bake the ensaimadas for 15–20 minutes. Remove from the oven, then brush with the remaining melted butter and sprinkle with caster sugar. Serve warm.

JAPAN & KOREA

The food of Japan is unique and the Japanese cooks' skill in preparing and serving fish is legendary. This is partly due to the fact that the country has abundant fish stocks and only limited land for grazing but also because the government banned the consumption of meat for many years, except by the sick, because it was believed to increase aggression. The 200-year ban on foreigners from 1640 also meant that food in Japan remained true to its origins and became exquisitely refined. Aesthetics are as important as taste to the Japanese, and even the humblest dish is served with great artistry. Korea, which borders China to the north, has a cuisine that features seven basic flavours – garlic, ginger, pepper, soy sauce, spring onions, sesame oil and toasted sesame seeds – producing delicious and surprisingly varied results.

MISO SOUP

This light soup is one of the most commonly eaten dishes in Japan, and it is usually served with every meal that includes rice. Miso paste is made from fermented soya beans and gives this soup its distinctive flavour.

SERVES 4

INGREDIENTS
½ packet silken tofu, drained weight about 150g/5oz
1 litre/1¾ pints/4 cups freshly made dashi or instant dashi
10g/¼oz dried wakame seaweed
60ml/4 tbsp white or red miso paste
2 spring onions (scallions), shredded, to garnish

1 Cut the tofu into 1cm/½in cubes. Bring the dashi to the boil, lower the heat and add the wakame seaweed. Simmer for 1–2 minutes.

2 Pour a little of the soup into a bowl and add the miso paste, stirring until it dissolves. Pour the mixture back into the pan.

3 Add the cubes of tofu and heat through for about 1 minute. Ladle the soup into warmed serving dishes and serve immediately, garnished with the shredded spring onions.

COOK'S TIP
When the stock begins to boil, reduce the heat at once and simmer gently. If boiled for too long, the delicate flavour of the soup will be lost.

Rice Triangles

Picnics are very popular in Japan and rice shapes – onigiri – are ideal picnic fare.
You can put anything you like in the rice, so you could invent your own onigiri.

Serves 4

Ingredients

1 salmon steak
15ml/1 tbsp salt
450g/1lb/4 cups freshly cooked sushi rice
4 umeboshi (pickled plums)
½ sheet nori seaweed, cut into four equal strips
white and black sesame seeds, for sprinkling

1 Grill the salmon steak for 4–5 minutes on each side, until the flesh flakes easily when it is tested with the tip of a sharp knife. Set aside to cool while you make other *onigiri*. When the salmon is cold, flake it, discarding any skin and bones.

2 Put the salt in a bowl. Spoon a quarter of the warm cooked rice into a small rice bowl. Make a hole in the middle of the rice and put in one umeboshi. Smooth the rice over to cover. Repeat with the remaining rice and umeboshi.

3 Wet the palms of both hands with cold water, then rub the salt evenly on to your palms. Tip one of the rice and umeboshi balls on to one hand. Use both hands to shape the rice into a triangular shape. Make three more triangles.

4 Mix the flaked salmon into the remaining rice, then shape it into triangles in the same way as for the umeboshi. Wrap a strip of nori around each of the umeboshi triangles. Sprinkle sesame seeds on the salmon triangles.

Simple Rolled Sushi

These simple rolls, known as hosomaki, *are an excellent way of learning the art of rolling sushi. They are very good for picnics and canapés and are always served cold.*

Makes 12 rolls or 72 slices

Ingredients
400g/14oz/2 cups sushi rice, soaked for 20 minutes in water
55ml/3½ tbsp rice vinegar
15ml/1 tbsp sugar
2.5ml/½ tsp salt
6 sheets nori seaweed
200g/7oz tuna, in one piece
200g/7oz salmon, in one piece
wasabi paste
½ cucumber, quartered lengthways and seeded
pickled ginger, to garnish (optional)
Japanese soy sauce, to serve

1 Drain the rice and place in a pan with 525ml/18fl oz/2¼ cups cold water. Cover, bring to the boil and cook for 20 minutes. In a separate pan, heat the vinegar, sugar and salt, stir well and cool. Add to the hot rice and set aside, covered, for about 20 minutes.

2 Cut the nori sheets in half lengthways. Cut the tuna and salmon into four long strips each. Place a sheet of nori, shiny side down, on a bamboo mat. Divide the rice into 12 equal portions. Spread one portion over the nori, leaving a 1cm/½in clear space at the top and bottom. Spread a little wasabi paste in a horizontal line along the middle of the rice and lay one strip of tuna on top.

3 Holding the mat and the edge of the nori nearest to you, roll up the nori and rice tightly into a cylinder with the tuna in the middle. Roll the sushi off the mat. Make 11 more rolls, four for each filling ingredient, but do not use wasabi with the cucumber. Cut each roll into six slices and stand them on a platter. Garnish with pickled ginger, if using, and serve with soy sauce.

Sashimi

This Japanese speciality – sliced raw fish – employs the cutting technique known in Japan as hira zukuri. *The perfectly cut fish is served with wasabi paste and soy sauce.*

SERVES 4

INGREDIENTS
2 fresh salmon fillets, skinned and any stray bones removed, about 400g/14oz in total
Japanese soy sauce and wasabi paste, to serve

FOR THE GARNISH
50g/2oz mooli (daikon), peeled
shiso leaves

Wrap the salmon in clear film (plastic wrap) and freeze for 10 minutes. Unwrap the fish and lay skinned side up with the thick end to your right and away from you. Use a long sharp knife and tilt it to the left. Slice carefully towards you, starting the cut from the point of the knife, then slide the slice away from the fillet, to the right. Always slice from the far side towards you.

Finely shred or grate the mooli and place it in a bowl of cold water. Leave to stand for about 5 minutes, then drain well.

Arrange the salmon slices on a serving platter, or divide equally among 4 serving plates.

Give guests their own platter, together with a garnish of mooli and shiso leaves. The fish is eaten dipped in soy sauce and wasabi paste.

COOK'S TIP
Salmon and tuna are among the most popular choices for sashimi, *although almost any type of fish can be used. If you are making* sashimi *for the first time, choose salmon or tuna and make sure you buy fish that is absolutely fresh.*

Assorted Tempura

Tempura is one of Japan's most famous and delicious dishes. Fish, rather than meat, is traditionally used, but choose any vegetable you like. The essence of really good tempura is that it should be cooked and served immediately.

SERVES 4–6

INGREDIENTS

1 small sweet potato, about 115g/4oz
8 large tiger prawns (jumbo shrimp)
1 small squid, cleaned
vegetable oil, for deep-frying
plain (all-purpose) flour, for coating
1 small carrot, cut into matchsticks
4 shiitake mushrooms, stalks removed
50g/2oz green beans, trimmed
1 red (bell) pepper, seeded and sliced into 2cm/³⁄₄in thick strips

FOR THE DIP

200ml/7fl oz/scant 1 cup water
45ml/3 tbsp mirin (sweet rice wine)
10g/¹⁄₄oz bonito flakes
45ml/3 tbsp Japanese soy sauce

FOR THE BATTER

1 egg
90ml/6 tbsp iced water
75g/3oz/³⁄₄ cup plain (all-purpose) flour
2.5ml/¹⁄₂ tsp baking powder
2 ice cubes

COOK'S TIP

Batter several carrots or beans at a time and deep fry in bunches. The mushrooms look best if only the undersides are dipped. Cut a cross in the upper side of the mushroom cap, if you like.

Make the dip. Put the water, mirin, bonito flakes and soy sauce in a pan. Bring to the boil, cool, then strain. Divide among 4–6 bowls. Slice the unpeeled sweet potato thinly. Put in a bowl with cold water to cover.

Peel the prawns, leaving the tails intact, and devein. Lay a prawn on its side. Make three or four diagonal slits, about two-thirds of the way in towards the back, leaving all the pieces attached. Repeat with the rest. Flatten with your fingers. Cut the body of the squid into 3cm/1¼in thick strips.

Make the batter. Put the egg in a large bowl, stir without beating and discard half. Add the water, flour and baking powder. Stir two or three times, leaving some flour unblended. Add the ice cubes.

Heat the oil in a deep-fryer to 185°C/ 365°F. Dust the prawns lightly with flour. Holding each in turn by the tail, dip them into the batter, then very carefully lower them into the hot oil; cook until golden. Fry the remaining prawns and the squid in the same way. Keep warm.

Reduce the temperature of the oil to 170°C/340°F. Drain the sweet potato and pat dry. Dip the vegetables into the batter and deep-fry (see Cook's Tip). Drain well, then keep warm. As soon as all the tempura are ready, serve with the dip.

GRILLED VEGETABLE STICKS

These kebabs are made with tofu, konnyaku – a type of Japanese gluten – and aubergine (eggplant). Soak the bamboo skewers in water overnight to prevent them burning.

SERVES 4

INGREDIENTS
1 × 285g/10¼oz packet tofu block
1 × 250g/9oz packet konnyaku
2 small aubergines (eggplant)
25ml/1½ tbsp toasted sesame oil

FOR THE YELLOW AND GREEN SAUCES
45ml/3 tbsp white miso
15ml/1 tbsp caster (superfine) sugar
5 young spinach leaves
2.5ml/½ tsp sansho
salt

FOR THE RED SAUCE
15ml/1 tbsp red miso
5ml/1 tsp caster (superfine) sugar
5ml/1 tsp mirin

TO GARNISH
pinch of white poppy seeds
15ml/1 tbsp toasted sesame seeds

Drain the liquid from the tofu packet and wrap the tofu in three layers of kitchen paper. Set a chopping board on top to press out the remaining liquid. Leave for 30 minutes until the excess liquid has been absorbed by the kitchen paper. Cut into eight 7.5 × 2 × 1cm/3 × ¾ × ½in slices.

Drain the liquid from the konnyaku. Cut it in half and put in a small pan with water to cover. Bring to the boil and cook for 5 minutes. Drain and cut it into eight 6 × 2 × 1cm/2½ × ¾ × ½in slices.

Cut the aubergines into two lengthways, then repeat with each half to make four flat slices. Soak in cold water for 15 minutes. Drain and pat dry.

4 To make the yellow sauce, mix the white miso and sugar in a pan, then cook over a low heat, stirring to dissolve the sugar. Remove from the heat. Place half the sauce in a small bowl.

5 Blanch the young spinach leaves in rapidly boiling water with a pinch of salt for 30 seconds and drain, then cool under running water. Squeeze out the water and chop finely. Transfer to a mortar and pound to a paste using a pestle. Mix the paste and sansho pepper into the bowl of yellow sauce to make the green sauce.

6 Put all the red sauce ingredients in a small pan and cook over a low heat, stirring constantly, until the sugar has dissolved. Remove from the heat.

7 Pierce the slices of tofu, konnyaku and aubergine with two bamboo skewers each. Heat the grill (broiler) to high. Brush the aubergine slices with sesame oil and grill (broil) for 7–8 minutes each side. Turn several times.

8 Grill the konnyaku and tofu slices for 3–5 minutes each side, or until lightly browned. Remove from the heat.

9 Spread the red miso sauce on the aubergine slices. Spread one side of the tofu slices with green sauce and one side of the konnyaku with the yellow miso sauce from the pan. Grill the slices for 1–2 minutes. Sprinkle the aubergines with poppy seeds. Sprinkle the konnyaku with sesame seeds and serve all together.

Straw Noodle Prawns & Sweet Ginger Dip

Prawns (shrimp) are a popular feature in Japanese cooking. Rarely are they more delicious than when wrapped in crispy noodles and seaweed.

SERVES 4–6

INGREDIENTS

85g/3oz somen noodles or vermicelli
2 sheets nori seaweed
12 large fresh prawn (shrimp) tails, peeled and deveined
vegetable oil, for deep-frying

FOR THE DIPPING SAUCE
90ml/6 tbsp soy sauce
30ml/2 tbsp sugar
2cm/¾in piece fresh root ginger, grated

1 Cover the somen noodles, if using, with boiling water and leave to soak for 1–2 minutes. Drain and dry thoroughly with kitchen paper. Cut the noodles into 7.5cm/3in lengths. If using vermicelli, cover with boiling water for 1–2 minutes to soften. Cut the nori into 1cm/½in strips, 5cm/2in long, and set aside. To make the dipping sauce, bring the soy sauce to the boil with the sugar and ginger. Simmer for 2–3 minutes, strain and cool.

2 Line up the noodles or vermicelli on a wooden board. Straighten each prawn by pushing a bamboo skewer through its length. Roll the prawns in the noodles so that the noodles stick and stand up around around each prawn. Moisten one end of the nori and wrap it around the noodles at the fat end of the prawn. Set aside.

3 Heat the vegetable oil in a deep-fryer, or wok fitted with a wire draining rack, to 180°C/350°F. Fry the prawns in the oil, two at a time, until the noodles or vermicelli are crisp and golden. To finish, cut off the bottom of the prawn (at the nori end) exposing a clean section of prawn. Drain well on kitchen paper and serve with the dipping sauce in a small dish.

CRAB & TOFU DUMPLINGS WITH DIPPING SAUCE

These little crab and ginger dumplings are traditionally served in Japan as a delicious side accompaniment.

MAKES 30

INGREDIENTS
115g/4oz frozen white crab meat, thawed
115g/4oz tofu, drained
1 egg yolk
30ml/2 tbsp rice flour or wheat flour
1.5ml/¼ tsp salt
30ml/2 tbsp finely chopped spring onion (scallion), green part only
2cm/¾in piece fresh root ginger, peeled and grated
10ml/2 tsp light soy sauce
vegetable oil, for deep-frying
50g/2oz mooli (daikon), finely grated

FOR THE DIPPING SAUCE
100ml/4fl oz/½ cup dashi or light vegetable stock
45ml/3 tbsp mirin, or 15ml/1 tbsp sugar
45ml/3 tbsp dark soy sauce

1 Squeeze as much moisture out of the crab meat as you can before using. Press the tofu through a fine strainer with the back of a tablespoon and combine with the crab meat in a bowl.

2 Add the egg yolk, rice flour, salt, spring onion, ginger and soy sauce to the tofu and crab meat, and stir to form a light paste. Set aside. To make the dipping sauce, combine the dashi or stock with the mirin or sugar and soy sauce.

3 Line a tray with kitchen paper. Heat the vegetable oil to 196°C/385°F. Shape the mixture to make thumb-size pieces. Fry six at a time for 1–2 minutes. Drain on the paper. Serve with the sauce and radish.

KIMCHI

No self-respecting Korean moves far without the beloved kimchi. *Chinese leaves are salted and flavoured with garlic, fresh root ginger and chilli to produce a pungently flavoured pickled cabbage. In the past, large stone pots were filled with kimchi, and buried in the ground to last through the winter months.*

SERVES 6–8

INGREDIENTS
675g/1½lb Chinese leaves (Chinese cabbage), shredded
2 hard pears, peeled and thinly sliced
60ml/4 tbsp salt
200ml/7fl oz/scant 1 cup water
4 spring onions (scallions), finely chopped
4 garlic cloves, crushed
2.5cm/1in piece fresh root ginger, peeled and finely chopped
10–15ml/2–3 tsp chilli powder

1 Place the shredded Chinese leaves and sliced pears in a large mixing bowl and sprinkle evenly with the salt. Mix well until thoroughly combined, then press down into the bowl.

2 Pour the water over the vegetables, then cover the bowl with a plate or clear film (plastic wrap) and leave overnight in a cool place. Next day, drain off the brine from the vegetables and set it aside.

3 Mix the brined vegetables with the spring onions, crushed garlic, fresh root ginger and chilli powder (wearing rubber gloves if you have sensitive skin). Then pack the mixture into a 900g/2lb jar or two smaller ones. Pour over the reserved brine to cover. Cover the jar with clear film (plastic wrap) and place in a warm place for 2–3 days, then store in the refrigerator.

COOK'S TIP
Kimchi can be stored in the refrigerator for several weeks. Do not keep longer than this.

Rolled Omelette

This is a firmly set, rolled omelette, cut into neat pieces and served cold. The texture should be smooth and soft, not leathery, and the flavour is sweet-savoury.

Serves 4

Ingredients
8 eggs
60ml/4 tbsp sugar
20ml/4 tsp Japanese soy sauce, plus extra to serve
90ml/6 tbsp sake or dry white wine
vegetable oil, for cooking
wasabi and a pickled ginger flower, to garnish

Put the eggs in a bowl and stir, using a pair of chopsticks and a cutting action. Combine the sugar, soy sauce and sake or wine in a small bowl, then stir into the eggs. Pour half the mixture into another bowl.

Heat a little oil in a frying pan, then wipe off the excess. Pour a quarter of the mixture from one bowl into the pan, tilting the pan to coat it thinly. When the edge has set, but the middle is moist, roll up the omelette towards you.

Moisten a piece of kitchen paper with oil and grease the empty side of the pan. Pour a third of the remaining egg into the pan. Lift the rolled egg up with your chopsticks and let the raw egg run underneath it. When the edge has set, roll up in the opposite direction, tilting the pan away from you.

Slide the roll towards you, grease the pan and pour in half the remaining mixture, letting the egg run under. When set, insert chopsticks in the side of the rolled omelette, then flip over towards the opposite side. Cook the remainder in the same way. Slide the roll so that its join is underneath. Cook for 10 seconds.

Slide the roll out on to a bamboo mat and roll up tightly, then press into a rectangular shape. Leave to cool. Cook the second batch in the same way. Slice the cold omelettes into 2.5cm/1in pieces, arrange on a platter and garnish with a little wasabi and with a pickled ginger flower. Serve with soy sauce.

MOOLI & CARROT SALAD

This dish, called namasu *in Japan, is essential for the New Year's celebration meal. The bright colour combination of white mooli and red carrot is particularly favoured by many Japanese as it is regarded as a symbol of happiness. Start preparations for this recipe the day before it is to be eaten.*

SERVES 4

INGREDIENTS
20cm/8in mooli (daikon)
2 carrots
5ml/1 tsp salt
45ml/3 tbsp caster (superfine) sugar
70ml/4½ tbsp rice vinegar
15ml/1 tbsp sesame seeds

1 Cut the mooli into three pieces, then thickly peel the skin. Peel the carrots and cut them into 5cm/2in pieces. Slice both vegetables very thinly lengthways then crossways to make very thin matchsticks. Alternatively, shred them with a grater.

2 Place the mooli and carrot in a mixing bowl. Sprinkle with the salt and mix well with your hands. Leave for about 30 minutes. Drain the vegetables in a strainer and gently squeeze out the excess liquid. Transfer to another mixing bowl.

3 Mix the sugar and rice vinegar together in a bowl. Stir well until the sugar has completely dissolved. Pour over the mooli and carrot, and leave for at least a day, mixing at least two to three times.

4 To serve, mix the two vegetables evenly and heap in the middle of a small bowl or a plate. Sprinkle with sesame seeds and serve.

FRIED AUBERGINE WITH MISO SAUCE

In nasu-miso, *stir-fried aubergine (eggplant) is coated in a rich miso sauce. Make sure the oil is smoking hot when adding the aubergine, so it does not absorb too much oil.*

SERVES 4

INGREDIENTS
2 large aubergines (eggplant)
1–2 dried red chillies, seeded
45ml/3 tbsp sake
45ml/3 tbsp mirin
45ml/3 tbsp caster (superfine) sugar
30ml/2 tbsp shoyu
45ml/3 tbsp red miso
90ml/6 tbsp sesame oil
salt

1 Cut the aubergines into bite-size pieces. Place in a colander, sprinkle with salt and leave for 30 minutes. Squeeze the aubergines. Chop the chillies into rings.

2 Mix the sake, mirin, sugar and shoyu in a cup. In a bowl, mix the red miso with 45ml/3 tbsp water to make a loose paste.

3 Heat the oil in a large pan; add the chilli. When the oil begins to smoke add the aubergine; stir-fry for 8 minutes. Lower the heat to medium.

4 Add the sake mixture to the pan, and stir for 2–3 minutes. Add the miso paste and cook, stirring, for another 2 minutes. Serve hot.

Pan-fried Tofu with Caramelized Sauce

Tofu in the West is often used as a meat substitute for vegetarians, as it was by Chinese Buddhist monks who brought vegetarian cookery into Japan. They invented many delicious and filling protein dishes from tofu and other soya bean products. This dish is a modern addition to that tradition.

SERVES 4

INGREDIENTS
2 × 285g/10¼oz packets tofu blocks
4 garlic cloves
10ml/2 tsp vegetable oil
50g/2oz/¼ cup butter, cut into 5 equal pieces
watercress, to garnish

FOR THE MARINADE
4 spring onions (scallions)
60ml/4 tbsp sake
60ml/4 tbsp shoyu (tamari or sashimi soy sauce, if available)
60ml/4 tbsp mirin

1 Unpack the tofu blocks and discard the liquid, then wrap in three layers of kitchen paper. Put a large plate or wooden chopping board on top as a weight and leave for 30 minutes to allow time for the excess liquid to be absorbed by the paper. This process makes the tofu firmer and, when cooked, it will crisp on the outside.

2 To make the marinade, chop the spring onions finely. Mix with the sake, shoyu and mirin in a ceramic or aluminium tray with sides or a wide, shallow bowl. Leave to stand for 15 minutes.

3 Slice the garlic very thinly to make garlic chips. Heat the vegetable oil in a frying pan and fry the garlic for a few moments until golden. Turn the chips frequently to prevent sticking and burning. Scoop them out on to kitchen paper, using a slotted spoon. Reserve the oil in the pan.

4 Unwrap the tofu. Slice one block horizontally in half, then cut each half into four pieces. Repeat with the other tofu block. Soak in the marinade for about 15 minutes.

5 Take out the marinated tofu and wipe off the excess marinade with kitchen paper. Reserve the marinade.

6 Reheat the oil in the frying pan and add one piece of butter. When the oil starts sizzling, reduce the heat to medium and add the pieces of tofu one by one. Cook in one layer, if possible.

7 Cover and cook until the edge of the tofu is browned and quite firm, approximately 5–8 minutes on each side. (If the edges burn but the centre is pale, reduce the heat.)

8 Pour the marinade into the pan. Cook for 2 minutes, or until the spring onion is very soft. Remove the tofu and arrange four pieces on each serving plate. Pour the thickened marinade and spring onion mixture over the tofu and top each piece with a piece of butter. Sprinkle with the garlic chips and garnish with watercress. Serve while still hot.

CHAP CHAE

This Korean stir-fry of mixed vegetables and noodles garnished attractively with the yellow and white egg shapes is typical of Korean cooking.

INGREDIENTS

225g/8oz rump (round) or sirloin steak
115g/4oz cellophane noodles, soaked for 20 minutes in hot water
4 Chinese dried mushrooms, soaked for 30 minutes in warm water
groundnut (peanut) oil, for stir-frying
2 eggs, separated
1 carrot, cut into matchsticks
1 onion, sliced
2 courgettes (zucchini) or ½ cucumber, cut into sticks
½ red (bell) pepper, seeded and cut into strips
4 button mushrooms, sliced
75g/3oz/1½ cups beansprouts, washed and drained
15ml/1 tbsp light soy sauce
salt and ground black pepper
sliced spring onions (scallions) and sesame seeds, to garnish

1 Put the steak in the freezer for about 10 minutes. Cut into thin slices and then into 5cm/2in strips. Mix the ingredients for the marinade in a shallow dish (see Cook's Tip), stir in the steak strips. Drain the noodles and cook in a pan of boiling water for 5 minutes. Drain, then snip into short lengths. Drain the mushrooms, cut off and discard the stems; slice the caps.

2 Heat the oil in a small frying pan. Beat the egg yolks and pour into the pan. When set, slide them on to a plate. Add the egg whites to the pan and cook until set. Cut both yolks and whites into diamond shapes and set aside.

3 Drain the beef. Heat the oil in a wok or large frying pan and stir-fry the beef until it changes colour. Add the carrot and onion and stir-fry for 2 minutes, then add the other vegetables, tossing them until just cooked. Add the noodles and season with soy sauce, salt and pepper. Cook for 1 minute. Spoon into a serving dish and garnish with egg, spring onions and sesame seeds.

Marinated Beef Steaks

Bulgogi *is a very popular dish for outdoor entertaining. Traditionally it would have been cooked on a Genghis Khan grill (broiler), which is shaped like the crown of a hat, but a ridged heavy frying pan or wok works almost as well.*

SERVES 3–4

INGREDIENTS
450g/1lb fillet of beef or rump (round) steak, in one piece
sesame oil, for frying

FOR THE MARINADE
150ml/¼ pint/⅔ cup dark soy sauce
30ml/2 tbsp sesame oil
30ml/2 tbsp sake or dry white wine
1 garlic clove, cut into thin slivers
15ml/1 tbsp sugar
30ml/2 tbsp crushed roasted sesame seeds
4 spring onions (scallions), cut into long lengths
salt and ground black pepper

1 Put the meat into the freezer until it is firm enough to slice very thinly and evenly. Arrange the slices of beef in a shallow glass dish.

2 Make the marinade. Mix the soy sauce, oil, sake or wine, garlic, sugar and sesame seeds in a bowl and add the spring onions. Season to taste.

3 Pour the marinade over the slices of beef and mix well. Cover the dish and transfer to the refrigerator. Chill for at least 3 hours or overnight.

4 Heat the merest slick of oil in a ridged heavy frying pan or wok. Drain the beef slices and fry over a high heat for a few seconds, turning once. Serve at once.

COOK'S TIP
Freezing the beef until it is firm allows the meat to be cut into wafer thin slices. This method is used by Japanese chefs when making sashimi.

SLICED SEARED BEEF

Japanese chefs use a cooking technique called tataki *to cook rare steak. They use a coal fire and sear a chunk of beef on long skewers, then plunge it into cold water to stop it cooking. Use a wire mesh grill over the heat source to cook this way.*

SERVES 4

INGREDIENTS
500g/1¼lb chunk of beef thigh (a long, thin chunk looks better than a thick, round chunk)
generous pinch of salt
10ml/2 tsp vegetable oil

FOR THE MARINADE
200ml/7fl oz/scant 1 cup rice vinegar
70ml/4½ tbsp sake
135ml/4½fl oz/scant ⅔ cup shoyu
15ml/1 tbsp caster (superfine) sugar
1 garlic clove, thinly sliced
1 small onion, thinly sliced
sansho

TO GARNISH
6 shiso leaves and shiso flowers (if available)
about 15cm/6in cucumber
½ lemon, thinly sliced
1 garlic clove, finely grated (optional)

Mix the marinade ingredients in a small pan and warm through until the sugar has dissolved. Remove from the heat and leave to cool.

Generously sprinkle the beef with the salt and rub well into the meat. Leave for 2–3 minutes, then rub the oil in evenly with your fingers.

Fill a large mixing bowl with plenty of cold water. Put a mesh grill (broiler) tray over the heat on the top of the stove, or heat a griddle to a high temperature. Sear the beef, turning frequently until about 5mm/¼in of the flesh in from the surface is cooked. Try not to burn grid marks on the meat. Immediately plunge the meat into the bowl of cold water for a few seconds to stop it from cooking further.

Wipe the meat with kitchen paper or a dishtowel and immerse fully in the marinade. Leave to marinate in a cool place for 1 day.

Next day, prepare the garnish. Chop the shiso leaves in half lengthways, then cut into very thin strips crossways. Slice the cucumber diagonally into 5mm/¼in thick oval shapes, then cut each oval into 5mm/¼in matchsticks. Scoop out the watery seed part first if using an ordinary salad cucumber.

Remove the meat from the marinade. Strain the remaining marinade through a sieve, reserving both the liquid and the marinated onion and garlic. Using a sharp knife, cut the beef thinly into slices of about 5mm/¼in thick.

Heap the cucumber sticks on a large serving plate and put the marinated onion and garlic on top. Arrange the beef slices as *sashimi*, leaning alongside or on the bed of cucumber and other vegetables, if you prefer. You can also either make a fan shape with the beef slices, or, if they are large enough, roll them.

Fluff the shiso strips and put on top of the beef. Garnish with some shiso flowers, if using. Scatter with the lemon slices, and serve with the reserved marinade in individual bowls.

To eat, take a few beef slices. Roll a slice with your choice of garnish, then dip it into the marinade. Add a little grated garlic, if you like.

COOK'S TIPS
• *If you don't have a mesh grill (broiler) or griddle, heat 15ml/1 tbsp vegetable oil in a hot frying pan to sear the beef. Wash all the oil from the meat and wipe off any excess with a kitchen paper.*
• *If preparing this dish ahead of time, spear the beef rolls with a cocktail stick (toothpick) to secure.*

Paper-thin Sliced Beef Cooked in Stock

The Japanese name for this dish, Shabu Shabu, *refers to "washing" the wafer-thin slices of beef in hot stock. Use a portable cooker to cook this meal at the table.*

SERVES 4

INGREDIENTS
600g/1lb 5oz boneless beef sirloin
2 thin leeks, trimmed and cut into 2 × 5cm/³⁄₄ × 2in strips
4 spring onions (scallions), quartered
8 shiitake mushrooms, stalks removed
175g/6oz oyster mushrooms, base part removed, torn into small pieces
½ head Chinese leaves (Chinese cabbage), base removed, cut into 5cm/2in squares
300g/11oz chrysanthemum leaves, halved
275g/10oz tofu, halved then cut in 2cm/³⁄₄in thick slices crossways
10 × 6cm/4 × 2½in kombu wiped with a damp cloth

FOR THE PONZU (CITRUS SAUCE)
juice of 1 lime made up to 120ml/4fl oz/½ cup with lemon juice
50ml/2fl oz/¼ cup rice vinegar
120ml/4fl oz/½ cup shoyu
20ml/4 tsp mirin
4 × 6cm/1½ × 2½in kombu
5g/⅛oz bonito flakes

FOR THE GOMA-DARE (SESAME SAUCE)
75g/3oz white sesame seeds
10ml/2 tsp caster (superfine) sugar
45ml/3 tbsp shoyu
15ml/1 tbsp sake
15ml/1 tbsp mirin
90ml/6 tbsp dashi stock

FOR THE CONDIMENTS
5–6cm/2–2½in mooli (daikon), trimmed and peeled
2 dried chillies, seeded and sliced
20 chives, finely snipped

1 Make the *ponzu*. Mix together the lime and lemon juice, vinegar, shoyu, mirin, dashi and bonito flakes in a glass jar and leave overnight. Strain and keep the liquid in the jar.

2 Make the *goma-dare*. Roast the sesame seeds in a dry frying pan on a low heat until the seeds pop. Grind the sesame seeds to form a smooth paste. Add the sugar and grind, then add the other ingredients, mixing well. Pour 30ml/2 tbsp into each of four small bowls, and put the rest in a jug (pitcher) or bowl.

3 Prepare the condiments. Pierce the cut ends of the mooli deeply 4–5 times with a skewer, then insert pieces of chilli. Leave for about 20 minutes, then finely grate the mooli into a sieve. Divide the pink mooli among four small bowls. Put the chives in another bowl.

4 Cut the meat into 1–2mm/¹⁄₁₆in thick slices, and place on a large serving plate. Arrange the vegetables and tofu on another large plate.

5 Fill a flameproof casserole three-quarters full of water and add the dashi. Bring everything to the table and heat the casserole.

6 Pour 45ml/3 tbsp *ponzu* into the grated mooli in each bowl, and add the chives to the bowls of *goma-dare*. When the water comes to the boil, remove the kombu and reduce the heat to medium-low. Add a handful of each ingredient except the beef to the casserole.

7 Each guest picks up a slice of beef using chopsticks and holds it in the stock for 3–10 seconds. Dip the beef into one of the sauces and eat. Remove the vegetables and other ingredients as they cook, and eat with the dipping sauces. Skim the surface occasionally.

COOK'S TIP
*Chrysanthemum leaves (shungiku) are the leaves of
the chrysanthemum vegetable, not the flower.*

SUKIYAKI

You will need a special cast-iron sukiyaki *pan and burner or a similar table-top cooker for this dish. It is great fun because guests can cook their own dinner in front of them, and then help themselves to the delicious morsels of food.*

SERVES 4

INGREDIENTS
1kg/2¼lb beef topside (pot roast), thinly sliced
lard, for cooking
4 leeks or spring onions (scallions), sliced diagonally into 1cm/½in pieces
bunch of chrysanthemum leaves, stems removed, chopped (optional)
bunch of enoki mushrooms, brown roots cut off (optional)
8 shiitake mushrooms, stalks removed
300g/11oz shirataki noodles, boiled for 2 minutes, drained and halved
2 pieces grilled tofu, about 10 × 7cm/4 × 2¾in, cut into 3cm/1¼in cubes
4 fresh eggs, to serve

FOR THE SUKIYAKI STOCK
100ml/3½fl oz/scant ½ cup mirin
45ml/3 tbsp sugar
105ml/7 tbsp Japanese soy sauce

FOR THE SEASONING MIX
200ml/7fl oz/scant 1 cup dashi or instant dashi
100ml/3½fl oz/scant ½ cup sake or dry white wine
15ml/1 tbsp Japanese soy sauce

WATCHPOINTS
- Eating raw eggs should be avoided by the very young, the elderly, pregnant women and those with a compromised immune system.
- Chrysanthemum leaves are the leaves of the vegetable, not the flower.

Make the sukiyaki stock. Pour the mirin into a pan and bring to the boil. Stir in the sugar and soy sauce, bring to the boil, then remove from the heat and set aside until required.

To make the seasoning mix, heat the dashi, sake or wine and soy sauce in a small pan. As soon as the mixture boils, remove from the heat and set aside.

Fan out the beef slices on a large serving plate. Put the lard for cooking on the same plate. Arrange all the remaining ingredients, except the eggs, on one or more large plates.

Stand the portable cooker on a suitably heavy mat to protect the dining table and ensure that it can be heated safely. Melt the lard, add three or four slices of beef and some leeks or spring onions, and then pour in the *sukiyaki* stock. Gradually add the remaining ingredients, except the eggs.

Place each egg in a ramekin and beat lightly with chopsticks. Place one before each diner. When the beef and vegetables are cooked, diners help themselves to whatever they fancy, dipping their chosen piece of meat, vegetable or grilled tofu in the raw egg before eating.

When the stock has thickened, gradually stir in the seasoning mix and carry on cooking until all the ingredients have been eaten.

Roasted & Marinated Pork

Yuan, *a sauce made from sake, shoyu, mirin and citrus fruit, is often used to marinate ingredients either before or after cooking. In this recipe, the sauce gives a delicate flavour to pork. If possible, leave the meat to marinate overnight.*

SERVES 4

INGREDIENTS
600g/1lb 5oz pork fillet
1 garlic clove, crushed
generous pinch of salt
4 spring onions (scallions), white part only, trimmed
10g/¼oz dried wakame, soaked in water for 20 minutes and drained
10cm/4in celery stick, trimmed and cut in half crossways

FOR THE *YUAN* SAUCE
105ml/7 tbsp shoyu
45ml/3 tbsp sake
60ml/4 tbsp mirin
1 lime, sliced into thin rings

1 Preheat the oven to 200°C/400°F/Gas 6. Rub the pork with crushed garlic and salt, and leave for 15 minutes.

2 Roast the pork for 20 minutes, then turn the meat over and reduce the oven temperature to 180°C/350°F/Gas 4. Cook for a further 20 minutes, or until the pork is cooked and there are no pink juices.

3 Meanwhile, mix the *yuan* sauce ingredients in a container that is big enough to hold the pork. When the meat is cooked, immediately put it in the sauce, and leave it to marinate for at least 2 hours, or overnight.

4 Cut the white part of the spring onions in half crossways, then in half lengthways. Remove the round cores, then lay the spring onion quarters flat on a chopping board. Slice them very thinly lengthways to make fine shreds.

5 Soak the spring onion shreds in a bowl of ice-cold water. Repeat with the remaining parts of the spring onions. When the shreds curl up, drain and gather them into a loose ball.

6 Cut the drained wakame into 2.5cm/1in squares or narrow strips. Slice the celery very thinly lengthways. Soak in cold water, then drain and gather together as before.

7 Remove the pork from the marinade and wipe with kitchen paper. Slice the meat very thinly. Strain the marinade and keep it in a gravy boat or jug (pitcher). Arrange the sliced pork on a large serving plate with the vegetables around it. Serve cold with the *yuan* sauce.

FIVE-FLAVOUR NOODLES

The Japanese name for this dish is Gomoku Yakisoba, *meaning five different ingredients; however, you can add as many different ingredients as you wish.*

SERVES 4

INGREDIENTS
300g/11oz dried Chinese thin egg noodles or 500g/1¼lb fresh yaki-soba noodles
200g/7oz lean boneless pork, thinly sliced
22.5ml/4½ tsp sunflower oil
10g/¼oz grated fresh root ginger
1 garlic clove, crushed
200g/7oz green cabbage, roughly chopped
115g/4oz/2 cups beansprouts
1 green (bell) pepper, seeded and cut into fine strips
1 red (bell) pepper, seeded and cut into fine strips
salt and ground black pepper
20ml/4 tsp nori seaweed, to garnish (optional)

FOR THE SEASONING
60ml/4 tbsp Worcestershire sauce
15ml/1 tbsp Japanese soy sauce
15ml/1 tbsp oyster sauce
15ml/1 tbsp sugar
2.5ml/½ tsp salt
ground white pepper

1 Cook the noodles according to the instructions on the packet. Drain well and set aside. Cut the pork into 3–4cm/1¼–1½in strips and season.

2 Heat 7.5ml/1½ tsp of the oil in a large wok or frying pan. Stir-fry the pork until just cooked; remove from the pan. Wipe the wok; heat the remaining oil. Stir-fry the ginger, garlic and cabbage for 1 minute. Add the beansprouts, stir until softened; add the peppers and stir-fry for 1 minute.

3 Return the pork to the pan and add the noodles. Stir in the seasoning; stir-fry for 2–3 minutes. Serve immediately, sprinkled with nori seaweed, if using.

Mung Bean Pancakes with Pork

Bindaeduk *is sometimes referred to as Korea's answer to the pizza, although it is really a beancake. The filling can include* kimchi *(pickled cabbage), carrot and ginger.*

SERVES 4–6

INGREDIENTS
225g/8oz/1¼ cups skinned, split mung beans
50g/2oz/⅓ cup glutinous rice
15ml/1 tbsp light soy sauce
15ml/1 tbsp roasted sesame seeds, crushed
2.5ml/½ tsp bicarbonate of soda (baking soda)
115g/4oz/½ cup beansprouts, blanched and dried
1 garlic clove, crushed
4 spring onions (scallions), chopped
115g/4oz cooked lean pork, shredded
30ml/2 tbsp sesame oil, plus extra for drizzling
salt and ground black pepper
fresh chives, to garnish
light soy sauce, to serve

1 Put the beans and rice in a bowl; pour in water to cover. Soak for 8 hours then tip into a sieve, rinse under cold water and drain. Process in a food processor to a batter the consistency of double (heavy) cream. Add the soy sauce, sesame seeds and bicarbonate of soda and process briefly. When ready to cook, tip the batter into a bowl and add the beansprouts, garlic, spring onions and pork. Season with salt and ground black pepper.

2 Heat about 10ml/2 tsp of the sesame oil in a large frying pan. Spoon or ladle in half the batter, and, using the back of a spoon, spread it into a thick pancake. Drizzle a little more sesame oil over, cover and cook until the underside is done. Turn the pancake over and cook for 3–4 minutes. Keep warm, and cook a second pancake. Place the pancakes on serving plates and garnish with chives. Cut into wedges and serve with soy sauce.

YAKITORI CHICKEN

These tasty little Japanese-style kebabs are flavoured with Japanese seven-spice powder. They are easy to eat and ideal for barbecues or parties. Make extra yakitori sauce if you would like to serve it with the kebabs.

SERVES 4

INGREDIENTS
6 boneless chicken thighs
bunch of spring onions (scallions)
seven-spice powder or paprika, to serve (optional)

FOR THE YAKITORI SAUCE
150ml/¼ pint/⅔ cup Japanese soy sauce
90g/3½oz/scant ½ cup sugar
25ml/1½ tbsp sake or dry white wine
15ml/1 tbsp plain (all-purpose) flour

1 Soak 12 bamboo skewers in water for at least 30 minutes to prevent them from scorching under the grill (broiler). Make the sauce. Stir the soy sauce, sugar and sake or wine into the flour in a small saucepan and bring to the boil, stirring. Lower the heat and simmer the mixture for 10 minutes, until the sauce is reduced by a third. Set aside until required.

2 Cut each chicken thigh into bite-size pieces and set aside. Cut the spring onions into 3cm/1¼in pieces. Preheat the grill or light the barbecue.

3 Thread the chicken and spring onions alternately on to the drained skewers. Grill (broil) under medium heat or cook on the barbecue for about 10 minutes, brushing several times with the sauce, until the chicken is cooked but still moist.

4 Serve with a little extra yakitori sauce, offering shichimi or paprika with the kebabs for guests to help themselves.

CHICKEN & EGG WITH RICE

Oyako-don, *the Japanese name for this dish means parent (oya), child (ko) and bowl (don); it is so called because it uses both chicken meat and egg. It is a classic dish and is eaten throughout the year.*

SERVES 4

INGREDIENTS
300g/11oz skinless boneless chicken breast portions
1 large mild onion, thinly sliced
200ml/7fl oz/scant 1 cup freshly made dashi or instant dashi
22.5ml/4½ tsp sugar
60ml/4 tbsp Japanese soy sauce
30ml/2 tbsp mirin
4 eggs, beaten
60ml/4 tbsp frozen peas, thawed
Japanese or Thai fragrant rice, to serve

1 Slice the chicken breast portions diagonally with a sharp knife, then cut the slices into 3cm/1¼in lengths.

2 Place the onion, dashi, sugar, soy sauce and mirin in a pan and bring to the boil. Add the chicken and cook over a medium heat for about 5 minutes, or until cooked. Skim off any scum that rises to the surface of the liquid.

3 Ladle a quarter of the chicken and stock mixture into a frying pan and heat until the liquid comes to the boil., Pour a quarter of the beaten egg over the mixture and sprinkle over 15ml/1 tbsp of the peas.

4 Cover and cook over a medium heat until the egg is just set. Slide the egg mixture on to a large plate and keep it warm while cooking the other omelettes in the same way. Transfer to serving dishes and serve with boiled rice.

POT-COOKED DUCK
& GREEN VEGETABLES

Prepare the ingredients for this dish, Kamo Nabe, *beforehand, so that the cooking can be done at the table. Use a flameproof casserole with a portable cooker.*

SERVES 4

INGREDIENTS
4 duck breast fillets, about 800g/1¾lb in total
8 large shiitake mushrooms, stalks removed, a cross cut into each cap
2 leeks, trimmed and cut diagonally into 6cm/2½in lengths
½ head Chinese leaves (Chinese cabbage), stalk removed and cut into large squares
500g/1¼lb chrysanthemum leaves, cut in half crossways

FOR THE STOCK
raw bones from 1 chicken, washed
1 egg shell
200ml/7fl oz/scant 1 cup short grain rice, washed and drained
120ml/4fl oz/½ cup sake
about 10ml/2 tsp coarse sea salt

FOR THE SAUCE
75ml/5 tbsp shoyu
30ml/2 tbsp sake
juice of 1 lime
8 white peppercorns, roughly crushed

FOR THE SOUP
130g/4½oz Chinese egg noodles, cooked and loosened
1 egg, beaten
1 bunch of chives, to garnish
ground white pepper, to serve

1 Make the stock. Put the bones into a pan three-quarters full of water. Bring to the boil then drain. Wash the pan and bones; return to the pan with the same amount of water and the egg shell. Bring to the boil. Simmer, uncovered, for 1 hour, skimming frequently. Remove the bones and shell. Add the rice, sake and salt; simmer for 30 minutes. Remove from the heat.

2 Heat a heavy frying pan until it is just smoking. Remove from the heat for about 1 minute, then add the duck breasts, skin-side down. Return to a medium heat and sear for 3–4 minutes, or until crisp. Turn over and sear the other side for about 1 minute. Remove from the heat.

3 When cool, wipe the duck fat with kitchen paper and cut the breast and skin into 5mm/¼in thick slices. Arrange on a large serving plate with all the prepared vegetables.

4 Heat through all the ingredients for the sauce in a small pan and transfer to a small jug (pitcher) or bowl.

5 Prepare four dipping bowls, four serving bowls and chopsticks. At the table, bring the pan of soup stock to the boil, then reduce to medium-low. Add half of the shiitake and leeks. Wait for 5 minutes and put in half of the stalk part of the Chinese leaves. Add half of the duck and cook for 1–2 minutes for rare or about 7 minutes for well-done meat.

6 Each person prepares some duck and vegetables in a serving bowl and drizzles over a little sauce. Add the soft part of the Chinese leaves and the chrysanthemum leaves to the stock as you eat. When the stock is less than a quarter of the pan's volume, top up with 3 parts water to 1 part sake.

7 When the duck has been eaten, bring the reduced stock to the boil. Skim the oil from the surface, and reduce the heat to medium. Add the noodles, cook for 1–2 minutes and check the seasoning. Add more salt if required. Pour in the beaten egg and swirl in the stock. Cover, turn off the heat, then leave to stand for 1 minute. Garnish with the snipped chives and serve with ground white pepper.

COOK'S TIP
Chrysanthemum leaves (shungiku) *are the leaves of the chrysanthemum vegetable, not the flower.*

SALMON TERYAKI

Sake Teryaki is a well-known Japanese dish, which uses a sweet and shiny sauce for marinating as well as for glazing the ingredients.

SERVES 4

INGREDIENTS
4 small salmon fillets with skin on, about 150g/5oz each
50g/2oz/¼ cup beansprouts, washed
50g/2oz mangetouts (snow peas), ends trimmed
20g/¾oz carrot, cut into thin strips
salt

FOR THE SAUCE
45ml/3 tbsp shoyu
45ml/3 tbsp sake
45ml/3 tbsp mirin
15ml/1 tbsp plus 10ml/2 tsp caster (superfine) sugar

1 Mix all the ingredients for the teriyaki sauce except for the 10ml/2 tsp sugar, in a pan. Heat to dissolve the sugar. Remove and leave to cool for an hour. Place the salmon fillet in a shallow glass or china dish and pour over the teriyaki sauce. Leave to marinate for 30 minutes.

2 Meanwhile, cook the beansprouts in lightly salted water for 1 minute. Add the mangetouts; cook for 1 minute. Add the carrot; cook for 1 minute. Drain the vegetables and keep warm.

3 Preheat the grill (broiler) to medium. Take the salmon fillet out of the sauce and pat dry with kitchen paper. Reserve the sauce. Lightly oil a grilling (broiling) tray. Grill (broil) the salmon for about 6 minutes, carefully turning once.

4 Heat the sauce with the remaining sugar. Brush over the salmon. Grill until the surface bubbles. Repeat on the other side. Heap the vegetables on to serving plates. Place the salmon on top and spoon over the rest of the sauce.

SALT-GRILLED MACKEREL

Shio-yaki means salt-grilled. In Japan, salt is applied to oily fish before cooking to draw out the flavours. Mackerel, garfish and snapper are the most popular choices.

SERVES 2

INGREDIENTS
2 small or 1 large mackerel, snapper or garfish, gutted, with head on
30ml/2 tbsp fine sea salt
15ml/1 tbsp wasabi powder
10ml/2 tsp water
1 carrot, peeled and shredded

FOR THE SOY GINGER DIP
60ml/4 tbsp dark soy sauce
30ml/2 tbsp sugar
2.5cm/1in piece fresh root ginger, peeled and finely grated

1 Rinse the fish under cold running water and dry well with kitchen paper. Slash the fish to the bone several times on each side. Salt the fish inside and out, rubbing well into the skin. Leave to stand for 40 minutes.

2 To make the soy ginger dip, place the soy sauce, sugar and ginger in a stainless steel pan. Simmer for 2–3 minutes, strain and cool. Measure the wasabi powder into a small cup, add the water and stir to make a stiff paste. Shape into a neat ball and place on a heap of shredded carrot.

3 Wash the fish in plenty of cold water to remove the salt. Secure each fish in a curved position before grilling (broiling). To do this, pass two bamboo skewers through the length of the fish, one above the eye and one below.

4 Preheat a grill (broiler) or barbecue to a medium heat and cook the fish for about 10–12 minutes, turning just once. It is customary to cook the fish plainly, but you may like to baste the skin with a little of the soy ginger dip part way through cooking.

Rolled Sardines with Plum Paste

Japanese cooks seek to taste and express the season in their cooking, and menus always include some seasonal ingredients. This dish, Iwashi No Umé Yaki, *is one of many recipes prepared to celebrate the arrival of the harvest, when the sardine season peaks in the autumn.*

SERVES 4

INGREDIENTS
8 sardines, cleaned and filleted
5ml/1 tsp salt
4 soft umeboshi (pickled plums), about 30g/1¼oz in total
5ml/1 tsp sake
5ml/1 tsp toasted sesame seeds
16 shiso leaves, cut in half lengthways
1 lime, thinly sliced, the centre hollowed out to make rings, to garnish

1 Carefully cut the sardine fillets in half lengthways and place them side by side in a large, shallow container. Sprinkle with salt on both sides.

2 Remove the stones (pits) from the umeboshi and put the fruit in a small mixing bowl with the sake and toasted sesame seeds. With the back of a fork, mash the umeboshi, mixing well to form a smooth paste.

3 Wipe the sardine fillets with kitchen paper. With a butter knife, spread some umeboshi paste thinly on to one of the sardine fillets, then press some shiso leaves on top. Roll up the sardine starting from the tail and pierce with a wooden cocktail stick (toothpick). Repeat to make 16 rolled sardines.

4 Preheat the grill (broiler) to high. Lay a sheet of foil on a baking tray and arrange the sardine rolls on this, spaced well apart to prevent sticking. Grill (broil) for 4–6 minutes on each side, or until golden brown, turning once. Lay a few lime rings on four individual plates and arrange the rolled sardines alongside. Serve immediately.

SIMMERED SQUID & MOOLI

Ika To Daikon Ni is a classic dish, the secret of which used to be handed down from
mother to daughter. Today, you are more likely to taste the real thing only at
restaurants, but some grandmothers still cook it for family reunions.

SERVES 4

INGREDIENTS
450g/1lb squid, cleaned, body and tentacles separated
about 1kg/2¼lb mooli (daikon), peeled
900ml/1½ pints/3¾ cups dashi stock
60ml/4 tbsp shoyu
45ml/3 tbsp sake
15ml/1 tbsp caster (superfine) sugar
30ml/2 tbsp mirin
grated rind of ¼ yuzu or lime, to garnish

1 Separate the triangular flaps from the squid body and cut into 1cm/½in strips.
Cut the body into 1cm/½in rings. Cut off and discard 2.5cm/1in from the thin
end of the tentacles. Chop the rest into 4cm/1½in lengths. Cut the mooli into
3cm/1¼in thick rounds and shave the edges of the sections with a sharp knife.
Plunge the slices into cold water. Drain just before cooking.

2 Put the mooli and squid in a heavy pan and pour on the dashi. Bring to the boil,
and cook for 5 minutes, skimming constantly. Reduce the heat to low and add
the shoyu, sake, sugar and mirin. Cover the surface with a circle of greaseproof
(waxed) paper cut 2.5cm/1in smaller than the lid of the pan and simmer for
45 minutes, shaking the pan occasionally. The liquid will reduce by about half.
Leave to stand for 5 minutes and serve hot in small bowls with a sprinkle of yuzu
or lime rind.

COOK'S TIP
Buy mooli that is at least 7.5cm/3in in diameter,
with a shiny, undamaged skin, and that sounds
dense and heavy when patted.

Sweet Azuki Bean Paste Jelly

In this summery dessert, a dark red kanten and sweet bean cube is captured in a clear jelly, and looks like a small stone trapped in a block of mountain ice.

Serves 12

Ingredients
200g/7oz can azuki beans
40g/1½oz/3 tbsp caster (superfine) sugar

For the jelly
2 × 5g/⅛oz sachets powdered agar agar
100g/3¾oz/scant 1 cup caster (superfine) sugar
rind of ¼ orange in one piece

1 Drain the beans, then tip into a pan over a medium heat. When steam begins to rise, reduce the heat to low.

2 Add the sugar one-third at a time, stirring constantly until the sugar has dissolved and the moisture evaporated. Remove from the heat.

3 Pour 450ml/¾ pint/scant 2 cups water into a small pan, and mix with 1 agar agar sachet. Stir until dissolved, then add 40g/1½oz of the sugar and the orange rind. Bring to the boil and cook for about 2 minutes, stirring constantly until the sugar has all dissolved. Remove from the heat and discard the orange rind.

4 Transfer 250ml/8fl oz/1 cup of the hot liquid into a 15 × 10cm/6 × 4in container to a depth of 1cm/½in. Leave at room temperature to set.

5 Add the bean paste to the agar agar liquid in the pan, and mix well. Move the pan on to a wet dishtowel and stir for 8 minutes.

6 Pour the bean and agar agar liquid into an 18 × 7.5 × 2cm/7 × 3 × ¾in container and leave to set for 1 hour at room temperature, then 1 hour in the refrigerator. Invert on to a chopping board covered with kitchen paper. Leave for 1 minute, then cut into 12 rectangular pieces.

7 Line 12 ramekins with clear film (plastic wrap). With a fork, cut the set agar agar block into 12 squares. Put a square in each ramekin, then place a bean and agar agar cube on top of each.

8 Pour 450ml/¾ pint/scant 2 cups water into a pan and mix with the remaining agar agar sachet. Bring to the boil, add the remaining sugar, then stir constantly until dissolved. Boil for a further 2 minutes then remove from the heat. Place the pan on a wet dishtowel to cool quickly and stir for 5 minutes, or until the liquid starts to thicken.

9 Ladle the liquid into the ramekins to cover the cubes. Twist the clear film at the top. Leave to set in the refrigerator for at least 1 hour. Carefully remove the ramekins and clear film and serve cold on serving plates.

GREEN TEA ICE CREAM

In the past, the Japanese did not end a meal with dessert, apart from some fruit. This custom is slowly changing and now many Japanese restaurants offer light desserts like water ices or ice cream. Here, ice cream is flavoured with matcha – the finest green powdered tea used in the famous Japanese tea ceremony. It gives the ice cream a sophisticated twist.

SERVES 4

INGREDIENTS
500ml/17fl oz carton good-quality vanilla ice cream
15ml/1 tbsp matcha
15ml/1 tbsp lukewarm water
seeds from ¼ pomegranate, to decorate (optional)

1 Soften the ice cream by transferring it to the refrigerator for 20–30 minutes. Do not allow it to melt.

2 Mix the matcha powder and lukewarm water in a cup and stir well to make a smooth paste.

3 Put half the ice cream into a mixing bowl. Add the matcha liquid and mix thoroughly with a rubber spatula, then add the rest of the ice cream. You can stop mixing at the stage when the ice cream looks a marbled dark green and white, or continue mixing until the ice cream is a uniform pale green. Put the bowl into the freezer.

4 After 1 hour, the ice cream is ready to serve. Scoop into individual glass cups, and top with a few pomegranate seeds to decorate, if you like.

COOK'S TIP
Matcha is powdered green tea, which is mainly used in the Japanese tea ceremony. When dissolved in boiling water, it produces a vivid green-coloured tea with a fragrant aroma. Matcha is available from Japanese and Asian stores.

Sweet Potato & Chestnut Candies

It is customary in Japan to offer special bean-paste candies with tea. The candies tend to be very sweet by themselves, but contrast well with Japanese green teas; in particular, large-leaf Sencha and Banch.

MAKES 18

INGREDIENTS
450g/1lb sweet potato, peeled and roughly chopped
1.5ml/¼ tsp salt
2 egg yolks
200g/7oz/1 cup sugar
60ml/4 tbsp water
75g/5 tbsp rice flour or plain wheat flour
5ml/1 tsp orange flower or rose water (optional)
200g/7oz canned chestnuts in heavy syrup, drained
caster (superfine) sugar, for dusting
2 strips candied angelica
10ml/2 tsp plum or apricot preserve
3–4 drops red food colouring

1 Place the sweet potatoes in a heavy pan, cover with cold water and add the salt. Bring to the boil and simmer until tender, about 20–25 minutes. Drain, return to the pan and mash. Place the egg yolks, sugar and water in a small bowl, then combine the flour and scented water if using. Add to the purée and stir over a gentle heat to thicken. Turn out on to a tray and cool.

2 To shape the sweet potato paste, place 10ml/2 tsp of the mixture into the centre of a wet cotton napkin or handkerchief. Enclose the paste in the cotton and twist into a nut shape. If the mixture sticks, ensure the fabric is properly wet.

3 To prepare the chestnuts, rinse away the syrup and dry. Roll the chestnuts in caster sugar and decorate with strips of angelica. To finish the sweet potato candies, colour the plum or apricot preserve with red colouring and decorate each one with a spot of colour. Serve in a Japanese lacquer box or on an open plate.

GREEN & YELLOW LAYERED CAKES

This colourful two-tone dessert is made by moulding contrasting mixtures in a small pouch. The Japanese title is derived from the preparation technique: chakin-shibori, *in which* chakin *means a pouch shape and* shibori *means a moulding action.*

MAKES 6

INGREDIENTS

FOR THE YOLK MIXTURE
6 small (US medium) hard-boiled (hard-cooked) eggs
50g/2oz/¼ cup sugar

FOR THE PEA MIXTURE
200g/7oz/1¾ cups frozen peas
40g/1½oz/3 tbsp sugar

1 Make the yolk mixture. Shell the eggs, cut them in half and scoop the yolks into a sieve placed over a bowl. Using a wooden spoon, press the yolks through the sieve. Add the sugar and mix well.

2 To make the pea mixture, cook the peas in lightly salted boiling water for about 3–4 minutes, until softened. Drain and place in a mortar, then crush with a pestle. Transfer the paste to a saucepan. Add the sugar and cook over a low heat until thick. Stir constantly so that the mixture does not burn.

3 Spread out the pea paste in a shallow dish so that it cools as quickly as possible. Divide both mixtures into six portions.

4 Wet a piece of muslin (cheesecloth) or thin cotton and wring it out well. Place a portion of the pea mixture on the cloth and put a similar amount of the yolk mixture on top. Wrap the mixture up and twist the top of the cloth to join the mixtures together and mark a spiral pattern on the top. Unwrap and place on a plate. Make five more cakes in the same way. Serve cold.

Sweet Aduki Bean Soup with Rice Cakes

Don't assume from the word soup that this is a savoury dish – Zenzai is actually a classic and popular Japanese dessert, served with the ready-to-eat rice cakes (mochi) that are sold in Japanese supermarkets. Serve with Japanese green tea.

SERVES 4

INGREDIENTS
165g/5½oz/scant 1 cup dried aduki beans
225g/8oz/generous 1 cup sugar
pinch of salt
4 ready-to-eat rice cakes (mochi)

1 Put the aduki beans in a strainer, wash under cold running water, then drain and tip into a large pan. Add 1 litre/1¾ pints/4 cups water and bring to the boil. Drain the aduki beans and return them to the rinsed out pan.

2 Add a further 1.2 litres/2 pints/5 cups water to the pan and bring to the boil, then add a further 1.2 litres/2 pints/5 cups water and bring to the boil again. Lower the heat and simmer for 30 minutes until the beans are soft.

3 Skim the surface of the broth regularly to remove any scum; if left, it would give the soup an unpleasant bitter taste.

4 When the beans are soft enough to be mashed between your fingers, add half the sugar and simmer for a further 20 minutes.

5 Add the remaining sugar and the salt to the pan, stirring until the sugar has completely dissolved.

6 Heat the grill (broiler), then grill (broil) both sides of the rice cakes until softened, but not browned. Add the rice cakes to the soup and bring to the boil. Serve the soup immediately in deep warmed bowls.

KABOCHA SQUASH CAKE

Yokan (cake) is a very sweet dessert often made with azuki beans. It is eaten at tea time with green tea. In this version, kabocha squash is used instead of azuki and the cake is served with fruits.

SERVES 4

INGREDIENTS
1 × 350g/12oz kabocha squash
30ml/2 tbsp plain (all-purpose) flour
15ml/1 tbsp cornflour (cornstarch)
10ml/2 tsp caster (superfine) sugar
1.5ml/¼ tsp salt
1.5ml/¼ tsp ground cinnamon
25ml/1½ tbsp water
2 egg yolks, beaten

TO SERVE
½ nashi (optional)
½ kaki (optional)

COOK'S TIP
Nashi are round, russet-coloured Japanese pears. Kaki, also known as Japanese persimmon, have a smooth, reddish-orange skin. Both fruits can be found in Japanese and Asian stores.

---

1 Cut off the hard part from the top and bottom of the kabocha, then cut it into 3–4 wedges. Scoop out the seeds with a spoon. Cut into big chunks.

2 Steam the kabocha in a covered steamer for about 15 minutes over a medium heat. Check if a chopstick can be pushed into the centre easily. Remove and set aside, covered, for 5 minutes.

3 Remove the skin from the kabocha. Mash the flesh and push it through a sieve using a wooden spoon, or use a food processor. Transfer the flesh to a mixing bowl, add the rest of the cake ingredients, and mix well.

4 Roll out a sushi mat. Dampen some muslin (cheesecloth) or a dishtowel with a little water and lay it on the mat. Spread the kabocha mixture evenly. Hold the nearest end and tightly roll up to the other end. Close both outer ends by rolling up or folding the muslin over.

5 Put the rolled kabocha in the mat back into the steamer for 5 minutes. Remove from the heat and leave to set for 5 minutes. If using the nashi and kaki, peel and trim it then slice very thinly lengthways.

6 Open the mat when the roll has cooled down. Cut the cake into 2.5cm/1in thick slices and serve cold on four small plates with the thinly sliced nashi and kaki, if using.

Sweet Pancakes

In Japan, the sweet bean paste is traditionally sandwiched between two pancakes to resemble a little gong, hence its name Dora Yaki; *"dora" meaning a gong. In this version the pancakes are folded to make a half gong.*

Makes 6–8 DORA YAKI PANCAKES

Ingredients
65g/2½oz/5 tbsp caster (superfine) sugar
3 large (US extra large) eggs, beaten
15ml/1 tbsp maple syrup or golden (corn) syrup
185g/6½oz/1⅔ cups plain (all-purpose) flour, sifted
5ml/1 tsp bicarbonate of soda (baking soda)
150ml/¼ pint/⅔ cup water
vegetable oil, for frying

For the paste
250g/9oz canned azuki beans
40g/1½oz/3 tbsp caster (superfine) sugar
pinch of salt

1 To make the sweet bean paste, put the canned azuki beans and its liquid into a pan, then heat over a medium heat. Add the sugar gradually and stir the pan vigorously. Cook over a low heat until the liquid has almost evaporated and the beans have become mushy. Add a pinch of salt and remove from the heat. Stir for 1 minute, then leave to cool.

2 Mix the sugar, eggs and syrup in a mixing bowl. Blend well until the sugar has dissolved, then add the flour to make a smooth batter. Cover the bowl and leave for 20 minutes.

3 Mix together the bicarbonate of soda and water in a cup and then mix this into the batter, stirring to combine well.

4 Heat a little oil in a small frying pan until very hot. Remove from the heat and wipe with kitchen paper. Return to a medium heat and ladle some batter into the centre. Make a small pancake about 13cm/5in in diameter and 5mm/¼in thick.

5 Cook for about 2–3 minutes on each side until golden brown. Reduce the heat if the outside begins to burn before the inside is cooked. Make a further 11–15 pancakes.

6 Take a pancake and spread about 30ml/2 tbsp of the sweet bean paste in the middle leaving about 2.5cm/1in around the edge. Cover with another pancake. Place on a tray and repeat until all the pancakes are used. Serve the filled pancakes warm or cold.

COOK'S TIP
You can make a half "gong" by folding a pancake in the middle and filling the inside with a little of the sweet azuki bean paste.

Shopping for Chinese & Asian Foods

Australia

Asian Supermarkets
  Pty Ltd
116 Charters Towers Road
Townsville
QLD 4810
Tel: (07) 4772 3997

PK Supermarkets Pty Ltd
369 Victoria Avenue
Chatswood
NSW 2067
Tel: (02) 9419 8822

Kongs Trading Pty Ltd
8 Kingscote Street
Kewdale
WA 6105
Tel: (08) 9353 3380

Duc Hung Long Asian
  Foodstore
95 The Crescent
Fairfield
NSW 2165
Tel: (02) 9728 1092

Exotic Asian Groceries
Cnr Market and
  Bermuda Streets
Mermaid Waters
QLD 4218
Tel: (07) 5572 8188

Saigon Asian Food
6 Cape Street
Dickson
ACT 2602
Tel: (02) 6247 4251

The Spice and Herb Asian
  Shop
200 Old Cleveland Road
Capalaba
QLD 4157
Tel: (07) 3245 5300

Sydney Fish Market Pty
  Ltd
Cnr Pyrmont Bridge Road
  and Bank Street
Pyrmont
NSW 2009
Tel: (02) 9660 1611

Harris Farm Markets
Sydney Markets
Flemongton
NSW 2140
Tel: (02) 9746 2055

Burlington Supermarkets
Chinatown Mall
Fortitude Valley
QLD 4006
Tel: (07) 3216 182

UK

Arigato
48–50 Brewer Street
London W1R 3HM
Tel: 020 7287 1722

Good Harvest Fish
  Market
14 Newport Place
London WC2H 7PR
Tel: 020 7437 0712

Golden Gate Cake Shop
13 Macclesfield Street
London W1V 7LH
Tel: 020 7287 9862

Golden Gate Supermarket
16 Newport Place
London WC2H 7JS
Tel: 020 7437 6266

Golden Gate Hong Kong
14 Lisle Street
London WC2 7BE
Tel: 020 7437 0014

Hong Kong Supermarket
62 High Street
London SW4 7UL
Tel: 020 7720 2069

Loon Fung Supermarket
42–44 Gerrard Street
London W1V 7LP
Tel: 020 7437 7332

New Peking Supermarket
59 Westbourne Grove
London W2 4UA
Tel: 020 7928 8770

Manila Supermarket
11–12 Hogarth Place
London SW5 0QT
Tel: 020 7373 8305

Miah, A. and Co
20 Magdalen Street
Norwich NR3 1HE
Tel: 01603 615395

Miura Japanese Foods
44 Coombe Road
Nr Kingston KT2 7AF
Tel: 020 8549 8076
also at
5 Limpsfield Road
Sanderstead
Surrey CR2 9LA
Tel: 020 8651 4498

Natural House
Japan Centre
212 Piccadilly
London W1V 9LD
Tel: 020 7434 4218

Newport Supermarket
28–29 Newport Court
London WC2H 7PQ
Tel: 020 7437 2386

Oriental City
399 Edgware Road
London NW9 0JJ
Tel: 020 8200 0009

Rum Wong
  Supermarket
London Road
Guildford
Surrey GU1 2AF
Tel: 01483 451568

S. W. Trading Ltd
Horn Lane
Greenwich
London SE10 0RT
Tel: 020 8293 9393

South-east Asian Hopewell
  Emporium
2f Dyne Road
London NW6 7XB
Tel: 020 7624 5473

Sri Thai
56 Shepherd's Bush Road
London W6 7PH
Tel: 020 7602 0621

T.K. Trading
Unit 6/7
The Chase Centre
Chase Road
London NW10 6QD
Tel: 020 8453 1001

Talad Thai Ltd
320 Upper Richmond
  Road
London SW15 6TL
Tel: 020 8789 8084

Tawana
18–20 Chepstow Road
London W2 5BD
Tel: 020 7221 6316

Wang Thai Supermarket
101 Kew Road
Richmond
Surrey TW9 2PN
Tel: 020 8332 2959

The Wing On Department
  Store (Hong Kong) Ltd
37–38 Margaret Street
London W1N 7FA
Tel: 020 7580 3677

Wing Yip
395 Edgware Road
London NW2 6LN
Tel: 020 7450 0422
also at
Oldham Road
Ancoats
Manchester M4 5HU
Tel: 0161 832 3215

and
375 Nechells Park Road
Nechells
Birmingham
B7 5NT
Tel: 0121 327 3838

EQUIPMENT
Neal Street East
5–7 Neal Street
London WC2 9PV
Tel: 020 7240 0135

Obhrai Cash and Carry
168 Ealing Road
Wembley
Middlesex HA0 4DQ
Tel: 020 8903 4450

Popat Store
138 Ealing Road
Wembley
Middlesex HA0 4PY
Tel: 020 8903 6797

GENERAL INFORMATION
Bart's Spices
York Road
Bedminster
Bristol BS3 4AD
Tel: 0117 977 3474

Fiddes Payne Spices Ltd
Unit 3B, Thorpe Way
Banbury
Oxfordshire OX16 8XL
Tel: 01295 253 888

Sharwood's Ethnic Food
  Bureau
Bury House
126–128 Cromwell Road
London SW7 4ET
Tel: 020 7373 4537

US

Ai Hoa
860 North Hill Street
Los Angeles, CA 90026
Tel: (213) 482-48

Asian Food Market
6450 Market Street
Upper Darby, PA 19082
Tel: (610) 352-4433

Asian Foods, Etc.
1375 Prince Avenue
Atlanta, GA 30341
Tel: (404) 543-8624

Asian Foods Ltd.
260-280 West Lehigh
   Avenue
Philadelphia, PA 19133
Tel: (215) 291-9500

Asian Market
2513 Stewart Avenue
Las Vegas, NV 89101
Tel: (702) 387-3373

Asian Market
18815 Eureka Road
South Gate, MI 48195
Fax: (734) 246-4795

Augusta Market
   Oriental Foods
2117 Martin Luther King
   Jr. Boulevard
Altanta, GA 30901
Tel: (706) 722-4988

Bangkok Market
4757 Melrose Avenue
Los Angeles, CA 90029
Tel: (203) 662-7990

Bharati Food &
   Spice Center
6163 Reynolds Road
   Suite G
Morrow, GA 30340
Tel: (770) 961-9007

Chinese Oriental Market
300 South Bruce Street
Las Vegas, NV 89101
Tel: (702) 382-7295

Daido
1385 16th Street
Fort Lee, NJ 07024
Tel: (201) 944-0020

DIHO Market
655 Pasquinelli Drive
Westmont, IL 60559
Tel: (630) 323-1668

First Asian Food Center
3420 East Ponce De
   Leon Avenue
Scottsdale, GA 30079
Tel: (404) 292-6508

Han Me Oriental Food
   & Gifts
2 E. Derenne Avenue
Savannah, GA 31405
Tel: (912) 355-6411

Hong Tan Oriental Food
2802 Capitol Street
Savannah, GA 31404
Tel: (404) 233-9184

The House of Rice Store
3221 North Hayden Road
Scottsdale, AZ 85251
Tel: (480) 947-6698

Huy Fong Foods Inc.
5001 Earle Avenue
Rosemead, CA 91770
Tel: (626) 286-8328
www.huyfong.com

Katagiri Speciality
224 East 59th Street
New York, NY 10022
Tel: (212) 755-3566
www.katagiri.com

Khanh Tam Oriental
   Market
4051 Buford Highway, NE
Atlanta, GA 30345
Tel: (404) 728-0393

Lotte
2030 Will Ross Court
Chamblee, GA 30341
Tel: (770) 454-7569

Maruwa Foods Company
   of America
1737 Post Street
San Francisco, CA 94115
Tel: (415) 563-1901
www.maruwa.com

May's American
   Oriental Market
422 West University
   Avenue
Saint Paul, MN 55103
Tel: (651) 293-1118
www.maysamoriental.
   qpg.com

Modern Thai Incorporated
135 Yacht Club Way #210
Hypuluxo, FL 33462
Tel: (888) THAI-8888

Norcross Oriental Market
6062 Norcross-Tucker
  Road
Chamblee, GA 30341
Tel: (770) 496-1656

Oriental Grocery
11827 Del Amo Boulevard
Cerritos, CA 90701
Tel: (310) 924-1029

Oriental Market
670 Central Park Avenue
Yonkers, NY 10013
Tel: (212) 349-1979

The Oriental Pantry
423 Great Road
Acton, MA 01720
Tel: (978) 264-4576

Pearl River Chinese
  Products Emporium
277 Canal Street
New York, NY
Tel: (212) 431-4770

Saigon Asian Market
10090 Central Avenue
Biloxi, MS 39532
Tel: (228) 392-8044

Sea Rance
3223 West Lake Avenue
Wilmette, IL 60091
Tel: (708) 256-4404

Siam Market
27266 East Baseline Street
Highland, CA 92346
Tel: (909) 862-8060

Spice Mahal
3621 Kirkwood Highway
Wilmington, DE
Tel: (302) 994-8144

Suruki Super Market
71 East 4th Avenue
San Mateo, CA 94401
Tel: (415) 347-5288

Sushma Emporium
480-A Blossom Hill Road
San Jose, CA
Tel: (408) 281-0392
www.indolink.com/SFO/
  sushma.html

TAJ International Foods
7334 Lee Highway
Chattanooga, TN 37421
Tel: (423) 892-0259

Thai Market
3297 Las Vegas Boulevard
Las Vegas, NV 89030
Tel: (702) 643-8080

Thai Market
916 Harrelson Street
Fort Walton Beach,
  FL 32547
Tel: (904) 863-2013

Thai Number One Market
5927 Cherry Avenue
Long Beach, CA 90805
Tel: (310) 422-6915

Thai-Lao Market
1721 West La Palma Avenue
Anaheim, CA 92801
Tel: (714) 535-2656

Unimart American and
  Asian Groceries
1201 Howard Street
San Francisco, CA 94103
Tel: (415) 431-0362

Yaohan
595 River Road
Edgewater, NJ 07020
Tel: (201) 941-9113

AUTHOR'S ACKNOWLEDGEMENTS

Sallie Morris would like to thank her family: Johnnie, Alex and James for their support; Beryl Castles for her help in typing the manuscript; Beth Ware for advice on recipes from the Philippines; Rupert Welchman for his advice on Japanese recipes; John Phengsiri at the Wang Thai Supermarket in Richmond; Bart's Spices Ltd; Cherry Valley Farms (Tel: 01472 371 271), who supplied ducklings for recipe testing; Ken the Fishman (Tel: 0860 240 213), and Magimix (Tel: 01483 427 411) for supplying a food processor, ice cream maker and electric steamer for recipe testing.

Deh-Ta Hsiung would like to thank Sallie Morris and Emi Kazuko for their advice and help in writing about South-east Asian and Japanese foods.

INDEX

J

Japanese pickles, 34
jellyfish, dried, 51
junket, almond curd, 137

K

kaffir limes, 66
kan shao green beans, 108
kimchi, 274
kobacho squash cake, 306–7
kombu, 36
konnayaku, 48

L

laksa lemak, 162–3
lamb, 54
    lamb satay, 212–13
    Mongolian firepot, 116–17
larp of Chiang Mai, 190
leche flan, 258
lemon grass, 65
    spicy pork with lemon grass
        and coconut, 224
lemon sauce, 82
lily buds, dried, 29
limes:
    hot chilli crab with ginger
        and lime, 166
    pickled, 35
lion's head meatballs, 119
liqueurs, 86–87
lobster, 59
    baked lobster with black
        beans, 135
lotus root, 29
luffa, 31
lychees, 39

M

mackerel, 57
    salt-grilled mackerel, 297
mangetouts, 31
mangoes, 40–1
    beef satay with spicy mango
        dip, 210–11
    mangoes with sticky rice, 203
mangosteen, 39
meat, 52, 54
    see also types of meat
mee goreng, Indian, 150
mint, 67
    green vegetable salad with
        coconut mint dip, 148
    pork balls with minted
        peanut sauce, 246–7
mirin, 86
miso, 48, 83
    fried aubergine with miso
        sauce, 277
    miso soup, 264
mohinga, 200–1
Mongolian firepot, 11,
    116–17
    steamboat, 152–3
mooli, 26
    mooli and carrot salad, 276
    simmered squid and
        mooli, 299
mu shu pork with eggs and
    wood ears, 118
mung bean flour, 14
mung bean noodles, 16
mung bean pancakes with
    pork, 291
mushrooms, 32–3
    Chinese mushrooms and
        bamboo shoots, 109

mu shu pork with eggs and
    wood ears, 118
mussaman curry, 186–7
mussels, 58
mustard, 73
mustard greens, 24

N

nasi goreng, 219
nonya spring roll pancake
    wrappers, 18
noodles, 15–17
    bamie goreng, 225
    Cantonese fried
        noodles, 114–15
    chap chae, 280
    five-flavour noodles, 290
    Indian mee goreng, 150
    pork and noodle broth with
        prawns, 235
    straw noodle prawns and
        sweet ginger dip, 272
    thamin lethok, 182–3
nori, 36
nuoc cham, 84
    cha gio and nuoc
        cham, 240–1
nuts, 42–3
    see also types of nut

O

oils, 76–77
onions, 27
    beef rendang with deep-fried
        onion, 222–3
orange peel, 66
oyster mushrooms, 32
oyster sauce, 80

rice cookers, 11

rice dumplings, 22

rice flour, 14

rice noodles, 16

rice papers, 20

  Vietnamese rice paper
rolls, 238–9

rice vermicelli, 16

  crispy fried rice
vermicelli, 188–9

rice vinegar, 78

S

salads:

  chicken, vegetable and chilli
salad, 252

  mooli and carrot salad, 276

  egg pancake salad
wrappers, 218

  exotic fruit salad, 257

  fruit and raw vegetable
gado gado, 216–17

  green papaya salad, 181

  green vegetable salad with
coconut mint dip, 148

  larp of Chiang Mai, 190

  sweet and sour salad, 215

  Thai beef salad, 185

  Thai fruit and vegetable salad
with coconut sauce, 180

salmon, 56

  rice triangles, 265

  salmon teryaki, 296

  sashimi, 267

salt and pepper prawns, 99

salt-grilled mackerel, 297

sambals, 83–4

  sambal goreng with
prawns, 229

sambal nanas, 149

sotong sambal, 164–5

spicy meatballs with chilli
sambal, 220–1

samosas, 146–7

sardines with plum paste,
rolled, 298

sashimi, 267

satay:

  beef satay with spicy mango
dip, 210–11

  chicken satay, 142–3

  lamb satay, 212–13

  sauces, 79–82

sausages *see* Chinese sausages

scallions *see* spring onions

scallops, 59

  dried, 50

sea bass, 55

sea bream, 56

sea cucumber, dried, 51

seaweed, 36–7

seaweed, crispy, 106

sesame baked fish with ginger
marinade, 158–9

sesame oil, 77

sesame paste, 83

sesame seeds, 43

seven-spice powder, 69

shallots, 27

shellfish, 58–9

  dried, 48–51

  ragout of shellfish with
basil, 198–9

  seafood chow mein, 132–3

  see also types of shellfish

shiso, 68

shitake mushrooms, 32

shrimp noodles, 15

shrimp paste, 83

shrimps:

  dried, 50

  see also prawns

Sichuan pepper, 72

silver ears, 33

Singapore sling, 169

sinigang, 256

snake beans, 31

snapper, 57

  sesame baked fish with ginger
marinade, 158–9

snowpeas, 31

sole, 57

sotong sambal, 164–5

soups:

  asparagus and crab
soup, 236

  Balinese vegetable soup, 207

  chicken wonton soup with
prawns, 206

  crispy wonton soup, 92–3

  ginger, chicken and coconut
soup, 172

  hot and sour prawn
soup, 173

  hot and sour soup, 90–1

  laksa lemak, 162–3

  miso soup, 264

  pork and noodle broth with
prawns, 235

  puchero, 248–9

  sweet and sour pork and
prawn soup, 234

  sweet aduki bean soup with
rice cakes, 305

soy sauce, 79

soya flour, 14

spare ribs with spicy salt and
pepper, deep fried, 120

spices and herbs, 60–73